FULL DISCLOSURE

FULL DISCLOSURE

REAL TALK ABOUT RAW EMOTIONS

Amy Edwards

PALMETTO
PUBLISHING

Charleston, SC
www.PalmettoPublishing.com

Full Disclosure

Copyright © 2022 by Amy Edwards

All rights reserved.

First Edition

Hardcover ISBN: 978-1-68515-524-7
Paperback ISBN: 978-1-68515-525-4

To my dad. You sure did leave me an amazing legacy. You left me your love for God, for His Word, for people, for the church, for family, and for all things sweet! Of all those things that you left me, there is only one that I can hold in my hands and that is one of your old Bibles. I cherish reading those old pages where you underlined, highlighted, or made notes to the side in your scrawling handwriting. Thank you for showing me how to do ministry. I love and miss you and cannot wait until the day where I get to eat some banana pudding with you in heaven!

Foreword

Before you begin your journey through this book, you will need a few tools: a Bible and a journal or notebook. In your journal, you will be answering questions at the end of every chapter, in the 'Making It Personal' section. Please do not to skip those questions. This book on its own cannot fix the emotional struggles that you face in your life. But, if you will commit to doing the hard work of cooperating, uncovering, exploring, implementing, praying, and obeying, I promise you will see progress. In the 'Making It Personal' section you will be asked some hard questions that will require your total honesty and transparency as we travel together through the volatile topic of emotions. Rest assured, I have answered every single one of them on my own personal journey through these pages. Believe me when I say that I am in no way an expert on this subject. But I am happy to tell you that I have made progress and have covered some ground while researching and writing on this topic. I am not where I want to be, but I sure am a lot farther than where I started. Now, it is your turn. Turn the page and you too can begin to get real about your raw emotions.

Table of Contents

Introduction

ello, allow me to introduce myself. My name is Amy and I have a split personality. First of all, there is Mrs. Amy. She is the nice, polite, sweet, and super spiritual pastor's wife. She doesn't interrupt and is very patient. She lets others go first and she prays and reads her Bible a lot. Mrs. Amy knows lots of Bible verses and is actively working on surrendering all those pesky problem areas in her life. Next, there is just plain old Amy. She is real and she has issues. Amy wants to please God, and she knows she needs to work on some things but often lacks the motivation to do so. She makes progress but she fails a lot too. Amy loves her people and does her best to do things for them every day, but she also can be selfish and often just wants five minutes of peace and quiet to herself. Amy can be impatient and often wishes people would just do the right thing, herself included. This girl loves to shop and spends too much, according to her husband. Decorating is her thing, along with clothes and matching jewelry. Oh, and she has a ridiculous penchant for throw pillows. (Don't ask why.) All things considered, Amy is a pretty decent gal. Then there is Darth Amy. Yes, she really does exist. She is a pistol, this one. She expects everyone to bow to her wishes and they'd better do it fast. She is notoriously impatient and cynical. She has very little compassion and can be downright hard-hearted. She is known for losing her cool and snapping at others. She has a nasty streak that comes out in cutting sarcastic one-liners at the most inopportune moments. Darth Amy can be very quick to judge others and has very little tolerance for weakness. Darth Amy stomps, huffs, puffs, and closes a cabinet drawer now and then with a little more force than necessary. Oh, and she rolls her eyes. A lot! She has extremely high expectations of herself and everyone else for that matter. When these expectations are not met, aggravation and anger, along with frustration and irritation, abound. Not a pretty picture, huh? I have a sneaking suspicion you know just what I am talking about because, not so deep inside, there is a Darth You too. In the pages of this book we will take a journey that brings us face to face with this black helmet-wearing, lightsaber-wielding nemesis that lives in all of us. Then we will drag her into the light as she kicks and screams and take a good long look at her, her ways, and her weaknesses. We will study her and we will study what God's Word has to say to her. Then we will work on making imperfect progress. Together. No more thinking we are doomed to be this way, that we will never get victory over it, or that we are destined to be a slave to these raw emotions forever. Nope. It is time for a change, a real, true-blue 'take it all the way to the grave with you' kind of change. Now's the time, today's the day. Let's get real about some our very raw emotions.

This book is a very different work for me. I typically write Bible studies and devotional books. This one is much more topical. My goal, as God has laid it on my heart, is to be as real as possible with you. The phrase that keeps going through my mind is this: full disclosure. If I have learned anything in all my writing, teaching, speaking, and counseling, it is that I help people the most when I get brutally honest and real. So, prepare to laugh, cry, be surprised, and even be disappointed with me. Yes, I am a pastor's wife, speaker, and an author, but as you will soon see, I am a woman just like you. And a highly hormonal one at that! But I am a woman who wants to win. I want to win this battle. I want to make progress and cover some ground instead of constantly doing the one step forward, two steps back dance.

This first three chapters will be a look at emotions in general. We will take some time to see what God says about emotions, His purpose for creating emotions, and how Jesus handled His emotions while on this earth. In each subsequent chapter will take an in depth look at one emotion at a time. You can read those chapters in order or skip around as you see fit. At the opening of each chapter, I will share a true, and sometimes embarrassing, story from my life that illustrates the emotion that will be discussed in that chapter. At the close of every chapter, there will be questions for you to answer. Let me encourage you to be as brutally honest with yourself as I am being with you. Remember, full disclosure. This is a judgment-free book. You don't judge me and I won't judge you. This book is a safe place for us both to pull these messy emotions out of the place where we have stuffed them and to work through them in a healthy and godly way.

So, here we go, me and you, on a journey through our emotions. It won't be an easy journey and it may get really difficult at times, but it will be well worth every step we take, I assure you. We will make many discoveries along the way. Some you will be proud of and some, ahem, we won't talk about those just yet. I am glad you are here. I have found in life that there are certain journeys that are always better when you travel with a friend.

CHAPTER ONE

Emotions – Part 1

Emotion – "a natural instinctive state of mind deriving from one's circumstances, mood, or relationships with others"

Emotions can be a lot like quicksand. You know the stuff that was always well hidden from the unsuspecting guy in the movies. But when he was walking along minding his own business, he stepped into a pit filled with the stuff. He wasn't very alarmed at first and thought he could just step out of it. But that was when he discovered that this stuff wasn't just around him. Oh no, it got on him and it got a hold of him and wouldn't let go. It sucked him down deeper and deeper until he finally began to desperately search for something strong and anchored that he could grab onto. If he could just reach out and grab it, he had hope enough and help enough to get out. If not, the pit would suck him under and completely consume him.

The purpose of this book is to give you something to grab onto when powerful and potentially destructive emotions threaten to suck you under. What can we grab onto? This book? No. Our willpower? No. The answer is God's Word. Allow me to use an illustration I have used many times while speaking at countless women's conferences. If you have heard me teach it, please read it anyway. It is the best illustration I have ever heard concerning emotions.

When I was growing up in the mountains of North Carolina, I worked every day at the daycare that my mom directed at the church where my father pastored. Being the director's daughter, I had the opportunity to work in every classroom and with every age group. The one classroom that everyone hated being assigned to was the dreaded toddler room. It was a nightmare. I mean, you don't even love your own kid when they are in the terrible twos, much less a room full of other people's toddler terrorists! But, every once in a while, I had to go assist in that dreaded place. The head teacher's name was Kathy. She ran a tight ship but she sure did love those kids, and they loved her back. This woman came up with an absolutely wonderful system that allowed her to take those little terrors on walks down the two-lane country road when the days got long and the kids grew restless. Now, one or two toddlers would be no problem, but this room had about ten in there. How on earth could two ladies take ten toddlers on a walk down a road where cars occasionally would pass? It really was a rather genius plan that centered around a jump rope.

Kathy took that jump rope and held the end of the rope. Her job was to lead the rag tag group down the road to the bridge. At the bridge the kids would get to pick up rocks and toss them into the stream below. This would keep them entertained for at least thirty minutes, which, for a toddler, is quite impressive. My job was to hold the other end of the rope and keep an eye on the hoodlums. The kids had a job too. Their job was to hold onto the rope with one hand and walk on the white line along the side of the road. If they let go of the rope and headed toward the middle of the road or the embankment, I would go get them and bring them back to the rope and the white line. Did the toddler see the danger in the middle of the road or along the banks of the stream? No. But I did. So, in my wisdom, I made them hold onto the rope and walk in obedience along the line.

Now, let's bring this illustration home. The toddlers are the perfect picture of our emotions. (Not a far stretch. They pitch fits, want their own way, and are totally unpredictable and out of control if left on their own.) The jump rope is God's Word. The emotions are supposed to hold onto the Word and walk in obedience. They are to remain hooked into truth at all times. The head teacher is Christ. His job is to lead us to our destination. Our job is to bring up the rear and keep an eye on the emotions. When they let go of truth and wander into dangerous territory, we are to go get them and bring them back to truth. We have to make the decision to police them and make sure they are walking in obedience. If the toddlers did what they were supposed to, they arrived at their destination and a fun time was had by all. The lead teacher had a good destination in mind for them. Making them walk in obedience was for their safety and their benefit, even if they didn't like it at the time. The same is true for our emotions. Walking in obedience to God's Word is for our good. Reigning in our emotions to the truth of God's Word is key to getting to our destination (which is a good one) safely.

Now, when one toddler refused to walk in obedience, the whole class had to stop and wait for them to get in line. Emotions are like that. When they get out of line, progress is halted, and we remain stuck waiting for the wayward emotion to get back into obedience. We won't get anywhere until we get these little devils back in line, hooked into truth and walking in obedience.

THE RIGHT AND WRONG OF IT

Before we go any further, we need to establish something very important. Emotions aren't bad. Emotions aren't wrong. One goal of this book is to change the way we view our emotions. Emotions are a gift from God. Now before you roll your eyes, I want you to remember when your child would run up to you and give you a dandelion with their chubby little hand. You loved that dandelion simply because of who gave it to you. In fact, that little dandelion had gone from a weed to a treasure in your eyes. The difference was your perspective. The dandelion didn't change; your view, or your perception, did.

Now I know anger doesn't feel good, and neither does sorrow, or disappointment, or grief. But just as a dandelion has healing properties, so do emotions. That's right. Dandelions are actually useful little things. In the hands of someone who knows how to use them, these 'weeds' can become quite powerful and beneficial. First of all, they can lower blood pressure. So can emotions when we allow ourselves to let them out in a healthy way instead of the infamous unhealthy blowup. Dandelions can also fight inflammation. Emotions that we allow ourselves to experience in a healthy way instead of stuffing them all down will stop our cases of emotional inflammation. Then lastly, dandelions can assist in leveling out blood sugar highs and lows. Oh my! When we learn to walk through our emotions in a Biblical manner, we will finally be able to level out our wild emotional swings as well.

What a difference perspective makes! Our emotions are not weeds that God placed to grow in the cracks of the sidewalks of our lives. They are gifts, treasures actually, that bring healing on this journey we call life.

THE BIRTH OF AN EMOTION

Interestingly, emotions don't just show up on our doorstep. They have a beginning. And that beginning is a thought. Our thoughts give birth to our emotions. For example, we start thinking negatively about a friend. Those thoughts, left unchecked, turn into emotions. Those emotions of anger, jealousy, competitiveness, and comparison then turn into some sort of action. We will eventually snap at them, slight them in some way, end the friendship, or gossip about them. Thought – emotion – action.

In order to ever try to reign in those emotions, we need to nip them in the bud. Left on their own, our thoughts will color our emotions and our perceptions. We cannot expect to have controlled emotions when our thoughts are wandering into some very sinful territory. God has given us some very clear-cut guidelines for our thoughts. Philippians 4:8 says, "Finally brethren, whatsoever things are true, whatsoever things are honest, whatsoever things are just, whatsoever things are pure, whatsoever things are lovely, whatsoever things are of good report; if there be any virtue, and if there be any praise, think on these things." In your journal, I want you to draw a large circle. Around that circle write the words 'true,' 'honest,' 'just,' 'pure,' 'lovely,' 'good report,' 'virtue,' and 'praise,' so that you have a type of corral with these words as fence posts.

Now, imagine that you have a container full of marbles that you pour out over the circle you drew in your journal. What would happen? The marbles would go all over the place and very few would stay in that circle. Those marbles represent your thoughts on a daily basis. God has given us the guidelines in Scripture, and they make a circle of obedience (or a corral of sorts) that our thoughts need to stay inside. When they wander out and are left unchecked, they take root and you now have a very dangerous and destructive thought pattern. These wayward thoughts will lead to an emotion, which will eventually let go of the rope. In both scenarios the thoughts and emotions had God's Word that they could have stayed within or held onto in obedience. You will find that throughout this book we will continually refer back to Scripture as our absolute and final authority. Like a willful two year old rebels against authority, so do we. Just like those toddlers wanted to go their own way, so do our thoughts and emotions. How many times do we feel like we *deserve* to feel or think a certain way? If we are honest, we think this a lot. *They did this, so I deserve to think those catty and petty thoughts about them. They didn't do or say this, so I'll show them by giving them the silent treatment.* Then, we find ourselves going going from being hurt to resenting them and possibly even to hating them. Not long after we can be found talking about them to anyone who will listen. Thought – emotion – action.

CAN I REALLY HAVE CERTAIN EMOTIONS WITHOUT THEM BEING WRONG?

The answer to that question is yes. The reason I know that is I have seen that. Not in me—goodness gracious no! But in the pages of Scripture. We know that God is sinless. We also know that Jesus, while on this earth in a human form, didn't sin either. But all throughout Scripture we see that every member of the Trinity expresses, feels, and experiences a vast array of emotions.

Don't believe me? Check it out. In Deuteronomy 1:34, God the Father shows anger. In 1 Kings 3:10, we see that the Lord is pleased. In Zephaniah 3:17, we see He experiences joy. In Genesis 6:6 and Ephesians 4:30, we see God and the Holy Spirit experience grief. In Mark 1:41, we see Jesus moved with compassion. In John 11:35, we see Jesus weeping. In John chapter 2, we see Jesus outraged at the money changers in the Temple. Then in Matthew 23:37, we see Jesus display great disappointment. And finally, on Calvary, we see Jesus as He displays the greatest love ever shown.

Yes, God feels. Jesus feels. The Holy Spirit feels. They have emotions, just like we do. After all, we are created in His image, so this really shouldn't surprise us. Yet, they experienced them, and still do experience them, without sin. If we are to be like Christ, then this is a goal we need to have. But it will take purpose, focus, very deliberate awareness, and action on our part. Hence, this book. My heart's desire is for me to walk through the emotions in life like Christ. And I just bet that is why you purchased this book. It is your heart's desire too, isn't it?

Making It Personal

Answer the following questions in your journal:

1. Write out Philippians 4:8 and 2 Corinthians 10:5.

2. If you haven't already, draw that circle we talked about earlier, surrounded by the words 'true,' 'honest,' 'just,' 'pure,' 'lovely,' 'good report,' 'virtue,' and 'praise.' Draw some marbles inside and at least three marbles outside. Label those on the outside with some sinful thoughts, or thought patterns, that you personally battle over and over again. Then spend some time journaling about those. Explore subjects like: when did that thought first begin to happen, what are the triggers for these thoughts, and what are the results in your behavior because of them. Lastly, confess them and deliberately, prayerfully, and carefully set out to change them.

3. What will bringing those sinful thoughts into captivity look like for you?

4. Why is making our thoughts obedient so important to our emotions?

5. Look back at the paragraph that describes the emotions that each member of the Trinity displays in Scripture. Choose one and read the verse, or read them all. Which one helps you the most and why?

6. What toddler (emotion) lets go of the rope the most often in your life?

7. When does this normally happen?

8. What is your thought process before this emotion?

9. What are your behaviors after this emotion?

10. Take some time and look up what the Bible has to say about that emotion and write out the verses on index cards that help you the most. All you have to do is type in 'Bible verses that talk about _____' on your internet browser. A whole list will pop up. The ones that minister to your heart about your particular emotion is your 'rope.' Target that emotion in prayer every day. Memorize those verses and watch the difference they will make.

CHAPTER TWO

Emotions – Part 2

Emotion – "a natural instinctive state of mind deriving from one's circumstances, mood, or relationships with others"

There are three reactions to an emotion. Reaction number one is to stuff and resent. Reaction number two is to stuff and blow. Reaction number three is to explode. Which is yours? Do you push down the emotion, say you shouldn't feel that way, refuse to acknowledge it, and then slowly begin the resentment simmer? Or do you stuff and stuff and stuff until you blow? Or are you the one one who just simply explodes with no stuffing at all? This person feels, and feels big. Everyone around them (and on social media) knows exactly how they are feeling at all times, whether they want to or not.

So, which is it? It is important that you are fully aware of which type of responder you are. Being in touch with your personality and your tendencies is very important on our journey together. If you are not willing to be brutally honest with yourself, you might as well put this book down. It won't do you any good until you are ready for some full disclosure of your own.

If you stuff and resent, you have a constant stream of talking in your head that sounds something like this: "I shouldn't feel this way. I am a terrible person. Sigh, I wish I would get it together. I wish they would or wouldn't _____. Why can't I be more like _____? Why can't they be more like _____? If only...." Sound familiar?

If you stuff and blow, your constant stream of talk sounds like this: "I cannot believe they did this again. How many times do I have to _____? This is ridiculous. One day I am going to give them a piece of my mind." And eventually that one day comes and regret always follows.

If you are an exploder, you have a constant stream of hateful chatter in your mind. You use the word 'deserve' a lot and you keep a scorecard ready in your back pocket at all times. You feel entitled to your explosion and that it is somehow earned. The mess and the fallout from your explosion is viewed as the other person's fault because they 'made' you explode because of their actions or inactions.

THE POWER OF 'AND'

What on earth do I mean by the power of the word 'and'? Many times, as stuffers, we feel we cannot possibly feel upset AND be a good Christian. How many times do we think, *I shouldn't feel this way?* But we do. Therefore, we do not explore that emotion, experience it, and then emerge from it better than we were before.

Explore – experience – emerge

That is a concept we need to get. We can feel something AND be a good Christian. We can be sad AND ok at the same time. We can miss someone AND be happy in our current circumstance. We can grieve AND move on. We can love someone AND let them go. We can cry AND be spiritual. We can be hurt AND be honest. We can be angry AND sin not. We can be disappointed AND godly. We can be frustrated AND humble. We can be devastated AND right with God. That is the power of 'and.'

The problem is, we have been operating under the 'or' principle. We think, *I am sad OR ok. I can miss someone OR be happy. I can grieve OR move on. I can be angry OR right with God. I can be disappointed OR godly. I can be frustrated OR humble. I can be devastated OR a good Christian.* See the difference?

God created emotions for us to explore, experience, and emerge from them with wisdom, maturity, and grace. He did not mean for us to deny them, ignore them, stuff them, and then explode them all over the place. That has Satan's fingerprints all over it. Instead of "I shouldn't feel this way," how about we say something like "I feel this way. Period. Now, why do I feel this way? What happened to cause this feeling? What are my behaviors as a result of this feeling? What does God's Word say about this feeling? What will I choose to do with this feeling? Can I be ok and have this feeling? Can I be right with God and have this feeling?" You get the idea. If we would be honest with ourselves, our people, and God, we could explore, experience, and emerge all without sin. What a concept!

My safe place to do this is my journal and my prayer time. Before I die, I will have to burn my journals! I am VERY honest in there. I work out my disagreements with my husband in there. I work through my hurts, disappointments, worries, fears, sorrows, and anger on those pages. I work through betrayals and devastations. I even work through petty daily frustrations in there. Why? It is safe. It gets the feelings out where I can see them and honestly examine them. Safely. Without sin and without repercussions and regret. I damage nothing on those pages. I STRONGLY recommend that you start journaling. If you aren't a writer, become one. You can even sit in your car or a closet and talk out your feelings. People may think you are crazy, but not as crazy as when you explode over a ridiculously small thing. Try it. It helps, I promise.

POWERFUL WORDS FROM PAUL

In the book of second Corinthians, the Apostle Paul, one of the greatest Christians of all time, writes a journal of sorts. He puts pen on paper and works through many of his own feelings. In reading the Scofield notes about the book, I ran across this: "The Epistle discloses the touching state of the great apostle at this time. It was one of physical weakness, weariness, and pain. But his spiritual burdens were greater. (Paul felt) anguish of heart over the distrust felt toward him by Jews and Jewish Christians." According to these notes, Paul was feeling weariness, physical pain, weakness, rejection, and despair. Ok, so we could say that Paul was an emotional wreck while writing this. All of these emotions compounded by physical pain spilled out on the pages of second Corinthians. I want you to listen to a verse that shows Paul's frustration. This verse doesn't reveal any sin, but instead, reveals great wisdom on his part. You will see that I picked some words out to emphasize. We will discuss why in a bit.

2 Corinthians 13:10: "**Therefore I** write these things being absent, **lest** being present **I** should use sharpness, according to the power which the Lord hath given me to edification, and not to destruction." I added bold to certain words for a reason. Paul shows us a man very much in tune with his own personal weaknesses. He said, "Therefore I _____ lest I _____." He chose to write out his feelings in a letter instead of talking to the people of this church in person *lest* he would sin in his sharpness. Interesting. Paul knew if he got to talking to these frustrating people in person, his emotion would cross over into sin. So, he chose to let it out in a non-sinful and controlled way. Perhaps we could learn from this great man. He was AWARE of his own sinful tendencies and then he made CONCESSION so he could avoid them. He beat Satan to the punch, so to speak.

Awareness of our own sinful tendencies is huge. I have counseled woman after woman who sat across the desk completely clueless as to the sin that was obviously ruling her life. She really didn't see it. I saw it. Her husband definitely saw it. Her kids saw it on a regular basis and so did her co-workers. Passersby may have even seen it. People on her social media even caught glimpses of it. But Satan had her completely blinded to it. If she ever did see some hint of it, she quickly renamed it or excused it. For the remainder of this book, I am begging you not to be that woman. *Be aware* of your sinful tendencies. *Be honest* with yourself and God about them. *Be proactive* concerning them.

When, if ever, have you done the 'Therefore I _____ lest I _____' concept laid out by Paul? Remember, having emotions isn't wrong. Emotions having you is.

CENTERSTAGE

Years ago, I went to see an orchestra perform. It was amazing how many instruments make up an orchestra. The conductor stood in front of all those instruments and each musician followed his lead, and a thing of beauty was the result. Each piece had the proper balance as they played together in perfect harmony. Every once in a while, however, there was a solo. All the other instruments fell silent as the violin, or the cello, or even the flute, had centerstage. Why? They were simply following the piece as it was written. But not one time did the conductor hand the cellist his baton and sit down. Not one time. Why? That wasn't the cellist's place. He may have had a solo, but he didn't get to conduct the whole orchestra.

So, what does this have to do with emotions? A lot, actually. Let's say each instrument is an emotion. The flute is joy. The light-hearted piccolo, well, that is laughter. The oboe is sorrow, the violin is sadness, and the cello could be grief. The bass drum would be frustration, and the crashing cymbals are fear for sure. The loud blast of the trumpet is anger, and the soothing harp is the emotion of calm or peace. God writes the musical scores or pieces of our lives, and we are the conductor of our emotions.

There will be times in the different pieces of our lives that anger, grief, hurt, disappointment, or any other emotion will have a solo. Sometimes it may be the sharp trumpet that plays centerstage. And that is ok. Anger is an honest emotion that we will have. Anger adds to the pieces of our lives just as a trumpet adds to the overall sound of an orchestra. In tandem with the other instruments, the trumpet adds depth and harmony. But if we, as the conductor, hand the trumpet the baton and sit down, we have a problem. Anger has gone from one instrument of many to the conductor of the whole orchestra! And that, ladies, is the difference between experiencing an emotion and sinning with an emotion. And that is what Jesus never did. He never allowed his anger to control Him.

Making It Personal

Answer the following questions in your journal:

1. Which of the following are your sinful tendencies?

   Harsh words   Hateful thoughts

   Impatient   Jealous

   Selfish/self-centered   Being a scorekeeper

   Greedy   Bitter

   Materialistic   Wallow in an
   emotion

   Discontent   Exploder

   Stuffer who resents   Stuffer who blows

   _____   _____

   _____   _____

2. What instruments of emotions have had solos in your life recently?

3. Describe a time when you allowed the instrument to conduct the whole orchestra.

4. How can you keep that from happening again?

5. How can journaling help you in releasing an emotion safely and without harm or sin?

6. Are you honest about your sin or do you deny, rename, or excuse it?

7. What sin has God shed some light on in this chapter?

8. What can you do, like Paul, to be proactive in making an adjustment so that you won't sin? Therefore I _____ lest I _____.

9. Describe the difference between you having an emotion and an emotion having you.

CHAPTER THREE

Emotions - Part 3

Emotion – "a natural instinctive state of mind deriving from one's circumstances, mood, or relationships with others"

I love to read. One of my favorite things to do as my girls were growing up was to curl up with them and read children's books. We have a long list of our favorites, but among the top was a book entitled Alexander and the Terrible, Horrible, No Good, Very Bad Day. In the story, Alexander had a day that was terrible from start to end. It started out with him waking up to find that he had accidentally gone to bed the night before with gum in his mouth and now he had gum in his hair. The day progressed from bad to worse as everything and anything that could go wrong did. The day ended with his nightlight not working and his favorite pajamas were in the laundry, of course. At the end of each terrible happening, Alexander decreed that he wanted to move to Australia. Apparently, Alexander believed that there were no terrible, horrible, no good, very bad days allowed in Australia. Every time I read this book, we would giggle and laugh and recount some of our own terrible, horrible, no good, very bad days. Even now when one of those days comes along and one of my girls declares, "This has been the worst day ever!" I always look at them and say, "Everyone has a bad day now and then. Even in Australia." Today we are going to look at the absolute worst *day ever recorded in history today. And then we are going to learn how we need to let go of our own 'Australia' misconceptions and comparisons.*

I wonder if there are some ladies reading this book and thinking the whole concept of having emotions, without sinning in that emotion, is downright impossible? You are thinking, *Sure, Mrs. Amy, Jesus felt and sinned not, but He is JESUS! I would be able to do that too, if I was sinless perfection in human form!* Come on, admit it, that thought did cross your mind! Well, allow me to introduce you to a human who experienced the whole gamut of human emotions and did so without sin. The Bible records that he experienced 'great grief,' sorrow, despair, rage, sadness, worry, fear, rejection, mistreatment, loss, hopelessness, immense physical pain, and even thoughts where he wished he were dead. And in all this, not one time did he sin. *Yeah, right,* you are thinking. But it is true. Allow me to introduce my friend, Job. For four months I have been studying his life, his experiences, his reactions, and his emotions. And guess what? Not one sin did I find. I did find a boatload of unfair and despair, however. Before we begin deep-diving into one emotion at a time, let's take a nice long walk through the book of Job and see how on earth he was able to walk through all those emotions without sinning, even once. I really need to know just how this is done. I desperately need some hope here. I need to know it is possible because I can't even walk through someone cutting me off in traffic without sin, much less face great loss and pain without it.

QUIET ON THE SET... AND ACTION!

Let's paint the backdrop of our story. Job is the oldest book of the Bible. Scholars say that the book covers about one to three years of time. At the opening, Job is seventy years old. After the book closes, Job lives for 140 more years. He is a very wealthy businessman; in fact, he is the wealthiest and most powerful man in the East. He is married and has seven sons and three daughters. In the opening of the book, his vast wealth is described in detail. Job is a man who loves God and lives according to His law. He is an obedient and responsible servant of God who raised his family in the ways of God. He also ran his business honestly and with great wisdom. In fact, the wisdom and wealth of Job was the stuff legends are made of. He was held in great esteem and honor by all who knew or had heard of him.

The book of Job is written almost like a play. There are scenes, actors, behind-the-scenes action, along with heroes and villains. The opening scene takes place in heaven and is between Satan and God. Satan prowls restlessly in front of God, and God asks him what the problem is. Satan responds that he has been walking around the earth looking for something to do. It is then that God actually suggests that he test Job. Satan gleefully agrees. (As the audience, we know this, but throughout the rest of the story we must watch Job suffer greatly due to the fact that he isn't privy to this scene at all.) Satan, it seems, is convinced that Job serves God simply because God has been good to him. Take away the good and the love and service unto God will cease is Satan's logic. So, Satan places all his money on this bet. It is a sure-fire win, he thinks. God, however, disagrees. And the divine wager of sorts was made. Satan leaves the presence of God and then throws his worst at the faithful servant of God.

What happens next is a most unbelievable turn of events. Job receives news that a group of rebels attacked his servants, killing all but one and then they made off with all his oxen and donkeys. Every last one of them. On the heels of that terrible news, I mean while that servant is still talking, in comes another servant with more terrible news. This guy gives horrific details about fire that fell from heaven and burned up every last sheep and all the servants too, except him, of course. While he is still giving that grim report, yet another servant comes and says a group of thieves attacked them and stole all the camels and murdered each one of the servants. Only he escaped. Then, along comes another servant carrying even more terrible news. This fellow has the worst news yet. His eyewitness account is of a 'great wind' that came and blew down Job's eldest son's house where all his children were gathered together for a meal. Oh. My. Word. In the space of six verses, Job loses everything. His entire business gone. His assets - all gone. His employees gone. His vast holdings gone. His children are all gone too. Everything gone and in just a few minutes of time. Can you even imagine?

We have all had a moment in time when everything changed. Some of us have even experienced a phone call or a text that took our normal away. It was in that moment of time that so many emotions hit us at once that we can't even begin to describe it in words. Everything changed. Nothing was the same. Gone was easy. Normal couldn't be tracked down with the FBI. But, just like Job, we discovered that that moment stretched out into days, weeks, months, and, for some of us, even years. The moment wasn't here and gone. Oh no. It was followed by many, many more terrible, even excruciating moments along the way. For Job, his moment lasted from one to three years! So, what was Job's reaction? How did he handle all that awful?

Job 1:20: "Then Job arose, and rent his mantle, and shaved his head, and fell down upon the ground, and worshipped." Umm, what? I get the ripping his clothes. I even get the falling on the ground. But where we expect to read that Job cursed God, raged in agony, threw things, or yelled and screamed at anyone and everyone, we read that he worshipped. Remember the 'power of and'? Job was in agony of spirit AND worshipped. He was in the throes of grief AND worshipped. He was at a total loss AND worshipped. This makes the difference between a REACTION and a RESPONSE. A reaction is a knee-jerk physical or verbal reaction to a happening. Something happens, then you react. The reaction can be volatile explosion or a slow burn or simmer. You see that person that wronged you and your reaction can be a loud yelling match or a sinking feeling, nausea, a spike in blood pressure, or a full-blown panic attack. Do you see the different aspects of a reaction? There can be physical reactions, verbal reactions, emotional reactions, and mental reactions.

A response, however, is a purposeful, thought-out, calm, cool, and collected moment after a happening. That's what we see with Job. He responded. Everything in him was screaming, "REACT!" Yet, what we read is a response. How? How on earth did Job worship after hearing such terrible news? The answer is found in the fact that Job had worshipped BEFORE the bottom dropped out. We read of Job sacrificing, praying, and worshipping before the bad news. We will never respond spiritually during the bad times if we haven't done so in the good times. Think of it like a tea bag. In that tea bag we have its contents. Tea is in that tea bag. We catch glimpses of it if we hold it up to the light, but otherwise it is pretty well hidden. But, when the hot water hits it, the contents of that tea bag come out for all to see. Job had worship packed in his 'tea bag.' He had humility in there too. He had an awareness of his place in the grand scheme of things. He had an awareness of God's sovereignty and His authority packed in there. And, because of this, we get to read in the next verse, "And (Job) said, Naked came I out of my mother's womb, and naked shall I return thither: the LORD gave, and the LORD hath taken away; blessed be the name of the LORD." Job knew his place. He knew where He fit in the grand scheme of things. He knew who God was and that God had the RIGHT to do whatever He chose to do. Because Job had bowed to the authority of God BEFORE the hot water hit, we see him being able to do so AFTER the hot water hit.

The reason we do not respond like Job is because our tea bags are full of sins such as selfishness, pride, ego, entitlement, greed, and bitterness. We haven't faithfully packed them full of a regular quiet time, or a prayer time that is disciplined, alive, and active. We haven't packed in obedience, surrender, and trusting Him with all our hearts. So, when the hot water of a trial comes, what has been packed in the tea bag, of our heart, will come out. If we want to respond well, we have to consciously choose to pack in things of the Spirit. Can we say that we are faithfully doing this on a daily basis?

Now you may be wondering how I know that Job didn't sin. Perhaps he pitched an unrecorded hissy fit. Well, verse 22 lets us know loud and clear that that wasn't the case. "In all this Job sinned not, nor charged God foolishly." Let me just stop a minute and say, "Wow." Just wow. IN ALL THIS Job sinned not. What ALL THIS are you IN right now? Can it be said that you aren't sinning in your 'all this'? Can that be said about me? The problem is, we think that our 'all this' is an excuse note or a hall pass, if you will, for sin. But if we look at the life and times of a man named Job, that way of thinking gets negated, doesn't it? If ever a person earned a hall pass for sin, it was this guy. But he deliberately responded by not thinking that way and therefore he didn't react that way.

You know, I bet that in the moments after all the servants came with their bad news, all the hosts of heaven and of hell held their breath. I am sure they had placed their bets as to Job's response.. What would this guy do? Would he remain true to his God or would he cave in under the immense pressure? Can't you just hear the deafening silence as they watched it all play out? Then as Job hits the ground, his worship, surrender, and praise ring loud and clear for all to hear. I can just imagine a holy whoop went up in heaven and nasty jeers echoed through the caverns of hell. Now, imagine that scene in your life. Which side has been cheering because of your reactions? If it has been a reaction instead of a response, we know exactly which side has been cheering, don't we? It is time for a game changer. It is time we start packing our tea bags wisely and we start making the deliberate choice to RESPOND and not react. It is time we understand that 'power of and' and incorporate it into our lives.

Scene change: Now we as the audience enter back into the courts of heaven for another meeting between God and Satan. Satan approaches the throne with a defiant tilt of his chin, and God has that sparkle in His eye of one who has won the match. God asks Satan how it is going with Job and I can almost see the traces of a victorious smile on His holy face. Satan whines that if he had been allowed to attack Job's physical body, he would have won the wager. So, God confidently gives him permission to do so, but he will not be allowed to take Job's life. Ha! Satan jauntily walks out of heaven with the full belief that Job is done for. But that gleam hasn't left God's eye. He knows the heart of his servant and His confidence in him never waivers. (This makes me wonder, have I ever given God that gleam of respect in His all-seeing eye? Or do I give Him reason to sadly shake His head instead?)

Just as Satan arranges for the worst possible events for Job earlier, he now cooks up the worst possible physical affliction for the man. Boils. Job is covered with boils from head to toe. Swollen, puss-filled boils. There is no position he can find that is comfortable. Forget relief or sleep. His face is so swollen, you can't recognize him. Fever and pain wrack his body day after day. It is extremely painful, extremely embarrassing, and extremely public. No hiding those disgusting boils that cover his body. His clothes would be rubbing them. Puss would be constantly running out of them. The man would literally stink. Yes, I think Satan picked the worst for this faithful servant of God. But Job still holds onto his faith in God even through this!

Satan's next blow is a below-the-belt move. Remember that the Bible records that in all this Job sinned not, *nor charged God foolishly*. That means he didn't blame God or get mad at Him. But, Job's wife on the other hand, didn't fare so well. She didn't overtly shake her fist at God, but she did give Job some pretty bad advice which gives us a glimpse into her heart. She advised Job to just 'curse God and die.' Why would she have said such a thing? This was something she had been doing for a while in her heart before she ever uttered a word. What was in her heart was now coming out in her speech. And so, it is with us. We don't overtly say, "I hate you, God." We don't wear a T-shirt that says, "Mad at God." But we walk around with that stamped on our heart. We 'charge God foolishly.' Thoughts of 'why didn't God' or 'why did God' or 'if God loved me then…' are allowed free rein in our mind. They swiftly turn to emotions that embitter us. Actions or words will follow as we become hard and cynical toward God. One bad decision after another becomes our normal, which will then lead to guilt, regret, or consequences which we will, of course, decide is all God's fault. See the cycle? None of us can blame the woman for being heartbroken. Let's face it, many times we have been that woman. She had buried ten children, lost it all, and was now watching her husband go through a disgusting physical torment right in front of her eyes. Remember, she wasn't privy to the heavenly battle going on. The difference between Job and his wife is the difference between a person having an emotion and a person allowing the emotion to have them. Job shows us it is possible, but she shows us what is probable if we do not make the decision to respond instead of react. Now we can add to Job's long list of miseries a strained relationship with his wife and the ensuing marital issues that always follow. A spouse that didn't understand or 'get' him was a particularly painful addition to Job's list. Can't you just see the smile on Satan's face?

OH GOD, WHY?

Another hardship for Job was all the unanswered questions that surrounded him while sitting on that ash heap covered in painful puss-filled boils. It's no surprise that the book of Job wins the award for the most 'whys' in Scripture. The word 'why' appears more times in this book than any other book in the Bible, and that is totally understandable given the circumstances. But never once does God answer even one of those whys, not even at the end of the book when He breaks His silence. We need to hear that and somehow come to terms with it. There are just some things that we will encounter and endure for which we will not get a heavenly explanation. We just won't. Sometimes we need to be able to be at peace with the words 'I don't know.' We need to rest in that reality. We need to stop raging at it. Please understand that I am preaching to myself here. God is a mystery. He is. We will never ever be able to figure Him out or even begin to understand His ways, and that brings us to the next scene.

Enter Job's so-called 'friends.' With these 'friends,' who needs enemies? At first, they start off alright. They all meet up at Job's ash pile, and for days they just sit and listen. This is always a great approach when someone we know is going through a hard time. Just be there and listen. But then these fellas open their all-knowing mouths and reveal just how much they don't know. Each one of them spends time kicking Job while he is down. They have used their vast wisdom about God to come to the conclusion that Job has committed some great and terrible sin. They never do get the memo about God and His ways being a mystery. They try to put him into a box. They think they have Him all figured out. They are the ones that go through life with an equation of 'do good + be good = get good' firmly affixed in their way of thinking. Along with that, they decide that 'do bad + be bad = get bad' also must be true. The only problem with such logic is that it simply isn't true. Yes, God blesses obedience, but force fitting Him into an equation is a very dangerous and faulty thing to do. God does what God does. Period. We cannot explain it or understand it. His ways are higher than ours and so are His thoughts. But what we can know is that He makes no mistakes; His ways are perfect, He is always in control, He is never late, and everything He does is out of love and for our good. Those truths we can bank on even when we don't understand, don't get, and don't see how it will ever make sense.

Poor Job has to endure the snide comments and the judgmental attitudes of his friends. They call Job everything under the sun. They even accuse him of doing terrible things such as starving widows and orphans. Job has done nothing to deserve such accusations, so now you can add being falsely accused to his list of hardships. This one, well it had to have been a particularly hard pill to swallow.

THE EMOTIONS OF JOB

Now, let's take a walk through the book and see some of the emotions that Job had that are recorded throughout his story. Remember, he feels each of these without any sin. In Job 6:4, we see he feels like God is against him. In Verses 8 and 9 of Chapter 6, he wants to die. In Verse 27 of the same chapter, he feels betrayed. In Chapter 7 we see he feels hopeless. In Chapter 9 we see Job experiencing fear. In Chapter 16 he feels targeted and attacked. Add all these feelings to the ones we have already seen of great grief, anger, sorrow, dejection, desperation, and shock and you have yourself quite a cocktail of emotions. But still no sin. Are you beginning to see that we can experience a massive gamut of emotions without wandering into sinful territory?

Imagine for a moment that God places you in a vehicle and says that you are to go to a certain destination a long way off. He says to stay on the road and not to veer off. So, off you go. On the way, you encounter curves, steep climbs, deep descents, potholes, and bumps—all while on the road He told you to stay on. Would God be angry that you hit a pothole or rounded a curve, or climbed a hill? No. He knew they were part of the assigned journey. They were factored in as part of the plan the whole time. So it is, with emotions. They are part of the pavement that makes up the journeys of life. But, if you hit the pothole and then back up and keep hitting it over and over, we have a problem. Or, if you had road rage along the way, He wouldn't very well be pleased. How about if you refused to head up the steep incline because it was too hard or wouldn't proceed around the curve because you couldn't see what was around the bend? You get the picture. Hitting the pothole, slowly making the way up the steep incline, carefully driving around the deep curve, patiently putting up with other drivers and their imperfections are all pictures of us experiencing the emotions we will encounter along life's way. *How do I do this?* you are probably wondering. Well, let's look at how Job did it.

DEFINING DECLARATIONS

One of the things that kept Job from crossing the line into sin is an action that we most definitely must learn to do. We see that Job makes something that I call 'declarations' while in the midst of these tumultuous emotions. Declarations are statements of truth that we make to ourselves when we FEEL the exact opposite. It is stating FACT when faced with overwhelming FEELINGS. The first declaration Job made he said twice. He stated it to his so-called friends. Yes, they needed to hear it, but Job needed to hear it more. Job looked at those judgmental men who were looking down their noses at him and stated, "I am not inferior to you." Babam! Job wasn't just stating this to them, he was stating this to himself. God didn't love those men any more than He did Job. No, they weren't covered in boils, but that didn't mean that they were any more loved and favored than poor old boil-covered Job. And this truth uncovers much of our struggle, doesn't it? Comparison is at the root of much of what fuels and what drives our sin in the hardships we face. Misery truly does love company, and when we feel alone in our misery while someone else is living it up in the lap of ease and luxury, it makes for an even more miserable misery. But Job's loud and clear declaration puts a balm of truth where it hurts. Job was not inferior to his friends. And we are not inferior to that beautiful size 4 woman on our social media feed either. Oh, you know the one. She has kids who have clean rooms and As on all their report cards. She has a husband who buys her flowers on a regular basis and surprises her with romantic date nights and getaways to exotic places. And her hair? It's perfect. She's the one I am talking about. We all have her in our lives. She takes photos of that six-hundred-calorie coffee she drinks with her devotions every morning, yet she somehow never gains weight. How is that possible? Maddening, isn't it? The truth is, you are not inferior to her. And neither am I.

Declaration number 2 is this: "Though he slay me, yet will I trust him." Job's simple but powerful statement here showed that he didn't allow his circumstances or mean-spirited friends to cause him to be suspicious of his God. He stood firm on the character and the identity of God no matter what he saw or what he experienced or what he felt at that moment. The character of God is revealed in the Scripture and will not change. Period. He is faithful. Period. He is good. Period. He makes no mistakes. Period. He loves me. Period. The list could go on and on. Search it out. Look up the attributes, names, character, and personality of your God. Go on, I dare you. Then stand on the facts that you find. Even when. Even if. Even then. Even though. Even through.

Later, Job declares, "I know my redeemer liveth." Even when He is silent. Even when I cannot understand Him, His ways, His thoughts, His actions, what He allows, or His silence. He is. End of story. He is alive and well during the silent seasons, and they will come to all of us. He lives in my stormy seasons. He lives in my harsh seasons. He lives. Job KNEW that even when he didn't feel that. Job's declarations weren't for the benefit of those terrible comforters sitting around him. Oh no, those statements of truth were war cries meant for the heart of Job and the ears of God. Try it sometime when the bottom drops out of your life and you feel despair and doubt creeping in all around you. Make some declarations out loud. Scream them out if you need to. Journal them, pray them, or whisper them as you cry. Whatever way that you do them, believe them and hold onto them for dear life. Even if it's the last thing you do, and it may be just that.

The final declaration we will look at is this: "but he knoweth the way that I take; when he hath tried me, I shall come forth as gold." Job has no idea what was going on behind the scenes in heaven, but man does it appear that he realizes something more was going on than what he could physically see. This declaration shows an amazing grasp of God's sovereignty. He knew God was in control, had a purpose, a plan, a reason, and a goal for it all. Oh, that we would grasp this in our own lives! God is sovereign. God has a plan for your life and not one wound will ever be wasted. Not one. Job shows immense determination to come out of this strong and with his faith intact. I SHALL come forth as gold. Do you hear the determination? Can you see him saying this through gritted teeth, jaw set in granite, and fists clinched by his side? My, my, the cheer that must have gone up in heaven! What a scene! What a thought!

Now we come to the last scene. Finally, God breaks the silence. It is important to note that not one time does God give Job an answer for all his questions. What He does do is ask some questions of Job. God takes Job on a tour of the deepest, darkest ocean. He takes him to the vast expanse of space and walks him through the many wonders of the animal kingdom. All the while asking Job questions he could never answer. Why? To give him a glimpse into that character and that sovereignty of God that he had held onto so tightly during his trial. Somewhere along the way, while Job was so busy defending himself from those terrible friends, he began to believe his own press, as they say. He was beginning to think a little too highly of himself. This is a very easy trap to fall into when you have been done wrong. Hear me well, *it is never harder to stay right than when you have been done wrong.* Read that again. We know enough to expect life to be hard. We do not expect life to be unfair, however. When this happens, and it will, we can cross over into sin in a mere heartbeat. Job was precariously close to crossing the line into prideful territory. God gives Job a none too gentle reminder of "Me God, you not."

Job has allowed anger to cross over into what we love to call 'righteous indignation.' The only problem is the definition of righteous indignation is 'being angry when GOD is done wrong.' It is NOT being angry when WE have been done wrong. Well, there goes all the wind out of our indignant sails, huh? Thankfully, God steps in before this could become bitterness, pride, and a whole boatload of other sins in Job's life.

Job, in typical Job style, repents and once again realizes his place in the grand scheme of things. He lays down his rights and realizes that God has the right to do whatever He wants to do or not do. God then instructs Job to pray for the very friends that have mocked and accused him. At the very moment when Job obeys and does this incredibly hard thing, God "turned the captivity of Job." This was absolutely vital to Job coming forth as gold. You see, I am sure he felt entitled to the hate. The anger felt justified, deserved even. It felt good to be mad. Mad feels better than sad. Ladies, please know that Job's captivity wouldn't have turned had he not turned his feelings of bitterness and anger over to God. Perhaps you believe that that person that wronged you is holding you captive. You feel the hurt or the situation has you trapped. But, if you are truly honest here, you can realize that your bitterness is what is keeping you locked up. The truth is, you have the key. The key to your freedom is to forgive and release the bitterness that is robbing you of so much.

You know the rest of the story. Job ends up with double the amount of wealth and power. He and his wife have seven more sons and three more daughters. The story ends by letting us know that Job lived for 140 more years. God actually did have a plan for Job, and it was a good one. Sure, it had some bumps along the way, some mighty big ones. But Job navigated the emotional minefield successfully and his story teaches us that we can too.

Making It Personal

Answer the following questions in your journal:

1. What did you think at first about the concept that we can fully experience an emotion without it being a sin?

2. What do you think about that concept now after seeing Job's journey?

3. Describe the difference between a reaction and a response.

4. Describe a time when you reacted.

5. Describe a time when you responded.

6. What deliberate choices and actions can help pack our tea bags so that the right things can come out in our hot water circumstances?

7. Describe the difference in having an emotion and an emotion having you.

8. When have you had an emotion and when has an emotion had you?

9. Do you have any unanswered questions that haunt you? If so, write them down followed by the statement, "I don't know." Lastly write, "God knows and that's enough."

10. What are 'declarations' and why are they important? Write out some declarations you need to declare and believe.

CHAPTER FOUR

Anger

Anger – "a strong feeling of annoyance, displeasure, or hostility excited by a sense of injury or insult"

It was a typical Monday morning. The house was dirty and my girls were doing anything but school, like they were supposed to. I found myself taking deep breaths. A lot of them. Everything they did threatened to send me over the edge. What was wrong with me? Noises irritated me beyond belief. I was walking around mad. As I cleaned toilets and showers with more vigor than necessary, it began to dawn on me that my fuse was getting pretty short and my reactions uncharacteristically grouchy. On so many days it seemed that the scoreboard read: Anger: 4, Amy: 0 or Frustration: 6, Amy: 0. And so on. You get the picture. My prayer time seemed to be spent asking God for a lot of forgiveness. Not to mention having to ask my people for the same thing. For the life of me, I couldn't understand what was happening with me. I seemed to be losing ground in the battle called emotions. Wasn't it supposed to be the other way around? Shouldn't I be gaining ground as I got older and wiser? I questioned if it had to do with the recent death of my father. I am not prone to sadness or crying, and I wondered if maybe I had suppressed grief and it had decided to come out as anger. That was the only explanation I could come up with. I was at a loss for the reason why I was living life mad. It was around that time that I went for a routine doctor's appointment at my integrative specialist. When he walked in carrying his laptop, he looked at me, then his computer, then at me again. He, almost fearfully, asked how I was doing. I wondered what his problem was until he went over my bloodwork numbers. It seemed my body was getting ready to enter into perimenopause. This is a period of time just before pre-menopause that can last anywhere from three months to ten years! It was early, but it was here, it seemed. He told me that my body had been experiencing what is called an 'estrogen dump.' Now I have always had high estrogen levels, hence the reason I go to this doctor. These high levels lead to terrible headaches around my period each month. But my levels this month, and the months leading up to this appointment, were off the charts. He told me that a normal estrogen count was around 100. Mine was well over 600! When I still didn't get it, he said, "Amy, estrogen is what we call the 'mad hormone.' How on earth are you functioning with this level? Your mad hormone has gone crazy." Great. As if it wasn't hard enough to control Darth Amy! She may as well have gone postal with these numbers! At that moment, it clicked. No wonder I had wanted to strangle people for the slightest thing. It all made sense now that I had gotten to the bottom of why I was so mad. Sometimes there is something going on inside of us, or around us, that extorts an honest emotion. This happens most with the emotion we call anger.

Anger seems to be everywhere right now. Sometimes I wonder if the whole world has too much estrogen! Rage is running rampant. Angry tirades and rants pop up all over social media. Viral videos appear with people screaming at one another while veins pop out on their neck and their face is cherry red. College kids are marching, protesting, and raging at society's 'norms' or laws and absolutes that have been around for centuries. Husbands are raging at wives and vice versa in angry arguments. Kids rage at parents while slamming their bedroom door. At work bosses rage at employees, and in the break room they rage right back to one another about their bosses. Roads are filled with drivers that rage at one another with often deadly results. News broadcasts are filled with stories of people whose rage has bubbled up and over, leading them to try and solve their problems with violence. Why are we all so mad?

Just like my body had too much of what is referred to as the mad hormone, it seems our world also has way too much mad. My mad came from an overabundance of estrogen. My body didn't know what to do with it. It was too much too fast. In order to address this, my doctor gave me an estrogen blocker and another pill that helps my body to dump the estrogen into my gut instead of my bloodstream. This is a much healthier and less destructive way to get rid of it. Too much estrogen in the bloodstream can lead to several types of cancer. It is necessary for me to try to get it out in a healthy way or there could be harmful consequences. Wouldn't it be nice if we could take a pill that would help us dump our anger in a healthy way instead of us dumping it all over the people around us?

Anger is sort of like the calories in our food. If we metabolize the calories, they are burned off and give us the energy we need to function. If, however, we do not metabolize the calories, they are stored as fat. This, as we all know, is not good. The same doctor told me at that same visit that my metabolism is at an all-time low. I already knew this, as my jeans had told me that that very morning when I struggled to button them. My body is gearing up for a change and it doesn't like it. At all! So, it is grabbing onto every Little Debbie and holding on for dear life. It doesn't want to let go, so it refuses to metabolize at a healthy rate.

So it is with our anger. If we do not metabolize it, then expect it to be stored up. Gobs of unsightly anger will build up in our lives just as cellulite on our thighs. Many of us have muffin-top anger. It rolls up and out of our spiritual pants we are trying to button. It spills out of our lives and we cannot seem to figure out where it comes from. It is there because we haven't burned it off. We haven't metabolized it at a healthy rate and now we see it in all its ugly glory.

This chapter is one of the most important ones in this book. If we can learn to process anger in a healthy way, our lives will be all the better for it. Anger isn't an emotion to be avoided, stuffed, or ignored. It is an honest emotion to be processed and experienced. So, let's dive into the deep, dark depths of our anger.

HOW WE PROCESS ANGER

The pop psychologists of today promote 'venting' as the healthiest way of processing anger. We will call this the 'blow-up' approach. This approach is not healthy for relationships, the people in the lane next to you, or the person in the checkout ahead of you. And, if truth be known, it isn't healthy for the person venting either. Venting, and the rants that are the result, cause much damage along the way. The person you just vented all over did not deserve such harsh treatment, nor did the innocent bystanders. Testimonies are ruined and you can forget mending a lot of those damaged fences. The blow-up is nothing more than a grown-up version of the infamous temper tantrum thrown by an angry toddler. Both of them are sinful, unpleasant, and harmful if left unchecked.

Another incorrect attempt at processing anger is the 'clam-up' approach. This one is, by far, the most popular in Christian circles. We stuff our anger, causing a slow simmer as opposed to the roiling boil of the blow-up approach. The problem is, this one silently eats away at us over time. Relationships are still damaged and fences will still need to be mended after the person silently withdraws and resentment inevitably sets in. Bitterness will be the end result of this approach.

DELETE THE WRONG

A healthy exercise in processing anger is to write out on a computer the wrong that was done to you. Write it ALL out, every last detail, including how you feel and what the wrong has done to you deep inside. Make sure to include all the ugly consequences and the fallout from the wrong committed. Then, hit the delete key. Delete each and every word. After staring at the blank screen for a time, go back and fill it back up, but this time with a prayer. The prayer should include choosing forgiveness and extending space and grace to the person who wronged you. This prayer needs to include how you are grateful for God hitting the delete key on your sins time and time again.

This is a great time to write out what I call 'head-to-toe prayers.' Some of you may be familiar with this concept, especially if you have the prayer journal *A Woman, A Warrior*, which I wrote. This approach to praying is an incredibly visual and impactful approach of praying over every part of you and every part of those that you love. Anger has the potential to harm so much of you. Thus, covering these with prayer will be vital to your victory over it. Head-to-toe prayers concerning anger might sound something like this:

> **Head** – Lord, I pray over my mind today. You know the anger I am feeling over _____. I do not want my thoughts to wander into sinful territory here. I want to think on things that are true, honest, just, pure, lovely, and of good report. I choose to think on things that have virtue and are filled with praise. I will not stew over this incident today. Help me to fill my thoughts with things that are pleasing to You every hour of this day.

> **Eyes** – Lord, I pray over my perceptions today. Help me not to go about this day looking for ways that this person will wrong me, or let me down. Help me not to replay the incident or rehash the argument in my mind's eye. Help my eyes not to center on me or think it's all about me. Help me to see things from their perspective. I choose to do this on purpose. Cause me to see my actions and hear my words from their point of view. Open my eyes, Lord, to MY sin in this situation.

> **Ears** – Lord, Satan will capitalize on my anger by telling me lies. He will use words like 'deserve,' 'I can't help it,' 'hate,' 'revenge,' 'unfair,' and 'hopeless,' among many

others. I choose not to listen to these lies but to go to Your Word for truth today. Guide me to the verses I need in this situation.

Shoulders – Lord, I cannot carry the load of this hurt or the load of fixing it. I lay this situation down at your feet along with all the fallout and the issues that spring up from it.

Heart – Lord, my heart is filled with anger right now. Anger is not sin, but it is a breeding ground for sin. I choose to 'be angry and sin not' today. I have anger, but anger will not have me. I choose to walk away from bitterness and hate and all the destruction they bring. I plead the blood of Jesus over my heart today.

Hands – Lord, my hands want revenge. They want to prove myself right. They want to point out the wrongs of the other person. They want to tear them down. Lord, these actions are not right in your sight. I take my hands off the situation and release this person to You. I choose to lift my hands up in prayer today. Take this situation, Lord. Not my will but Thine be done.

Knees – Lord, I make my anger bow to You today. I bow to You today. I surrender to handling this anger in the way You show me in Scripture. I choose kindness. I choose forgiveness. I choose patience. I choose meekness. I choose surrender to Your will and Your way on this.

Feet – I pray that every step I take today will leave behind footprints of peace. I will not be swift to run to mischief. I pray that every step I take will be the steps You order for me. I will walk in obedience.

After writing those prayers out, place them with your Bible and daily pray them as you meet with God each day. These prayers are not meant to be prayed one time. These will need to be prayed daily, and on some days, several times a day.

WHEN YOU ARE ONE BIG BALL OF EMOTIONS

Another exercise to help us see and process our anger is to visualize the statement we have all heard before: 'I am one big ball of emotions.' Picture yourself walking around in a large circle with a softball in your hands held out in front of you. Now picture that circle being filled with all the people in your life milling about within that circle. Occasionally that ball in front of you will be bumped into, but not much, because it is a small and manageable ball. You have probably guessed by now that the ball represents your emotions, namely, anger, in this chapter. Now imagine that you have been wronged and you trade that softball in for a kickball instead. You go back to walking around in that circle with those same people, and you begin to notice that people bump into your mad a whole lot more. Why is that? Because it is 'out there' more than the softball used to be. You can still manage that kickball and go through life completing your tasks, but it is more difficult than before. Now picture taking an air pump, and each time you rehearse and nurse that anger, you pump and fill that kickball with more and more air. Eventually, you are walking around that same circle with those same people, holding one of those massive exercise balls in your hands. People cannot even see you anymore. All they see is the anger that is now controlling you. In fact, you cannot even interact with those people because you have to focus on managing the mad that has so much of you. You cannot open your arms to give or to receive a hug. The overly large ball of mad takes all your time and effort and energy. You have a hard time seeing around the ball, and your hands find it extremely difficult to complete the required tasks due to the large ball they have to manage. As you try to go about your daily walk around that circle, people cannot help but bump into that ball. And you feel each and every bone-jarring bump clear down to your soul. This is a very clear mental image of what living mad looks like. Each person reading this book has had a season in their life when this has been their reality. Including me.

INFLAMED ANGER

Now let's bring this illustration home. What size ball are you walking around the circle of your life carrying? Is it the healthy and manageable sized softball, the inflamed kickball, or the overly inflated exercise ball? It is important that you know because this will help you know how to proceed. Painful events are going to happen, and kickballs will be our realities from time to time. Having an inflamed ball of emotions isn't wrong. Experiencing anger isn't wrong. When we have been misused or abused, we will find ourselves with a kickball in our hands—and that is ok. When that is our reality, we must learn to make kickball concessions for a season. This means we need to give ourselves and others a little more space and alter our steps a bit for the time being. Our arms need to work together more efficiently in order to handle the kickball and continue to complete our daily tasks. Being aware of the kickball is key to being able to manage life with a kickball reality for a while. This managing includes lots of head-to-toe prayers, journaling, seeking godly counsel, and a daily surrendering of our 'rights.' It means that you may have to have some honest conversations with the people in your circle so that they can better understand and pray for you. Each day you will need to pick up your responsibility to respond in such a way that lines up with Scripture and that is pleasing to the Lord. Managing anger in a healthy way includes a targeted Bible study as you look up verses on anger, bitterness, forgiveness, grace, and mercy. Lastly, it will include a daily choice to respond instead of react. Responses are prayerful and careful. Reactions are quick and destructive. Responses are God-centered and God-controlled. Reactions are flesh-centered and controlled by the feelings of the moment. Remember, the kickball isn't sin. Feeling anger isn't sin. Anger is a God-created emotion that can be experienced and traveled through without sin. But keeping this truth front and center in your mind will help you navigate your anger more successfully. This will require you to process, or metabolize, your mad on purpose.

ANGER GOALS

Here's an exercise that can help you to manage the anger you are feeling. Take a journal or a notebook and write out why you are mad and the name of the person with whom you are angry. In the days that follow, write out your anger goals. Such as: Today my GOAL for my anger is _____. The steps I will take today to reach my goal today are _____, _____, and _____. Then write out a prayer asking God to help you to take those steps in order to reach your goal. Write out a verse concerning your goal or a necessary step that you must take in order to reach that goal. That evening, write a synopsis of your day and record how you did concerning your steps and reaching your goal. You may even want to give yourself a grade. Confess any shortcomings that led to sin that day and then close the book on your anger for the night.

INFLATED ANGER

Now let's leave the kickball-sized anger and visit the exercise ball of overly inflated anger. This ball has been pumped up over and over again, and this is where we cross over into sin. The kickball is a picture of inflamed anger, which is a natural response to hurt or being done wrong, much like a bruise on your shin from when you hit the corner of the coffee table. Then there is inflated anger that has been nursed and rehearsed over and over again. You can bet this anger will eventually be dispersed over time. Bitterness, scorekeeping, fault finding, and pride fill this big ball. Selfishness and self-centeredness are pumped into this ball as we decide we have no fault and *deserve* something much better. It is full of 'why me,' 'what about me,' and 'it's all about me' sentiments. It is full of misconceptions and misperceptions as we view life through distorted lenses colored by this powerful and destructive emotion we call anger. It is also pumped full of lies. Lies about what they really meant by that comment, how you are completely sinless in that conflict, and how it is all their fault. Lies that use the word 'right' and 'deserve' are pumped in over and over again as you seethe at the very thought of what they did to you. This ball is decorated with question marks as unanswered questions help to pump it up. Why did this happen to you? How could God allow this? Why did this person treat you this way? What do you do now? How can you possibly get over this? I am sure many of you reading this can relate to many of these unanswered questions.

Pumping that ball full of air is a picture of what I call 'reactionary sins.' These are sins that happen in reaction to the sins of another. You start off in the 'right,' but it doesn't take long before you are failing to be 'righteous.' I want to tell you something that may surprise you. God isn't concerned with who is 'right' in the conflict you are facing. He cares about you being 'righteous' in that conflict. He isn't keeping score with who 'wins' the war raging between you and another person. He is watching to see if you will 'win' the battle between the flesh and the spirit. So, we must ask ourselves this question, "I may be right, but am I being righteous?" Now remember, righteous indignation is being angry at GOD being done wrong, not us being done wrong. So, don't try to throw that term around and feel justified in your sinful exercise-ball moments. Deflating the ball will take a deliberate course of action. First of all, you have to realize that you really are carrying that ball around and living life mad. Next, you will need to confess the sin that has been pumped into it. You will then have to unscrew the air valve by choosing to let the anger go. The next steps you take are the same ones outlined earlier for the inflamed anger. This is the way you reverse the nurse, rehearse, and disperse pattern you have slipped into. In order to release the *emotion* of anger, you must first release the *thoughts* of anger, otherwise victory cannot be achieved.

FIVE-STEP PROCESS FOR HANDLING WHAT IS HANDLING YOU

In his book *Anger: Taming a Powerful Emotion*, Gary Chapman lays out five steps for dealing with anger. They are as follows:

1. Consciously acknowledge to yourself that you are angry.

2. Restrain your immediate reaction.

3. Locate the focus of your anger.

4. Analyze your options.

5. Take constructive action.

First, we must consciously acknowledge that we are angry. As Christians, many times we feel it is a sin to be angry, therefore we deny that we are angry. We will not say a thing to the person we are mad at, and we act as if everything is ok. We feel that is the spiritual thing to do. The problem with that is stored and stuffed anger festers. Sadly, the anger comes out in other ways toward other people in our lives who are completely innocent. We must begin honestly acknowledging the fact that we are angry. Then it is incredibly important to do a little self-analysis, as well as a situational analysis. Is what you are feeling definitive anger, that is, anger that is real from a real wrong, or is your anger perceived anger? Perceived anger is anger we feel when we perceive we have been done wrong. We often THINK a person should have done or said this or that, and when they do not, we feel anger. We EXPECT life to be this and we get that instead. We feel slighted and then along comes the anger. This is perceived anger. An example of this in Scripture is Naaman. He expected to be treated one way, and when he was asked by a servant to dip in the dirty Jordan seven times, he exploded. If we are completely honest with ourselves, we will realize a huge percentage of our anger falls into this category of perceived anger. Letting go of our perceived slights will greatly benefit our relationships with others and with God. Once you have discovered that it is definitive anger from a true wrong, you can proceed to the second step.

Next, we must restrain our immediate reaction. No matter if it is stuffing, exploding, withdrawing, or attacking, these immediate knee-jerk reactions will be harmful in the end. The split second after you admit that you are angry, you must decide to stop doing what you have always done in response to anger. In this moment, you must make a purposeful decision to respond and not react. This may be the most moment of your lifetime.

Thirdly, we need to locate the true focus of our anger. As stated earlier, many times innocent bystanders bear the brunt of our misguided anger. Ask yourself, "Am I really angry at this person or thing, or is it something or someone else that I am angry at but refusing to acknowledge?" You may be surprised to find that your spouse isn't the person you are really upset with. It may be your boss, your friend, or perhaps something from your past that has recently reared its ugly head again.

Analyzing my options is the next step I must take. I am angry, now what? What are my options in this situation? I can talk to them, I can cover it in prayer, I can choose to let it go, I can search Scripture to see what God says I need to do in this situation, or I can seek godly counsel. Sometimes the options are limited, as the person I am angry with may not even be in my life anymore. Many times, the answer is to simply pray and choose to love the person as Christ loves us. In some instances, biblical confrontation is the answer. If so, follow the procedure in Matthew 18:15–17. The way the church treated a heathen man and a publican was with kindness, hoping to reach them with the gospel of Christ. They were not mean, uncivil, or hateful to those outside of the church. However, they did not receive them into their inner circle or trust them with their safety or their hearts.

They were on guard but not unkind. Later, we will have tips on confronting someone in this chapter.

Lastly, choose what will be the most *constructive* course of action. Will this be beneficial for the other person? Will this help them? Will this build up our relationship or tear it apart? Will this drive a wedge or will this build a bridge? Will this person receive what I have to say? Will this please God or will it just make me feel better? After prayerfully going through these five steps, you will be able to come to the conclusion that will be of most benefit to everyone involved.

THE ORDER OF ANGER

The first stage of anger is what I call the *'view' stage*. We perceive a wrong-doing. We see a slight. Once again, this wrong may be real or imagined. It could be as real as a drunk driver killing a family member or as imagined as a wife being upset that her husband does not do something the way her father did. Deciding if our lenses are distorted is a huge step in dismantling anger at perceived wrongs. Ask yourself, "Am I looking at this person through distorted lenses or am I seeing them or their action clearly?"

The next stage of anger is call the *'stew' stage*. In this stage we think and rethink, play and replay the wrong that was done to us, whether it was real or imagined. We have that conversation or relive that event over and over and over again. We say what we really want to say to them and give them a piece of our mind in our mind, and nobody is the wiser. The stew stage takes place completely in our minds.

We then move on from the 'stew' stage to the *'brew' stage*. This stage takes place in our hearts. Now our emotions get involved and we put them on the back burner on simmer. It doesn't take long before we begin to seethe in our hearts and the hurt and the mad consume us. This emotion eventually comes to a slow boil and every once in a while spills out in other areas of our lives as we begin to live our lives mad. We find ourselves snapping at others and overreacting at small things here and there. We may have digestive issues, our blood pressure elevates, and we often have trouble sleeping at night.

Then comes the final stage of our anger. This stage is called *"spew" stage*. In the brew stage, others will catch glimpses of our anger here and there. But in the spew stage, it isn't just a glimpse; it is out there for all the world to see or hear. Imagine shaking a bottle of soda and then opening the lid. That's spew. The sad thing is, even if the wrong was real, sin is placed on our account in the stew, brew, and spew stages. If our perception is colored with unrealistic expectations and selfishness, even our view can be sinful. How we respond in our anger is of utmost importance to God. It is possible to navigate great hurt and great wrong without entering into great sin. These stages of anger can last a day or even decades. Just remember, anger is designed to be a pit stop along life's way, not a destination where we unpack our bags and set up camp. Just how much of our journey through life this anger has permission to consume is entirely up to us.

WHEN YOU ARE ANGRY AT YOUR SPOUSE

Love and uncontrolled anger cannot peacefully coexist. Love and unprocessed anger cannot peacefully coexist either. Here are some steps to follow when you are angry at your spouse. Remember, before we begin, are your lenses clear? Are you perceiving your mate's actions accurately? Have you communicated with them your expectations? Are they the one with whom you are really angry? Or is it someone or something else? The answers to these questions are key to how you proceed.

Step one in handling anger in a marriage is to declare that you are angry. Stop sweeping the anger under the spiritual rug. Stop hiding behind your personality and following the lack of anger-management habits of your personality or upbringing. Admit you are angry and then analyze if it is real or perceived anger.

Step two is to decide to talk about it in a healthy and productive manner. Communication is key to resolving marital anger. Your spouse must know about your anger if the problem is ever going to be fixed. The silent treatment is no treatment at all. In fact, it is sin, if you want to be honest about it. The Bible doesn't say if a brother offends you, stop talking to them, give them the cold shoulder, and make them squirm. Half of communication is the receiving or the listening to what is being communicated. This means the way you communicate and the how of your communication is of utmost importance. To learn more about this, read *The Marriage Ring*, written by my husband and me. This book is available at www.pbckannapolis.org and contains entire chapters devoted to this topic.

Step three is to define what is acceptable when you express your anger. There must be a mutual understanding of what is acceptable when arguing. When disagreements happen in a marriage, and they will, there must be some 'fight rules' clearly laid out. Once again, these are explained at length in *The Marriage Ring*.

Step four is to discover the details before you jump to conclusions. Listen, listen, listen, and then listen some more. Force yourself to see things from the other person's perspective. They have one and it is a valid perspective.

Step five is to determine to resolve the conflict instead of winning an argument. When someone 'wins,' the other one 'loses.' And the marriage will be the ultimate loser in the end.

Step six is to display grace as you say something positive about your spouse, not just focus on the negative. Pepper your confrontation with kindness and sweetness.

SOMETHING TO TRY

Write on the front of an index card the following:

> *I am angry about something and I need your help talking it out. Don't worry, I will not attack you. Is now a good time to talk?*

This is called a conflict card, as described by Gary Chapman. Place this card in a place, like the kitchen drawer or a desk drawer. Before you pick it up and approach your spouse, you will need to have prayed and journaled and sought out the true source of your anger. Do not pick up the card if you are out of control or feel as if you will lose your cool.

After reading your side of the card, hand your spouse the card so they can look at the back. On the back have these steps written out:

1. *Listen to my spouse without interrupting.*

2. *Listen again as I ask them to repeat what they just said.*

3. *Listen one more time as I ask them any questions I may have.*

4. *Walk over to their side and look at what I did or said, or what I didn't do or say, from their point of view.*

5. *Express understanding of their anger, hurt, or disappointment.*

6. *Share any information that they may not know in order to clear up the situation. *Do not do this before steps 1–5 are completed.*

7. *Confess and apologize for any wrong doing that I am responsible for.*

8. *Walk away from the conflict and do not bring it up again.*

This approach also works great with children. You may wish to write one in words that they can grasp and have it in the drawer alongside the one for you and your spouse. I know this may seem a little childish for you and your spouse, but it works. Eventually, you will no longer need the card, as the proper way to handle a conflict will have been ingrained in you. And think, you will have modeled a wonderful way to process anger to your children! If angry outbursts or silent seething is an issue in your marriage, this is a must try.

FINAL THOUGHTS

Proverbs 14:29 says, "He that is slow to wrath is of great understanding, but he that is hasty of spirit exalteth folly." I hope this chapter has helped to slow down your wrath and enabled and equipped you to be the person described in Proverbs 16:32: "He that is slow to anger is better than the mighty; and he that ruleth his spirit than he that taketh a city." Understanding and disarming our anger is one of the most empowering things we can ever do. The emotion of anger is the most powerful emotion we will experience. Learning the power over it truly makes us mighty through Christ.

In learning to process our anger properly we can finally "Let all bitterness and anger, and clamor, and evil speaking be put away from you, with all malice" (Ephesians 4:31).

Now, it is your turn. It is time to put into practice all you have learned in this chapter. This "Making It Personal" will take quite a bit longer than the others in this book. Take the time. These exercises are what will slow down your wrath and cause you to be mighty as you properly process your anger so that you can finally put away your anger.

Making It Personal

Answer the following questions in your journal:

1. How have you typically processed anger in the past? Do you blow up or clam up?

2. Are you carrying around a softball, a kickball, or an exercise ball of anger right now?

3. What, or who, is making you angry?

4. According to what you have learned in this chapter, how do you need to proceed?

5. Choose one, or more, of the following in order to process your anger:

   *Delete the anger exercise.

   *Write out your own 'head to toe' prayers about your anger and daily pray them.

   *Write out anger goals, along with the steps it will take each day, to reach them. Each evening, journal how you did and give yourself a daily grade.

   *Copy down and follow the five steps of processing anger by Gary Chapman.

   *Begin journaling how you have fallen into the view, stew, brew, and spew cycle in the past. Be on the lookout for how you are currently exhibiting these stages and journal through it.

*Try the conflict card with your spouse or children.

6. Write out the one or ones you have chosen and then get to work on it in your own journal or notebook.

7. Write out a prayer from your heart concerning your anger.

CHAPTER FIVE

Rejection

Rejection – "the dismissing or refusing of a proposal or idea. The spurning of a person's affections"

I t happened many years ago, but I remember it like it was yesterday. I had been dating the perfect guy, who I was convinced was my Mr. Right. You see, I had graduated from a large Christian university, and my plan had been to find my Mr. Right there and marry, like my sisters had done. It had only taken them a year to do so, but all I ended up with was a degree. Although I appreciated my degree, I really would rather have had that coveted MRS degree, all things considered. After graduation, I returned home not sure of where I fit or who I was. My tiny church boasted no singles program, and I taught in a Christian school with no options anywhere of that good-looking single guy that I had been dreaming of. Then, out of nowhere, he appeared as if by magic. In he walked to my tiny little church one Sunday night. It was like a scene in the movies. Honestly, girls, a spotlight shone behind him and a chorus of angels began singing in the background. Time stopped and we were the only two people in the room. My stomach dropped almost as much as my jaw. Man, oh man, was he cute! And bonus, he had a flashy sports car to boot, not those ridiculous 4 × 4 trucks the local rednecks drove around. Did I mention that he was also a Christian university graduate who had a great job, with goals and aspirations *that made all those small-town boys appear very small-town indeed? This was it! What I had been longing for had finally fallen into my lap! My family loved him. His family loved me. I found myself grinning like a fool and walking around on cloud nine. So, this was love. This was my dream come true. We settled into a relationship soon after that Sunday night introduction, and my destiny unfolded before me. In my mind I could foresee him climbing up that corporate ladder, and my future held a beautiful home and two perfect kids that I would chauffeur around to the soccer games and ballet recitals. Seriously, that was what I had in my head. As a result, I relaxed. I exhaled. The waiting had been worth it. God had my miracle walk right into that little church in the middle of nowhere, and I felt like the country mouse dating the city mouse. He was perfect. Until he wasn't. There were warning bells, faint at first, then louder as we went along our way. Those goals and dreams he had were his gods, I discovered, and that sports car would never be traded in for a more practical minivan one day. In hindsight, I see I was blinded by how lucky I felt to have caught such a big fish in such a small pond. So, I did what every other girl on the planet has done at one point or another—I made excuses for those aggravating little warning bells. I turned a blind eye to what was becoming glaringly obvious. Then came the day when I went to spend a weekend with his family. The warning bells turned into full-blown fire truck sirens. His mother was going to be a rather large and a rather overbearing fly in the ointment of our perfect happily ever after. But he was so perfect, I reasoned. What with that charming smile that made me go weak in the knees and that oh so perfect hair! Surely, his mother wouldn't be that bad, would she? I could fix that mama's boy I saw when he was around her, couldn't I? And we could move really far away from that controlling mama I had caught a glimpse of, couldn't we? Time marched on and soon there was no Amy left. I morphed into what I felt this perfect guy wanted. I completely lost myself in the new of this relationship. I found myself desperate to please him and was consumed with the fear of losing him. Then, my worst fear happened. It was a Sunday night, on my doorstep. I had gone out of town for the weekend with some friends and had been miserable the whole time. I talked about him nonstop and hoped he was as lonely and lovesick as I was. It was torture being separated from the one who gave you the only reason for living. In reality, my poor friends were the only other ones miserable that weekend, and they must have been glad to be rid of me by that fateful Sunday night. Sure enough, he came over as soon as I called him, but not for the reason I was hoping for. I smiled when I heard his flashy little car in my driveway. So, he did miss me! Boy, was I wrong! His weekend, unlike mine, had been wonderful, as he had been a carefree bachelor with no clingy or needy girlfriend to tie him down. He dropped me like a hot potato without a warning. Country mouse, it seemed, no longer amused city mouse. And country mouse was completely devastated. The tears of disbelief, shock, and embarrassment coursed down my cheeks for weeks after that fateful night. I had never been dumped before and felt the strong need to apologize to each and every boyfriend that I had put through this. Rejection is an incredibly painful thing. Not only did he walk out of my life but so did all my carefully constructed plans and dreams. That, I think, was even more painful than seeing him walk away. Because my newfound normal and my new identity walked out that door with him. The pain of his rejection took my breath away. It felt like a knife had literally pierced my heart and it would never ever be the same again.*

THANKS, BUT NO THANKS

Rejection. We will all deal with it at some point. Some cases may be slight and some much more destructive and devastating, but all rejections—large or small—hurt. We have many avenues in which we can encounter rejection, such as relationships with husbands, boyfriends, friends, parents, children, coworkers, bosses, and even within the church walls. Rejection comes in the form of betrayal, abandonment, or even a simple "we didn't feel you were the right candidate for the job" email. The thing that makes rejection so awful is that someone looked at you and said, "Thanks, but no thanks." And that stinks. Sometimes the rejection that we deal with isn't even real; it is the fear of rejection, or even perceived rejection, that casts a deep, dark shadow in our lives and our relationships. According to counselors and therapists, rejection is one of the most painful experiences in the human existence. In fact, when MRI scans were done on patients who were asked to recount rejections in their lives, the same neural pathways lit up as when patients actually experienced physical pain. This has led doctors to believe that rejection can actually cause physical trauma and pain. Therefore, as Christians, we need to pull it out of the closet and deal with it. Rejection, and the pain it causes, is a very real thing. That's what this chapter is all about.

I am absolutely positive that if I gave you the space, each person reading this book could fill that space with a painful rejection story from your past. Chances are, you have never dealt with the emotional fallout of that painful rejection properly. In fact, you probably felt like that terrible moment was yesterday when you thought about it just now. You may have been able to recall even the smallest detail, such as the outfit you were wearing or a particular sight, sound, or smell from that moment of intense pain. If the truth were told, you could close your eyes and be right back to that time and that place of intense pain in your life. Am I right? So, what makes rejection so incredibly painful?

There are several answers to that question. First of all, rejection gives voice to our worst fears. What you were so afraid would happen, did. Secondly, it validates what you have been saying in your head all along. Statements such as "I am worthless, unimportant, unlovely, unlovable, and not good enough" were given credibility by a person you trusted. You were afraid that these feelings were true and that person just proved it when they treated you badly. What they said was nothing new—you had been saying it to yourself for a long time. It is just extremely disturbing to hear it from a voice other than your own. Thirdly, rejection hits a tender spot. Imagine you have a bad bruise on your leg and you bang that exact spot against the coffee table. It hurts more due to the fact that the spot has already been injured. That is exactly what rejection does. It finds a bruised spot and hones in on it.

TYPES OF REJECTION

There are two main types of rejection. The first one is real rejection. This is a real event of rejection happening in your life. The husband does, in fact, walk out the door. The boss actually chooses the coworker over you for the promotion. The best friend does drop you like a hot potato. The father really does walk away from his daughter. This very real rejection brings much devastation and fallout along with it. The second type of rejection is perceived rejection. This type is much more difficult and complicated to explain. Perceived rejection is based on deep-seated fears, often as a result of a real rejection in one's past. Imagine, if you will, wearing sunglasses that have red lenses in them. Everything you look at appears red. That isn't the way things really are, but to you, they are as red as red can be. Your perception is distorted. Everyone's actions look red. Their motives are red, their words filtered through red, and their actions are, once again, red. Perceived rejection is fueled by fear of rejection, which is often brought on by a real rejection. See the vicious and very destructive cycle? Many a woman walks around with this very real stronghold in place. And, in most cases, she doesn't even know it. In some instances, the fear of rejection and the resulting perceived rejection will actually lead someone to reject the other person first. They will do this so that they won't be rejected first. This person will do anything to avoid the pain of rejection, even walking away from a loving and healthy relationship. You may actually know a woman like this. She goes through friendship after friendship and relationship after relationship, repeating the same destructive cycle.

How do you know if this is you? To find out, let's ask ourselves some tough questions. Do you play the worst-case scenario in your mind, picturing your husband leaving you, the boyfriend dumping you, or the friend betraying you? Do you distance yourself from others when the relationship gets too close? Do you have walls built around your heart in order to protect yourself from hurt? Do you become overly clingy or needy in relationship after relationship? The sad thing is, each of us could probably answer yes to at least one of those questions to some degree or another.

All of this could be avoided if we would only unpack the baggage rejection dumps on our doorstep, in a healthy and godly way. Unfortunately, most women stuff it down and pretend like it isn't there, and meanwhile the baggage gets bigger and heavier by the day.

Many women deal with something called self-rejection. This comes from a form of self-hate and results in an almost constant stream of negative self-talk that plays in the woman's mind over and over and over again. It is based on how she views herself. This kind of negativity paints those lenses a darker shade of red. Her negative self-perception is what she assigns to everyone else in her life. The way she sees herself is how she thinks everyone else sees her too. What is so sad is that this isn't truth. It is all based upon lies from Satan. This kind of thinking is often hidden, like a slow leak behind a wall or under the floor. It goes unnoticed, but over time, extensive damage is done.

Let's unpack the fear of rejection a little further. There are two main avenues the fear of rejection travels down. The first one is the fear of abandonment. This one is pretty obvious. The fear of being alone, left behind, or tossed aside runs deep in all of us. This is particularly painful when another person is chosen instead of you, as in the case of an affair. The second one is not as obvious. It is the fear of losing your identity. When researching this, I admit, I didn't get this one until I studied it out further. But I have found that it really does make sense. As women, we identify with our role. We are mother, wife, daughter, or girlfriend. Remember how I morphed into who I thought my boyfriend wanted me to be? I did so, in order to keep him. To lose the identity as his girlfriend meant more to me than actually losing him as a person. Upon looking back at that doomed relationship, I see that I didn't really love him so much as I loved the *idea* of him, the security of having him, and the enjoyment of the role of girlfriend. When a breakup or divorce happens, the role of girlfriend or wife is taken away forcefully. We no longer know who we are. We tend to lose ourselves in relationships, and the thought of that role no longer defining us is terrifying.

When the husband leaves, he takes with him our role and our identity as wife. When the child turns their back, they take with them our role as mother. When the boyfriend chooses another, he destroys our identity as girlfriend. When s father walks out, he takes our identity as a cherished daughter with him. In every case, we are left alone, worthless, useless, and a faceless nobody.

When we attach our identity to someone else, our insecurity finds a breeding ground in which to grow, just like a virus in a Petri dish or mold in a damp basement. If our definer (the other person in the relationship) is removed, then we feel our value, our validation, our very reason for being is removed as well. It is becoming increasingly obvious that we desperately need to unpack all this baggage that gets dumped on our doorstep when rejection rings our doorbell. In order to do so properly, we have to have an absolute, an unchanging truth to go by. This must be Scripture. Not another person. Not our feelings. Not circumstances. The fact of who we are, our worth, our value, and our validation must be found within in the pages of God's Word. What does He say about us? Who does He say we are? Those truths remain constant, steady, and sure no matter what our circumstances may be. So, for the remainder of this chapter, we will focus heavily on Scripture to define us in the light of truth. We will also listen to the voice of God in our rejections and see how God can weave them into the tapestry of our lives and somehow create beauty out of them, as only He can.

Always remember: The person that rejected you is not your definer; they are a defector. The only person who can be your definer is your Designer.

According to Scripture:

1. I am His child (John 1:12).

2. I am His friend (John 15:15).

3. I am justified and redeemed (Romans 3:24).

4. I am free (Romans 6:6).

5. I am accepted (Ephesians 1:6).

6. I am forgiven (Psalm 103:12).

7. I am clean (John 15:3).

8. I can do what I need to do (Philippians 4:13).

9. I am safe (Psalm 59:16).

10. I am loved (Romans 8:38–39).

11. I am complete (Colossians 2:10).

12. I am worth much (Psalm 139:14–16).

13. I am royalty (John 1:12).

14. I am blessed (Psalm 34:8).

These are FACTS and must be taken as such. They cannot be based upon feeling or circumstances. They are constant, steady, and sure. These facts must never be tied to how someone else treats us. They are based upon truth and upon Christ. This means they will not come and go or change when someone else begins to treat us badly.

Not only do I need to be secure in who I am but I must also be sure about who God is. According to Scripture, God is:

1. All powerful (Jeremiah 32:17)

2. All knowing (Isaiah 46:9–10)

3. Ever present (Psalm 139:7–10)

4. Faithful (2 Timothy 2:13)

5. Good (Psalm 34:8)

6. Just (Deuteronomy 32:4)

7. Merciful and compassionate (Romans 9:15–16)

8. Love (1 John 4:8–10)

9. Holy (Revelation 4:8b)

10. Worthy (Revelation 4:11).

REALITY CHECK

So, let's imagine we have just suffered a painful rejection. We feel worthless and like no one loves us or cares about us. If we take some time to unpack each of those feelings and hold them up to the truth of God's word, then we will see them for what they really are—lies from Satan. We are hurt but not hopeless. We are in pain but not destroyed. We are suffering but not forgotten. The truth is God loves us, we are worth much in His sight, and we are never ever alone. These truths will help us to weather many a painful rejection and come out on the other side a stronger and wiser woman.

Here's a passage of Scripture to make sure you have packed in that baggage rejection drops at your door: "But we have this treasure in earthen vessels, that the excellency of the power may be of God, and not of us. We are troubled on every side, yet not distressed; we are perplexed, but not in despair; persecuted, but not forsaken; cast down, but not destroyed" (2 Corinthians 4:8–9). Hallelujah! Did you see that? That suitcase may hold trouble, but distress isn't allowed in there. You may be perplexed and surrounded with unanswered questions, but despair can't have you. You may find persecution among the articles of that baggage, but never ever will you find forsakenness! You may be down, but girls, you are not destroyed!

According to these verses, God's people will encounter trouble, persecution, unanswered questions, and being tossed aside. We are living among sinful, selfish, and fallen people who will treat us accordingly. Expect it. But don't let it have the power to destroy you. That's not truth. It doesn't have permission from your Heavenly Father to destroy you. You may need to look in the mirror and say those verses over and over again. I have learned in my deepest heartaches that my prayer time tends to sound more like war cries than requests. I have shouted to the heavens with tears streaming down my face, "God, You are good! You have not made a mistake and You have not forsaken me!" During painful and devastating times of rejection, you will need to grit your teeth, pick yourself up by your faith straps, and declare truth. Rejection will either bring you to a place of lies or truth. The choice is yours. You may not have had the power to choose in this rejection, but you do have the power to choose what to do with that rejection.

Ephesians 4:19 says, "And to know the love of Christ, which passeth knowledge, that ye might be filled with all the fulness of God." Girls, are we full? Are we really? Or are we so empty of love that we run from person to person with our cup saying, "Can you fill me up, please?" And when they fail, we run to another and another and another. Fullness can come only from the love of Christ. I am reminded of the woman at the well. She had tried one relationship after another. She had been married five times and was currently living with a man when she came across Christ at the well. Rejection was her mantra. She had tried it all. But when she met Jesus, the Bible says she left her water pot and went into town to tell the men all about Him. She left her water pot. Why? It was filled! She no longer needed to keep searching. Leaving that water pot was a symbolic picture of her no longer searching to be filled from anyone other than Christ. It is also important to note that she went and told the very men she had gone to for her filling. She needed to show them where they could find their filling. She finally saw them as broken. She saw them for what they were—needy individuals who were imperfect humans and had no power to fill her. What a picture! Girls, it is time we put down our water pots at His feet, for He alone can fill us. That person who hurt you doesn't have permission to destroy you, or complete you, for that matter. That best friend can neither fill you nor empty you. What a difference this realization would make when we encounter rejections in this life. Yes, they will still hurt, but those rejections would just be a temporary casting down, instead of a permanent destruction.

Now, before we end this chapter, I want to include a list of what I call Rejection Rules. These rules are truths that we can take with us on this journey called life. Our journey is going to be filled with interactions with sinful people who will do sinful things. This means life will be ripe with rejection opportunities. If we have these rules firmly in place, we should be able to handle these rejections with far more grace than if we do not.

REJECTION RULES

1. Present rejection does not equal future rejection.

2. Rejection doesn't label me. It can actually enable me!

3. My current 'no' can lead to an even greater 'yes.'

4. Instead of looking at this rejection as harming me, it may be arming me for something I cannot yet see.

5. Instead of asking 'Why?' I will ask 'What?' What do you want me to learn from this, Lord?

6. I will not react to my rejection. I will prayerfully respond instead.

7. Rejection doesn't define me. Rejection is meant to refine me.

8. Rejection is a temporary stop at that nasty gas station bathroom. It is not your final destination.

9. Rejection doesn't have to be all destructive. It can be constructive, if I let it.

10. Rejection, like everything in my life, will be what I make it.

PRAYER

God, please help me as I navigate through this painful time of rejection. I know You were rejected by Your family, Your friends, those You loved so much, and even those You were so desperately trying to help. You are rejected every time a sinner refuses to call out to You for salvation. You understand exactly how I feel. Your rejection doesn't mean You are worthless and neither does mine. You love me and that is enough. Thank you that You will never ever leave me or forsake me. I choose You today. I put my water pot down at Your feet. You alone can fill me. Thank You for being my safe place.

Making It Personal

Answer the following questions in your journal:

1. Write out a rejection from your past.

2. What can I learn or what have I learned from this past rejection?

3. How did I contribute to the breakdown in the relationship?

4. What adjustments do I need to make in my current or future relationships based upon the mistakes I made in the past?

5. What lies did I unpack from my rejection baggage while reading this chapter?

6. What truths do I need to believe in order to replace the lies in that baggage?

7. What rejection rules do I need to incorporate in my present situation?

8. Write out the emotions this rejection made you feel and then the declarations of truth you choose to believe instead. An example has been done for you.

Emotion	Declaration
No one loves me.	God always has and always will love me.

CHAPTER SIX

Fear and Anxiety

Fear – "an unpleasant emotion caused by the belief that someone or something is dangerous, likely to cause pain, or a threat"

Anxiety – "a feeling of worry, nervousness, or unease, typically about an imminent event or something with an uncertain outcome"

Way back, a long time ago, when I was a little girl, I delighted in going to my grandmother's house for a Friday night sleepover. She would make me some of her famous chicken and dumplings for supper, and there were always buckwheat pancakes for breakfast. On those Friday nights, I loved to snuggle down in that freezing cold room under a stack of quilts so heavy it was difficult to roll over. But there was one thing about those Friday night sleepovers at my grandmother's house I didn't like. She did not have a nightlight. And trust me when I say that room was dark. Pitch black to be exact. So little eight-year-old Amy would lie there and imagine some pretty scary things in that cold dark room. Finally, when I couldn't stand it any longer, I would struggle to get out from under all those heavy quilts and slip out into that freezing cold room. Ever so slowly I would feel my way across the room until I came to the light switch in the hallway. I would then flip on the hall light so that I could have just a little crack of that comforting light to pierce through the darkness. Quick as a wink, I would jump back into that warm bed after carefully cracking the door just so. A contented sigh could be heard as all was right in my eight-year-old world. Then, it would happen. My grandmother would get up and turn off that hall light. Once again, I would be plunged into darkness. Drat! After what seemed like an eternity, waiting for her to finally fall asleep, I would sneak out and flip on that switch once again. Victory was mine! I was sure of it. She just had to be asleep by now. Then, just before I could fall asleep, my grandmother would flip off the switch again. Double drat! This battle of the wills, or really battle of the fears, would go on for hours every Friday night. And you know what? She always won. Not once did I ever fall asleep with the hall light on. You see, we were two scared little peas in a pod. I found out later that my grandmother had a deep fear of the house catching on fire, so to leave a light on was just tempting her worst fear to happen. She would check, double-check, and triple-check to see if the stove was off. She would then move on to the appliances and would make the rounds double-checking to make sure that each and every one was unplugged. The plug would have its own little ashtray to lie in so it didn't touch the carpet. And the heat had to be completely off, no matter how cold it was outside. Here I was longing for a little light to give me some relief from the darkness when she was longing for the darkness to keep her safe from the threat the light represented. You see, what I looked at as scary, she looked at as safe, and what she looked at as threatening was what I looked to for comfort. Fear is most definitely in the eye of the beholder. When talking about fear, perception is everything.

We all face fear. We all feel it, walk through it, and even dread it. But some of us are more prone to feel it more often and more deeply than others. The world is a scary place and filled with scary possibilities. How can we filter out the fear? The answer to that question is to have faith. Faith and fear cannot coexist. When one is in control the other flees. The antidote for recurring fear is recurring trust. Psalm 47:7–8 says, "For God is the King of all the earth: sing ye praises with understanding. God reigneth over the heathen: God sitteth upon the throne of his holiness." And there it is. The answer to all our deep, dark fears. God reigns. God is in control. God is over it all and He is still on the throne. In other words, God is good at being God. God is sovereign. God has a plan and He has not been caught off guard in your situation.

Psalm 139:7–12 says, "Whither shall I go from thy spirit? Or whither shall I flee from thy presence? If I ascend up into heaven, thou art there; if I make my bed in hell, behold, thou art there; if I take the wings of the morning, and dwell in the uttermost parts of the sea, Even there shall thy hand lead me, and thy right hand shall hold me." This is a promise that God will be with us *even there*. No matter where life takes you, God is with you. You will never ever be alone. Even in a cancer treatment center. Even in a nursing home admitting office, even in a divorce court, even in a drug rehab facility, and even when walking into a funeral home to plan the funeral of your loved one. God is with you even there. The same God who reigns over it all and holds it all in His hands, holds your hand and walks beside you down the dark and winding path when you cannot see what's around the bend. Trusting in this truth will go a long way in quelling our fears along life's way.

Romans 8:38–39 says, "For I am persuaded, that neither death, nor life, nor angels, nor principalities, nor powers, nor things present, nor things to come, nor height, nor depth, nor any other creature, shall be able to separate us from the love of God, which is in Christ Jesus our Lord." Read those verses again because they hold the key that will unlock the door of the assurance we so need in fearful times. There are some things that we can be persuaded about. When life is full of question marks, there are a few exclamation points I can bank on. This is one of them. I am loved! Nothing can separate me from the love of God! Even when it is my loved one that has died. Even when our loved one gets a scary diagnosis and we have to travel down a hard road watching them get worse and worse. And even when we hold their hand as they breathe their last breath. Not even death can separate me from the love of God. Life and all that it will bring—the disappointments, frustrations, blow-ups, and messy situations—can't separate me from the love of God either. Angels? (Even the scary ones that do Satan's work.) They cannot separate me from the love of God either. Principalities and powers cannot drive a wedge between us either, no matter what position they hold. How about the nasty now and now or the scary unknown? Can they separate me from the love of God? The answer is a resounding 'no.' Think about this for a moment. There is no unknown to God. God doesn't have anything that He doesn't foresee or foreknow. That is an amazing and a very calming thought. The reason we can count on this constant and unfailing love in a very changing and sinful world is that this love 'is in Christ Jesus our Lord.' It isn't in us, our achievements, our perfection, our works, or our approval and acceptance from others. Grabbing onto this truth will help us to cope with all the changes, hardships, and the failures of other people in our lives.

THE GRAPES OF FEAR

On those Friday night sleepovers at my grandmother's house, I loved to play with a decoration she had on her coffee table. She had a set of those old-fashioned scales that would dip down on one side if it was heavier or hover up higher if that side was lighter. I absolutely loved that thing. My grandmother kept artificial grapes on both sides of that scale. My pastime was to go around the house and compare the weights of different objects I could find. I would guess which would be heavier and then place the items on the scale to see what the result would be. Another thing I loved to do was to pull the grapes off their plastic clusters and see how many grapes it would take to make the other cluster heavier or lighter. I would sneak and pull them off and then plink! I would drop it down on the scale and wait to see what would happen because of my action.

I kind of picture our fears this way. Imagine a scale in front of you and on the table below it are two piles of artificial grapes. One pile represents our faith and the other our fear. Imagine placing a fear grape on the scale, causing it to dip down lower. Plink! Now, we have a choice. Do we pile more and more fear on that side, or do we deliberately choose to plink down a faith grape on the other side in order to balance it out? That decision is made by us a million times a day. In fact, if you listen closely enough, you may hear 'plink, plink, plink!' as you go about your day. When we indulge in the 'what ifs' or the many worst-case-scenario thoughts, we are adding grapes to our fear scale. When we wring our hands or get our hands overly involved trying to fix, manipulate, or control the outcome, we have added to the fear side. When we mull over the scary thoughts, rehearsing them over and over again, another fear grape gets plinked down on the scale. But there is another choice we can make. We can choose faith as we study Scripture, memorize verses, pray big prayers, and go throughout your day listening to podcasts and messages. We can choose to do a Bible study on a needed topic, digging deeper into the Word. We can determine to be faithful with our daily quiet time. We can choose to listen to godly music throughout the day, being careful to keep our thoughts and conversations centered on praise and thanksgiving. All of these actions and choices are effectively adding grapes to the faith side of the scale. If we could actually see our faith vs fear scale, what would yours look like? Are your thoughts and actions, along with your words and behaviors, feeding the faith side or the fear side? Think back to your day yesterday. What did you do to add grapes of fear or grapes of faith to your scale? What can you do today to make sure you add more to the faith side so that it outweighs the fear that is threatening you?

KEY TRUTHS IN OVERCOMING FEAR

In order to add some hefty weight to our faith side, we are going to have to have a firm grasp on some key truths. First of all, we have to have a firm grasp on the *identity of God.* Many Christians worship an idea of God. They feel He is more of a cosmic genie in a bottle or a Santa Clause–type god. The fact is, those ideas are false and are not supported by Scripture at all. These ideas will lead to disappointment and disillusionment when things go wrong and He doesn't bail you out of your trouble. Other Christians have a very small view of God. One where He is uninvolved or simply cannot do very much at all. This type of thinking will obviously lead us down a path of fear. Still others view God as uncaring and unloving. They choose to look at God as an angry 'man upstairs' who is holding a cane, ready to bop his misbehaving children on the head when they step out of line. Once again, fear will be the destination due to this type of distorted view of God. The truth is, not one of these perceptions of God is an accurate one.

One way to combat the trap of falsely perceiving God is to be so acquainted with the reality of His identity that the falsehoods pedaled by Satan and society will stand out easily. Spend some time studying the names of God. His names reveal His identity. Something I do every day to begin my prayer time is to praise God for two or three of His attributes or characteristics. I have a list of these in alphabetical order in my prayer journal. I also have a list of His names written down. You can easily pull these up on the internet and print off a list. I begin my prayer time praising Him for who He is and thanking Him for being that attribute. When I have a need, I call on that name in prayer. For example, when I have a need that only He can provide, I cry out to Jehovah Jireh, which means 'The God Who Provides.' Do you see how that would help you to get to know the REAL God of the scriptures? Realizing who God really is will help you to see Him as all powerful, ever present, and all knowing. This will go a long way in fighting your fears effectively.

The next thing we have to have nailed down is the *ability of God*. Studying the miracles of God, the amazing ways He fought battles for His children, and the way He empowered His children, or answered prayers, will fill your arsenal when fear comes calling. Realizing that your issue or situation is well within His ability to take care of will make your fear seem small as your faith is settled. The *reality* that 'God can' will soothe and calm us even when the situation we are facing doesn't change. Trusting in His person, as discussed earlier, helps us to reconcile this when God doesn't fix the issue right away. Understanding that He *is* love and that He *cannot* not love helps me know that when He doesn't answer a prayer the way I want, there is a reason behind that 'no.' This answer comes out of His love for me. There is a reason I don't see, and a fact I do not know. Yes, God is all powerful, but God is love and He is right and He is faithful too. Many Christians think of God's power as a blank check for them to get everything they want. This simply isn't true. God's power is something He will use when He chooses to do so. His choice to do so, or not, will never be wrong. Once again, this goes back to His identity. The older I get, the more I realize that this realization is absolutely vital to our Christian walk. Everything goes back to having that firmly nailed down. When faced with a scary situation, travel through Scripture with His children who faced scary situations of their own. Join Jochebed at the banks of the Nile. Walk with Gideon as he faced a massive army with only three hundred men. Climb in the wagon with Deborah and Barak as they rode toward the battle. Kneel down with David as he stooped to pick up those five smooth stones. Immerse yourself in the stories of God's amazing power. Be filled with wonder at the wonders He has done and watch your fear get smaller and smaller.

The third fact that we have to have nailed down is the *authority of God*. In other words, we not only have to know who God is and what God can do, we also need to be aware of His right to do whatever He chooses to do. God is God of all. God is over all. And God is right in it all. This one is harder than the other two. Why? Because nailing this one down means we have to realize that God has the right to tell me 'no' and still be right. Ouch! No wonder this one is harder!

Here's how this works in real life. Let's say that your loved one begins having some very scary symptoms and tests have to be run. Fear threatens to choke the life out of you. You have more questions than you have answers. You are googling every possibility, and you are becoming consumed with dread. How can these three facts help you as you are drowning in fear? You decide to look in the mirror and declare, "I will trust in the PERSON of God." This is realizing God is still good even if your loved one has cancer. Then you declare, "I will trust in the POWER of God." This is realizing that God is bigger than a diagnosis and that He is the one that decides what happens in the life of your loved one. Finally, you look in that same mirror and declare, "I will trust in the PREEMINENCE of God." This is realizing that no matter the result of those tests and no matter what happens in the end, God is right and He has the right to walk you and your loved one down whatever road He chooses. That is easy typing but very hard living. Nailing this down is the difference between being consumed with fear and just experiencing fear.

POWERFUL PEACE

Have you ever wondered where your peace went? Boy, I sure have! I mean, where is this peace that surpasses understanding when I am pacing the floor, wringing my hands, or tossing and turning long into the night? Did God promise something that doesn't exist? Was He just taunting us or dangling the proverbial carrot in front of our noses that He knew we could never reach? In order to answer those questions, we need to dive into Philippians 4:6–8. Take a moment and read those verses. In order to get to that promised peace, we have to do something. We have to be careful for nothing. That word 'careful' means "to be anxious about." God is telling us not to be anxious about anything. How on earth can we do that in a world full of change, chaos, criminals, and cancer? The next line tells us exactly how. "… but in everything by prayer and supplication with thanksgiving let your requests be made known unto God." That 'but' shows us it is a trade-off. It isn't wrong to experience anxiousness, but it is our choice what to do with it. When anxiety creeps in, and it will, we can choose prayer. And not just any prayer. This prayer needs to be peppered with honesty, relinquishing, and plenty of praise and thanksgiving. Most of us have a harder time with those last ingredients when fear looms large. The last thing we want to do is praise when panic grips us. But that praise is key. It is absolutely vital to receiving that powerful peace that is promised. Praise Him for those three facts we just talked about. His identity, His ability, and His authority. Lay out your honest requests and spill out your fears, then praise, praise, praise. Thank Him despite the scary situation. Sing to Him. Quote Scripture about Him. Then He will give that peace. That's a promise that you can take to the bank. He might not give an answer yet, but He will give peace in the meantime. (And, boy, isn't the meantime mean?)

Now, in order to keep that peace, Verse 8 has to happen, and we have talked about it already. Making sure your thoughts stay in that circle of obedience will be of paramount importance. If you do not filter your thoughts through the true, honest, just, pure, lovely, good report, virtue, and praise stipulations, then you can kiss your peace bye-bye. Our peace doesn't just 'wear off'; it usually is worn out by the disobedient thoughts. Those thoughts chip away at that heavenly peace a bit at a time until it is gone.

Our thoughts are kind of like shopping at Walmart. When you are there, you pass a lot of aisles and shelves. But you get to choose what you pick out and put in your cart. You cannot help what you pass along the way in aisle 3, but you don't have to put all the items in aisle 3 in your cart! You may have to walk down that aisle and see those needed items, but all those other items need your cooperation and permission to get inside your cart. In life, there are a vast array of thoughts on the shelves of our minds and situations. There are all kinds of prepackaged thoughts that wear labels like: guilt, regret, worst-case scenarios, control, manipulation, bitterness, what if, if only, why can't, how could, where's God, and what about me. There are boxes upon boxes of thoughts filled with insecurity, fear, hate, blame, comparison, competition, and scorekeeping, all calling your name as you wheel your cart down the aisle. These thoughts are brightly packaged and appealing to the eye. They are right in the middle of the shelves and very easily accessible. Why, all you have to do is reach out and take them. But then you notice that up, higher on the shelves are thoughts filled with praise. You have to reach your hands up for those. They aren't packaged for attention; in fact, they are rather plain looking. They do not call attention to themselves. But as you reach upward, you notice you must look upward and put forth more effort in order to attain those items. That seems fitting for praise, doesn't it? Then you happen to notice that on the bottom shelf are rows and rows of thanksgiving thoughts. No, not turkey and dressing but grateful thoughts. And in order to get those, you must bow down low. But my oh my, are they the ones to take home with us!

So, what has been in your thought cart lately? Do you need to do a different type of thought shopping than you have been recently? If you want to defeat the foe of fear, this will be a must.

WHICH PATH WILL WE TAKE?

We get to choose the path our mind will wander down. Picture yourself standing at a crossroads in the woods. Down one path there is a sign that reads, "Fear." The path is dark and lined with gnarled trees, some leaning precariously to one side, as if they could fall over at any moment. The limbs tear at your clothes and hair as you walk down that path. Briars grab at your feet and legs painfully as you try to cover some ground. Roots cause you to trip and fall, bringing injury along your way. Now, you find yourself limping along, wondering why it is so hard on this path God put you on. The only problem with that line of thinking is that wasn't the path He chose for you. There was another one labeled 'Faith' that you could have gone down. It too was lined with trees. It was still dark and the path still winding, but the trees were so different. Towering oaks represented the strength of God, beautiful maples that offered shade and a cool place to bring your burdens and find rest, and billowing willows bowed low in reverent worship of their Maker. Majestic evergreens lined the path and revealed the sufficiency of God even in the cold, harsh seasons that we go through. These evergreens also teach that there is beauty to be found even in the ugly seasons of life. What a difference taking the path of faith would have made in your situation! Before you take another step along the path you are on, make sure it is the path marked 'faith.'

YOU STEER WHERE YOU STARE

At the time of this writing, my oldest daughter, Sarah, is learning to drive. I have had many a close call with a mailbox of late. She tends to hug the white line and keeps her mother on praying ground! On several occasions, I have had to warn her of the truth: you steer where you stare. Notice it the next time you are in the car. If your gaze goes to the left, your car will eventually head in that direction. So it is, with fear. If we begin to focus on the scary part of our situation, we will head into fear territory.

Some folks in the Bible can attest to this painful truth. Just ask the twelve spies who were assigned the task of heading into Canaan. Ten of them focused on the fearful giants. They measured themselves against the towering men and found themselves too short. But two of them stared at their God and measured the giants against Him instead. They discovered that the giants came up short! This is what gave them the faith to say, "Charge!" when everyone else screamed, "Retreat!" What are we measuring our big, bad, scary fear up against? Are we holding it up to us and finding we come up short or are we holding it up against an immeasurable God instead? If you have been steering into your fears lately, it is because that's where you have been staring. Change your stare and you will change your steer.

TYPES OF FEAR

You may be surprised to know there are several different types of fear in the pages of Scripture. The first type of fear has a flashy new name, FOMO. But, as it turns out, 'fear of missing out' is not a new phenomenon at all, no matter what Webster's says. It is actually the fear that got Eve to take a bite of the forbidden fruit. She was afraid she was missing out on something amazing. God was holding out on her, so she opened her mouth and bit into a world of hurt. And so it goes with us, when we fall into the old FOMO trap. Is God holding out on me? Why doesn't He give me what she has? If only….Why can't I….If I had….The cure for FOMO is GIMP (grateful in my present). I made that one up myself. Exercising gratefulness for what you have, where you are, whom you are with, and what you get to do will be key in defeating the foe of FOMO.

Abram fell prey to the second type of fear. It is the 'what if' fear. This fear made him do an unimaginable thing… twice. He was so afraid of the area kings killing him for his beautiful wife that he asked her to lie for him and claim that she was his sister. Each time, she was forcibly taken and put into a harem. Can you imagine if you and your husband were walking down a dark alley and as some rough men approached you, the love of your life asked you to just let them do whatever they wanted to you so he wouldn't get beaten up? Jaw-dropping, isn't it? Abram. The father of the faith, a patriarch for Pete's sake, just tossed Sarai, his bride, off to the side in order to save his own hide. That's what 'what if' fears will do to us. They make us lose our moral compass, our courage, and our sense of right and wrong. They make us treat others callously, causing much relational damage along the way. What ifs will cause us, like Abram, to throw something precious away. They cause us to stop trusting God and start trusting ourselves. The result, also like Abram, will be a mess. Honestly, I do not think Sarai ever looked at her husband the same again. Something precious died on the altar of the 'what if.' The cure for a bad case of the 'what ifs' is to focus on 'what is' instead. God is what is. His power is what is. His control is what is. His will is what is. His plan is what is. So is His sovereignty, His providence, and His preeminence.

Sarai became entangled with the 'will it ever happen' fear. God had assigned her a task called 'wait.' Don't you hate that assignment? I sure do. It is a particularly harsh season for any person, especially for a controlling and manipulative female. Let's all just go ahead and plead guilty here. She began to stare at her very real circumstances. Menopause. Old age. A barren womb. Empty arms and an empty crib equaled an empty promise in her eyes. This type of fear goes from doubting if the request will be answered to doubting God Himself. Now, in Sarai's defense, her circumstances were very real and very much in her face. She physically could not bear a child. But God. Sarai made a mistake we often do in our waiting times fraught with fear. She discounted God's ability to be God. She took Him and His power out of the equation. Her equation read: empty arms + empty crib = empty promise. So, she set out to right the wrong God had done her. She logically came up with a solution to her problem. Oh girls, we are all guilty of this one! Fear fed her unbelief, which then fueled her actions. The cure for this fear is faith, but not just any faith will do. It will take the 'even when the chips are down' kind of faith. This is the kind of faith that holds steady in the darkest hours before the break of dawn.

Moses displayed the fear of 'I can't'. At the burning bush, God gave him his marching orders. They included facing his fear, his failure, and his foes. Not a fun assignment. Moses had been running and hiding for forty years. That's a long time. Then God said it was time to try again. Moses had tried to help the Israelites all those years earlier and failed. Miserably. Now he was just supposed to march in there and face his demons? His response was the same as ours. 'I am not good enough.' 'I am not able.' 'I am not a good speaker.' 'I am not capable to stand before Pharaoh.' 'I am not brave enough.' 'I am not powerful enough.' God's answer to all of Moses' "I am nots" was simply "I AM." Moses said, "I am scared. I am weak. I am a failure." God said, "I AM not." God's identity was Moses's answer for his identity crisis. When we feel insecure, afraid, less than, and not enough, He is our answer too. He is the vine and we are the branches. When hooked into Him, He flows through us. That vine enables the branch to do what it never could on its own. Whatever it is you are facing and you feel like you can't or you aren't enough, the truth is, you are right. Just like that branch, apart from the vine, cannot bear fruit, you cannot do what it is you are facing alone. But hooked into the Great I AM, nothing is impossible. In Christ, stutterers become orators, feeble failures become fearless, and the weak become warriors. The cure for the 'I can't' fear is to realize you are actually having an identity crisis. You are trying to be the Vine. And, well, you can't. Be a branch. That's the answer. Be a branch that's hooked into the Vine and then you will find an 'I can' in your future. Still don't believe me? Philippians 4:13 proves what I am saying is true. I can through Christ, my Vine. You can, through Christ. Those words, 'through Christ,' make all the difference. If you struggle with 'I can't' insecurity, write the words 'be a branch' on an index card and keep it where you can see it. It will help in the battle against this type of fear. Whatever it is that you are needing, the

Great I AM is it. He 'am' it. No, that is not a typo. 'Am' means the current state of being. When God gave Moses His name at the bush that day, He was thinking ahead in time to each and every child of His who would need God to be and to help them be. He currently is the state of whatever it is you need so desperately. What a God!

A CLEAR VIEW OF FEAR

I think many of us view fear as unfair. We have bought into the lie that if we are saved, we shouldn't have to face fearful things. But nowhere in Scripture does God say life is fair and will be without fear. The fact we need to learn is that fear is a part of the human existence. It will be an ingredient in our lives. So, now what? Now we need to strive to see fear clear. I know that isn't proper grammar, but it is proper theology. Scripture does teach that fearful things have permission to enter into our lives, but they are on a leash. And on the other end of that leash is God. Job's scary time had permission to take his children, his wealth, and his health. But as it strained at the leash and tried to take his life, God held firmly onto the other end. It could not take his life, no matter how hard it tried. There was a limit, a line in the sand, if you will, where God said, "No further."

Daniel had to experience being thrown into the lions' den and sealed in with no way out. Pretty scary, huh? The lions had permission to stalk around him but not to devour. Once again, the line in the sand was drawn. Joseph's life was fraught with fearful moments. God granted permission for a pit and a prison in his life. But he kept him from being killed by his brothers and from rotting away in that prison. That pit and that prison paved the way to the palace. And as for Daniel, he was brought back up to see the light of another day.

David was promised a throne. What he didn't know was that there would be years of running for his life and hiding in caves before he ever sat on it. God allowed javelins to be hurled, but He never allowed them to hit their mark. Girls, what I am trying to say is, whatever it is that you are afraid of only has permission to come so far. There is a line drawn in the sand of your life where God says 'enough.' And when God said, 'enough,' those hateful brothers, horrible diseases, vengeful kings, sharp javelins, and even hungry lions bowed to His command. Your scary thing bows too. No matter what it is. That, my friend, is a very empowering thought. Realizing that hateful people, diseases, prowling devourers, and even death must bow can give you confidence and calm in the middle of chaos.

Making It Personal

Answer the following questions in your journal:

1. Look up the following verses on fear and write out the ones that speak to you and your situation on index cards:

Isaiah 41:10	Philippians 4:6–7	Psalm 56:3
2 Timothy 1:7	Deuteronomy 31:6	Psalm 34:4
Matthew 6:25–34	1 Peter 5:7	1 John 4;18
Isaiah 35:4	John 14:27	Psalm 23:4
Psalm 27:1		

2. Have you been plunking down grapes of fear or faith in your life recently?

3. Describe how having a firm grasp of God's identity, ability, and authority can assist us in the fight with fear.

4. According to Philippians 4:6–8, what key ingredient needs to be in our prayers?

5. Earlier we talked about our 'thought cart.' We get to choose what thoughts we put in that cart. Thoughts of praise, thanksgiving, and worship were among the thoughts we can choose to put in there. Write out several praise, thanksgiving, or worship thoughts that you want to place in that cart.

6. Describe a time when you took the path of fear in your life.

7. Describe a time when you took the path of faith in your life.

8. What does the phrase 'You steer where you stare' have to do with fear?

9. Which type(s) of the four types of fears tend to be a battle for you.

10. Go back and look up the cure for the fear that you named and write it out.

11. In the section 'A Clear View of Fear,' we talked about Job, Daniel, Joseph, and David all going through scary times. We also talked about how scary times, people, or things have permission to go only so far in our lives. God holds tightly to their leash. Describe how that truth can help you when you are facing your own scary situation.

CHAPTER SEVEN

Disappointment

*Disappointment – "sadness or displeasure caused by
the nonfulfillment of one's hopes or expectations"*

Several years ago, my family and I decided to go on a cruise for our yearly vacation. Well, I decided we should go on a cruise for our yearly vacation. It seemed all my friends had the time of their lives on those floating vacations. Their pictures on social media were filled with smiles, fancy outfits, delicious dining, and exotic beaches that lured me to want the same. I wanted to post those amazing pictures and smile those freshly tanned happy and carefree smiles. So, book it we did. We picked the month of March. Nothing much happens in March, except you are ready for spring, and spring isn't ready to come. So, why not go to the Bahamas and find it early? We chose Charleston, SC, as our port because of its close proximity to us, and off we went. Unfortunately, nothing went as expected. We expected warm weather; we got freezing cold temperatures and an icy wind that went right through you. We expected other families like us onboard. We got a bunch of scantily clad, drunk-as-a-skunk spring breakers. We expected smooth sailing. We got choppy waters that made my daughter Anna and me terribly seasick. Disappointment abounded on the 'SS Tragedy,' as my husband dubbed it. Oh, did I mention that it was my birthday? I had such high expectations for that day. It was to be a warm, sunny one, and I was to be sitting soaking up that sun while *the sea breeze whipped my hair and the sparkling ocean greeted me. My reality was a birthday spent confined to a tiny room where if I stayed perfectly still with my eyes closed, I might not throw up. Not quite what I expected. There were no fancy dinners, no fancy dresses, no freshly tanned smiles on that floating birthday of disappointment. But I will say all was not lost. I had a couple of dear friends that had arranged for me to have a delicious birthday cake served at dinner. Even though I didn't get to eat it that night, their thoughtfulness reached all the way out to the middle of the ocean. And you know what? About halfway through the week, the sun did start shining and the temperatures did warm up. And we did get a few hours of warm sun on a Bahama beach. We did laugh and we did make hilarious memories that we still talk about today. And I did get about a million lesson illustrations from that experience! But we had to sail through the rough seas of disappointment before we ever got to those warm white sands and crystal-clear water that is a color that words cannot properly describe.*

Welcome to the chapter we can *all* relate to. Disappointment is woven all throughout our lives. We think we will get sunny skies and smooth sailing, and we get icy cold winds and churning waters. Disappointments happen when we set sail on ships that we could name 'SS Marriage,' 'SS Parenting,' 'SS New Job,' or 'SS Golden Years.' We climb on board with smiles and bags that we roll behind us filled with high expectations, only to find that our realities are far from what we thought they would be. Hello, disappointment! That gap between our expectations and our reality is a very fertile place packed with soil that will grow anything that is planted in it. We can choose to plant seeds of anger, sorrow, bitterness, or resentment. Or we can plant seeds of trust, hope, personal growth, and maturity. We do not get to choose the disappointments we will face in life, but we do get to choose how we react to them.

For instance, on that wretched boat I was telling you about, we had finally reached the first island on which we could disembark. Half Moon Cay, as described by Google, is a "tiny private island in the Bahamas accessible by cruise ship. It is known for the long, crescent-shaped Half Moon Beach. Luxury cabanas dot the beachfront, which gives way to trail-lined country rich in birdlife. Half Moon Lagoon Aqua Park has water slides and playgrounds. Stingray Cove, a lagoon enclosure, is home to tame stingrays." Ah, paradise! I had made it through the worst of the seasickness and was so looking forward to ground beneath my feet that didn't sway. We were sitting on deck and I was trying to eat dry toast when the captain came over the intercom and announced that due to inclement weather and unsafe conditions, we could not stop at our scheduled destination. Instead, we were to enjoy 'another fun day at sea.' I well remember my family as they each turned and almost fearfully looked at me. I could tell they were expecting a meltdown. But something inside me snapped. I dissolved into laughter. Tears coursed down my face as I laughed until my sides ached. I mean, you couldn't make this stuff up. It kept getting worse and worse. It was actually comical. That was the moment the whole journey changed. After that morning sitting at that table, the trip became fun. We made the best of it. We played shuffleboard, we slid down water slides, we ate molten lava cakes, and as I said earlier, we finally did get to the most beautiful beach I have ever seen. For as long as I live, I will never ever forget that journey. It sure did take many unexpected twists and turns and forced us to cover some very rough waters. But in the end, it took us somewhere amazing.

You see, in life's disappointments, there is a planned destination. God always has a reason and a plan. The Captain of our vessel has a charted course for our lives and He knows all about the unexpected twists and turns that lie ahead. What we do with them as we sit on the deck of our lives is up to us, however. It is my prayer that the remainder of this chapter will equip each of us, not only with healthy expectations but also with healthy responses when those expectations are not met and we are plunged into disappointment.

GREAT EXPECTATIONS

The pesky gap between our expectation and our reality is a very real problem. It can take away all our joy and satisfaction, along with our fulfillment and peace. We have to learn to deal effectively with this gap if we are going to have any lasting peace of mind and satisfaction in this life. The first thing we have to do in navigating through disappointment is to make sure that our expectations are realistic.

Unrealistic expectations are at the root of most of our sinful responses to our disappointments along life's way. For example, when we climbed on board the vessel named 'SS Marriage,' did we expect our husbands to fix us, fill us, and make us happy? Did we climb aboard with Hallmark expectations and get an ESPN reality? Let's be honest, many of us did. When we had that child, did we have a Gerber baby expectation and get a Chucky reality? If you don't know who Chucky is, consider yourself blessed. Inspecting and adjusting our expectations will be key in navigating the choppy waters of disappointment. Ask yourself the following questions:

1. Am I being selfish, self-centered, or self-absorbed?

2. Do I expect everything to revolve around me?

3. Do I place more importance on my needs being met than I do on the needs of others being met?

4. Is the expectation that I have healthy and realistic?

5. Am I placing too much responsibility on another person?

6. Do I think another person or a happening can make me happy or fix me?

7. Have I prayed about this expectation?

8. Am I open to adjusting this expectation?

9. What does Scripture say about this expectation?

10. How do I need to adjust this expectation to make it more realistic?

Once we adjust our expectations, we need to examine our communication concerning our, now healthy, expectations. Many times in our lives, we slip into the role of a teacher who hands out impossible assignments to others. But when we hand them their assignments, more often than not, they are a blank sheet of paper. What do I mean? We never communicate clearly what it is we are expecting. Terri Chappell says it this way: "People cannot read your thought bubbles." Don't you just love that? So often we assign our husband to fill an expectation, but we never ever communicate it clearly to him. We just wish, hope, and expect, only to get disappointed, frustrated, aggravated, and discontent as a result. Sound familiar?

If we had only clearly communicated our expectation to him, everything could have been different. For example, if you had said, "Honey, I would really love to go to the beach this year for vacation, instead of the mountains again. Do you think we could possibly look at rentals tonight after the kids are in bed, and see if we can afford it?" Or "Honey, can we afford to call the repairman for the sink in the laundry room? It is really starting to leak a lot and I know you are too busy to fix it." This kind of clear communication is a lot healthier than assigning him the responsibility to read invisible thought bubbles that he cannot possibly understand.

RESPONDING TO DISAPPOINTMENT

God has a design for everything in our lives, even our disappointments. He has a providential plan for each one of our disappointing seasons of life. His plan is to turn them into blessings. Romans 8:28 says, "And we know that all things work together for good to them that love God, to them who are the called according to His purpose." Disappointments are some of our 'all things.' Even the most heartbreaking, disappointing nos can lead to God's greater yeses. The frustrating closed doors can lead to even better open ones. The painful seasons can deepen our trust and increase our spiritual maturity. Absolutely nothing is wasted with God.

There are six steps that we need to take when faced with disappointment.

1. *Be on the lookout for selfishness.* In Scripture, Martha shows us a person who didn't handle disappointment well. When she looked out of that hot, messy kitchen trying to find Mary, she herself was a hot mess. She took one look at Mary and disappointment turned into white, hot rage. Disappointment has the nasty habit of quickly turning into other destructive and harmful emotions in our lives. Martha stomped, yes stomped, up to Jesus and accused Him of not caring. How often do we do the same thing? Someone else lets us down and we get angry at Jesus! We somehow, in our twisted way of thinking, feel that HE is the one who hurt us. Martha felt she was entitled to Mary's time and effort. She felt that Mary should put the same level of importance on the kitchen tasks as she herself did. In other words, she felt that everything revolved around her. Her desires and wishes were most important. Selfishness abounds in the fertile soil of disappointment. Be on the lookout for it!

2. *Stay focused.* Martha had gotten her priorities all mixed up. Somehow kitchen service found its way to the top of her list, over living room worship. Whenever that happens, we will become exhausted, short tempered, and frazzled. Misplaced priorities will lead us to find ourselves in the same, exact frazzled state as Martha found herself in on that fateful day in the living room. We must stay focused and keep the main thing the main thing. Prioritizing our relationship with God, our quiet time, our prayer time, our worship, and our recharging will be key to weathering life's disappointments. Not only did Martha focus on the kitchen works instead of living room worship but she also focused on another person and how little they were doing in *comparison* to her. The unfairness of it all irked Martha to no end. She was working hard*er* than Mary. Watch out for those 'er' words. Words like prettier, skinnier, richer, happier, and luckier, to name a few. The comparison trap will lead

us to lose focus every time. We will begin to look at others and what they are doing, or not doing, and, as a result, our focus will be off of our Savior. We must stay focused, especially during our disappointments.

3. *Worship on purpose.* When disappointment creeps in and we are struggling with aggravation, anger, frustration, and resentment, we must deliberately choose to worship God for His identity, His very person, and not just what He can do for us or what He can give to us. Focus on HIM, not IT. Focus on who He is and how He is worthy of worship and praise, *even* when we are disappointed.

4. *Choose acceptance rather than accusations.* It is very important that we come to terms with the fact that God will sometimes zig when we think He should zag. If we would ever learn to stop raging and start resting in our Rock, our disappointments wouldn't rock our world quite so bad. Martha, it seems, forgot her place. She actually stomped into the living room and fussed at Jesus! Have you ever stomped into the throne room and told God, a thing or two? Or maybe you didn't actually stomp and finger-point; maybe you just seethed and judged and distanced yourself from Him. Forgetting our place is a sure-fire way to get stuck in our disappointment for a lot longer than we have to. Allowing for God to see things we don't and understand much more than we do is vital to navigating disappointment in a healthy and godly way. A quick and easy way to adjust our attitudes during this time is to physically kneel in prayer, if possible. Kneeling shows an attitude of worship and respect. It physically shows that you are aware of your place while showing a holy awareness of His place. Try it sometime and see if it doesn't assist you when struggling with the authority of God when He made a different call than you would have.

5. *Be eternally minded, not temporally distracted.* Isaiah 55:8–9 lets us know that God's thoughts and ways are not ours. They are heavenly thoughts and ways. They are 'see the end from the beginning' thoughts and ways. They are 'know what's best' thoughts and ways. One way we can more easily make this adjustment is to ask God to help you look at the situation from a 'heaven's-eye view.' Force yourself to see this through His eyes and not just your own viewpoint. Ask for God to help you with this. Then practice what you preach by praying a heartfelt prayer of "not my will but Thine be done." You see, this is exactly what Jesus did in the garden. His view was awful. He saw the pain, sorrow, and suffering of the cross. God the Father saw the salvation, redemption, victory, and healing of the cross. Aren't we all glad that Jesus bowed to the Father's-eye view? Perhaps your situation has an eternal perspective you haven't considered. Why not pray for God to help you see it, and even if you don't see it, to surrender to Him through it? J. Vernon McGee said, "This is God's universe, and God does things His way. You may have a better way, but you don't have a universe." That puts it in proper perspective, doesn't it?

6. *Have a goal to glorify Christ.* I have a sneaking suspicion that all of Martha's cooking and cleaning was not for the glory of Jesus. Simply put, it was for the glory of Martha. Martha was a perfectionist and a people pleaser. She wanted everyone to be impressed with her flawless meal and her perfectly clean house. She was a glory hog. Ever been one of those? Motives matter. A lot. When we want the glory, we will become very frustrated when it goes elsewhere. When plans go awry and schedules go astray, are you overly agitated? When you do not get to control the situation, does it drive you crazy? If so, we have revealed the true root of the problem. You would like to control life and the situations around you. You would like the glory, the ease, the comfort, the ok, the normal, the known, along with a hefty dose of the expected, please. When this is the

case, we have made nothing about God and His plan or His glory. Our focus, our drive, our intention, and our motivation become all about you and yours. Ouch! That one hits close to home. The unknown isn't so scary when we think about Jeremiah 33:3: "Call unto me, and I will answer thee, and show thee great and might things, WHICH THOU KNOWEST NOT." That last part I emphasized on purpose. Just because we do not know the outcome doesn't mean it is a bad one. Perhaps it is a great and mighty one. God has plans for us that are good and filled with peace. He has an expected end, not *our* expected end, but *His*. When I was little, I used to read the chapter books where you could choose which ending you wanted to read. The author would say, if you want this ending, go to page _____. But if you want this ending, go to page _____. I got to pick the ending. That was nice as a third grader, but this isn't third grade anymore. We do not get to control our ending. But we do get to choose to leave the ending in His hands and trust Him with it.

In Acts 3:1–7, we read about a lame man who asked Peter and John for alms as he was sitting at the Temple. He was at the right place—the Temple. He asked the right people—the disciples. But he asked for the wrong thing—alms. He asked for a temporary fix, a fix that wouldn't really fix him. It would give him a tiny amount of money for a short amount of time. It would be here today and gone tomorrow. It wouldn't fix his inability to work so he could get enough alms for himself. What Peter and John gave him was the fix he truly needed. They healed the issue that kept him from working and earning alms for himself. That was a far better fix!

So many times, I think that we go to our church (the Temple) and ask our fellow church members or pastor (the disciples) to help us pray for a very small fix (some alms). This fix would make our disappointment go away temporarily but would fail to truly fulfill us or benefit us eternally. God isn't interested in our temporary comfort and ease. He is, however, very interested in our eternal benefit. Sometimes we are going to be asked to take our unmet expectation to the Lord and lay it down on the altar labeled trust. In so doing, we are learning the importance of leaving the ending, and the writing thereof, completely up to Him. He is the one who gets to pick the ending, not us. As I said, this isn't a third-grade 'pick your ending' chapter book anymore. This is life. This is your story. This is my story. And the stakes have never been higher.

IT'S ALL ABOUT PERSPECTIVE

Many times, we are guilty of following Christ for what He can do for us, not for who He is to us. We seek His hands, not His heart. This is exactly what Judas did. His belief was that Jesus was worth what He could do to benefit him. That's why when Mary, Martha's sister, was anointing the feet of Jesus with an extravagant (not to mention expensive) display, Judas balked. He saw it as a waste. He missed the whole point. Mary had lavished her treasure on Jesus simply because He was worthy of it. He was worth more to her than this valuable earthly treasure. Even if it was her dowry and her one ticket to marriage. Jesus was worth every drop, in her opinion. And so, she poured it all out. She held nothing back. Being single at her age would have been, not only disappointing, it would have been devastating. But once Jesus became her treasure instead of her hopes and dreams of marriage, everything changed. Her perspective was forever changed. Unfortunately, this perspective change never happened for Judas. The ointment Mary had poured out was worth approximately $30,000 which was an entire year's wages! Judas ended up selling Jesus for thirty pieces of silver. Big difference. In today's currency, that could possibly be around $300. As you can see, it is all about perspective. Jesus didn't give Judas what he felt he should have. He wasn't performing the way Judas expected. He was expecting an earthly kingdom, a powerful position, and prestige. What he got was healing lepers, feeding hungry multitudes, and blessing children for Pete's sake. What a disappointment. What a waste of his time and energy. So, he bailed, for less than a fraction of what Mary lavished on

His feet. He cut his losses and moved on. Mary, on the other hand, realized that even though Jesus wasn't doing things the way she thought he would, he was worth everything she had.

How about you? What worth have you assigned to Jesus? Does this worth hold fast even when you do not get what you want? When our goals, dreams, and aspirations begin to line up with Christ's Kingdom agenda, we will find ourselves filled with peace, rest, joy, and fulfillment. Even when we are in the middle of our deepest disappointments. Unfortunately, most of us lose our joy during these 'less than' moments. In fact, we have told Satan he can hold onto our joy until God gives us our way. You see, Judas had ideas of how all this was supposed to unfold and he lost his joy, his mission, and his fulfillment as his way and God's way drifted further and further apart. You see he hung his happy on what Jesus could do for him. In fact, that was the extent of his whole relationship with Jesus. He followed Jesus the whole time because of what he thought the Messiah could do to benefit him. He never made his relationship with Jesus personal. He never had a clue as to who Jesus really was. He followed a role he assigned to Jesus. How can you know if this is you? Take a listen to your prayers. Are you praying 'my will be done in heaven' or 'Thy will be done on earth as it is in heaven'? If our prayer times are full of us bossing God around and our days are filled with manipulation trying to make happen what we think should happen, we are guilty of having a Judas mentality. Understanding and accepting that God has the right to tell me 'no' and still be right is key to retaining the joy, the mission, and the fulfillment that God has for us, even in trying and disappointing circumstances.

STANDING ON THE BANKS OF DISOBEDIENCE

Welcome to Amyland, population 1. Amyland is a place literally built on great expectations. In Amyland, I not only like to call the shots, I expect to call the shots. I like to sit in the director's chair and bark orders to the people on my stage. I like to pick and choose the characters, setting, and scene changes (if there are any, because in Amyland, change isn't really popular). Scripts are very popular and I alone have permission to write them. Unfortunately, no one on the stage of my life ever seems to read from them! They just don't get that I want them to enter here, do this there, or say that then. They never seem to pay attention to when they are supposed to enter and exit either. And someone keeps changing the scenery and adding suspenseful plots when I am not looking! I have a sneaking suspicion that you have your own 'land' complete with unread scripts that you really worked hard on, as well.

There's a man in Scripture that we have mentioned earlier who I am convinced had a land like my Amyland. His name was Naaman, so we will call the place that he loved Naamanland.. He had an unexpected scene change in his life called leprosy. Talk about a doozy! He dealt with the difficult and disappointing on a daily basis until the day he heard from his little maid that there was help to be found back in her home country. So, he packed his bags full of those famous Naamanland expectations and headed out. He knew just how it would all go down too – maybe some mystical anointing oil, or some special prayer or a chant or some such. None of that happened. Instead a *servant* giving him the direction to dip in the dirty Jordan River was definitely not in his bag of expectations that he had brought along for the trip. His response? The same as ours. How dare you ask this of me! Who do you think you are? Don't you know who I am? You see, Naaman was used to sitting in the director's chair and so are we.

Obedience is the daily practice of trusting God. It is trust in the trenches. It is faith with work boots on. It is hard. And I hate to be the one to break it to you, but it's supposed to be. God designed it that way on purpose. In the end, God rewarded Naaman's obedience, after he got over his fit of rage and pride and surrendered to do life the way God said. All these years later, God still rewards obedience, especially when it involves us laying down our expectations and hurts and picking up obedience instead. This will require us to get out of the director's chair and off the banks of disobedience. It will require us to dip and bow down under what God is wanting us to get under. But the result will be worth it. Just ask Naaman.

Sometimes, as in Naaman's case, the disappointment can stretch out for quite some time. I wonder how long he had had to deal with the intense pain and discomfort of leprosy? I wonder what disfigurement had happened and the shame he had felt as a result? When disappointments last for a long period of time, it can be particularly hard to remain obedient.

1 Peter 5:19 says, "But the God of all grace, who hath called us unto his eternal glory by Christ Jesus, after that ye have suffered awhile, make you perfect, stablish, strengthen, settle you." Let's break this verse down in order to get some help during the long disappointments.

Who: God of all Grace

What: A calling

When: A while

Why: To perfect you

How: Suffering

Result: You will be strengthened, stablished, and settled

This breakdown shows us exactly why God allows us to go through disappointments. He calls us to suffer for a while in order to perfect, strengthen, settle, and stablish you. The definition of stablish is "to set fast, to turn resolutely in a certain direction, to confirm, to strengthen, to steadfastly set."

Ok, so when we go through a harsh, difficult, disappointing season, we can understand from this verse that God has allowed the disappointment to be our reality for a season in order to bring us into our calling. This calling is not one that is supposed to leave us the same, but rather it will lead us to a place of growing,maturing, learning, and stretching.God is trying to 'turn us resolutely' toward Him and His ways instead of us selfishly and stubbornly clinging to our own. He is trying to make us stronger, get us settled, and set us fast on some truths. He is trying to confirm some things we have heard about Him but haven't personally learned through experience yet. When we cooperate with Him instead of fighting against Him, we can actually shorten these seasons, and I am all for that! But, in order to do so, we will have to bow to God and His ways, even the hard ones. Naaman had to bow in order to dip. He had to bend in order to get under that muddy water that would eventually heal him. Want to shorten a disappointing season? Try humbly bowing to God while you are in it.

BEAUTY IN THE BROKEN

Sometimes we aren't just disappointed; we are damaged, devastated, and almost destroyed. Sometimes we aren't just broken by disappointment; we are shattered. In Japan, there is a practice, an art really, called *kintsukuroi*. It is when a master artist takes a piece of broken vessel and repairs it along the broken edges with liquid gold or silver. The broken vessel is then much more beautiful and of much greater value in the end. But it has to go through a breaking first. In our brokenness, we all surrender—to something. We can surrender to the hate, the enemy and his lies, the circumstances, and the bitterness, or we can surrender to the Master who made us and isn't finished with us yet. Could He be repairing us in such a way that we will be more beautiful and far more precious after the breaking? I believe so.

Making It Personal

Answer the following questions in your journal:

Take a few minutes and apply the questions from earlier in this chapter to the following areas of your life where you are experiencing disappointment: past, marriage, parenting, job, health, appearance, finances, friendship, ministry, or relationship with God.

1. Am I being selfish, self-centered, or self-absorbed?

2. Do I expect everything to revolve around me?

3. Do I place more importance on my needs being met than I do on the needs of others being met?

4. Is the expectation that I have healthy and realistic?

5. Am I placing too much responsibility on another person?

6. Do I think another person or a happening can make me happy or fix me?

7. Have I prayed about this expectation?

8. Am I open to adjusting this expectation?

9. What does Scripture say about this expectation?

10. How do I need to adjust this expectation to make it more realistic?

Write out what you discovered during this exercise.

What would you say are three of your greatest disappointments?

Apply the principles from 1 Peter 5:19 to" one of those disappointments.

1 Peter 5:19 says, "But the God of all grace, who hath called us unto his eternal glory by Christ Jesus, after that ye have suffered awhile, make you perfect, stablish, strengthen, settle you."

What does this verse reveal to you about that disappointment?

Write out what this verse can mean in your future disappointments.

CHAPTER EIGHT

Discouragement

*Discouragement – "a loss of confidence or enthusiasm;
dispiritedness; a feeling of having lost hope"*

Standing in the checkout line at Walmart, I never expected to sink to the lowest point of discouragement in my life, but that is just what happened. You see, my husband and I had been trying to have a baby for over two years. Finally, the day came when we got that positive pregnancy test. We were over the moon, excited, as we had trusted God for this miracle. We had deliberately not chosen the route of medicine and doctors. We had believed God would give us what He had promised to both of us in various verses along the way. We had testified and had praised God for this miracle. We just knew that everything would be wonderful, and in nine months we would hold that promised miracle in our hands. Yes, sir, believing and obedience to God would bring its rewards. We were living proof of that, until we weren't. It all happened so fast. One minute I was at work and the next I was at home with my feet up, trying to prevent a miscarriage that had no place in my plan. Unfortunately, the miscarriage would not be prevented. As I lay on that cold ultrasound table, I heard the words I never thought I would hear. "Your baby has no heartbeat. The pregnancy has ended." What? But we had been faithful to God. We had been obedient. We had waited and had believed. A numbness settled over me for the next few days and I remember very little about *them except that moment in the Walmart checkout line. I remember that moment very clearly. We had just walked out of the outpatient center and were on the way home. They had instructed us to pick up a certain medication that I would need, so we stopped by the store on the way home. I wanted to get out and move around a bit, so I went in the store with my husband. As we stood in that checkout line, I remember everything sounding very far away. Except one sound. The one sound I heard loud and clear was of a mother with her four children, harshly yelling at one of them. Her face was angry and contorted as she loudly berated her child over and over again. The child's face, I do not remember. But the angry mother's face is forever etched in my mind. I hated her in that moment. She had four children and didn't even care about them. I just wanted one. In my mind she obviously wasn't a good person, and here I was, a Christian trying to serve God. What good was it doing me? Was He even real? Did He even care? Did I even matter to Him? What was the use? Tears of discouragement coursed down my cheeks as we drove home to our little house with no nursery and what felt like no hope at all.*

Discouragement is a spiritual battle that we must all choose to fight. Not choosing to fight is choosing to lose the battle altogether. Take Tamar, for example. She was the daughter of the mighty King David, but that didn't stop her from being horribly attacked and raped by her own half-brother, Amnon. After he had had his way with her, he despised her and literally threw her out the door, locking it after her. Tamar was understandably shattered and shaken. She violently ripped her virginal robes and put ashes on her head before stumbling home with tears coursing down her cheeks. That's when she came across her dear full brother, Absalom. He took one look at her and knew exactly what had happened. He told her to hush and not worry about it. To add insult to that injury, her own father, the king of the land, did nothing once he heard about it. Not. One. Thing. She felt about as worthless as one could feel. No hope. No help. No reason. No purpose. Those ashes she had placed on her head had more worth than she did. Her life was nothing but a pile of ashes. Her hopes and dreams, her plans and her future had all gone up in smoke. All because of the selfish and sinful act of another. One of the saddest verses in Scripture is 2 Samuel 13:20: "… So, Tamar remained desolate in her brother Absalom's house." Isn't that the saddest verse ever? We know what happened before the 'so.' But it is what is after the 'so' that is so heartbreaking. We want to read more about her. We want to see that she rose up out of those ashes and moved on. We want to read that she found healing and help and hope. We so want to know that Tamar was OK. But she wasn't. She remained desolate. The word 'desolate' means "to stun, to grow numb, that is to devastate, stupefy, to destroy, to waste." Boy, doesn't that summarize discouragement! Doesn't that show us exactly what it feels like to lose all hope?

The truth is we will all be stunned and devastated in this thing called life. We will all be disappointed and hurt, and let down, and mistreated. We will all think that things will go this way and they go that way instead. We will all go through those numb times when we can't even cry and we feel absolutely nothing at all. You would think would be a blessing, but no, it is its own kind of torment. But there is another truth as well. We don't have to remain desolate. We can get up and out of Absalom's house and our own personal ash heap. We can trust God to give us 'beauty for ashes,' as it says in Isaiah. We can trust in Him when we can trust in no one else. We can win the battle of discouragement, but it will be a fight. We do not have to remain desolate in the ashes of our discouragement. We can rise up and step out of our ash heap, but the choice to do so is completely up to us.

WARNING: DISCOURAGEMENT AHEAD

There are several things we need to be on the lookout for during discouraging seasons. These are some warning lights on the dashboard of our lives.

1. Watch out for a negative inward focus. Throughout the day, even if you are silent, there is a never-ending stream of self-talk happening in your head. Just as with regular conversation, this talk can be positive or negative. Negative self-talk will have a profound impact on our outlook on life. A constant stream of 'woe is me,'

'why me,' or 'what about me' will quickly cause us to feel and live hopeless. Brick by negative brick we construct a stronghold in our mind. We will begin to look at everything in a negative light, even going so far as to assign negative actions and motives to the people around us. We will then have negatively painted lenses over our eyes. Every action and detail of our life will take on that negative hue, even when in reality that is not the case. Controlling our self-talk and choosing to be positive will be key in overcoming the battle of discouragement.

2. Watch out for a poor testimony. All that negativity on the inside will come out on the outside. As the saying goes, 'garbage in, garbage out.' If you notice others pulling away or telling you to try to 'look at the bright side' or 'lighten up' or 'don't be such a negative Nellie,' you need to pay attention. The warning light is on. Your testimony is taking a beating and others are noticing. Where you used to talk about God, you now talk about your problems. Where you used to glorify Him, you now glorify doom and gloom.

3. Watch out for self-destructive actions. Seasons of discouragement are ripe for all kinds of self-destruction. Addictions, self-harm, bad habits, and harmful behavioral cycles love to get their start in this fertile soil. Unfortunately, some of us have had a ringside seat to the life of a person we love going into a self-destruct mode. One harmful decision after another leads to a life of bondage and consequences. When someone is in this mode, they are blinded to reality, to consequences, and to the long-term effects of their choices. All they see is the discouragement and how that temporal choice or behavior gives them a tiny bit of satisfaction or relief, at least for a few minutes. Discouragement left untended will rob its victim of the ability to see the big picture and of the clarity of thinking.

4. Watch out for a desire to disengage. This happens when you walk away from goals, relationships, jobs, aspirations, faith, conviction, or even from life itself. What's the use? Why even try? These are the questions that plague you. These questions are voiced from Satan, who is the ultimate liar. He is very good at making those lies sound like our voice when, in reality, it is him all along. He isn't satisfied with you being down. He wants you out. Out of the marriage. Out of the job. Out of the friendship. Out of the church. Out of fellowship with God. Out of the family. Out of life. For good. God never had 'remained desolate' in mind for Tamar. He had good plans. He had an expected end. He had so much more for her that she never realized because she disengaged from life.

Psalm 27:13 says, "I had fainted, unless I had believed to see the goodness of the LORD in the land of the living." If you are feeling faint, it is because you have stopped believing that God has good for you *in* the land of the *living*. That means here and now. On this earth. In this life. God is good. God is for you, and He has good plans concerning you.

Discouragement thrives in loneliness. Satan is also really good at illusions. He can make it appear as if you are alone, when in fact, you aren't. He can make you feel isolated, forgotten, worthless, and useless. Just in case you were wondering, God hasn't forgotten you. Want proof? Take a look at Psalm 139:17–18: "How precious also are Thy thoughts unto me, O God! How great is the sum of them! If I should count them, they are more in number than the sand: when I awake, I am still with Thee." God hasn't forgotten about you. In fact, He thinks about you more than there are grains of sand on the earth! Try to wrap your mind around that. To help you picture it, there are an estimated seven quintillion five hundred quadrillion grains of sand on the earth! Written out, that number looks like this: 7,500,000,000,000,000,000. And He thinks about you *more* than that! If you lived to be seventy-five years old, that means the God of Heaven thinks about you at least two hundred seventy-three trillion, nine hundred seventy-two billion, six hundred million times per day! Wow! Making ourselves focus on the truth and the facts presented in God's Word will go a long way in getting you up and out of those ashes. Maybe this is how David 'encouraged himself in the Lord.' Retraining our thinking to focus on just how very much God thinks about us is the single most important thing we can do when we are discouraged.

My daughter Anna has a 'Thomas the Train' track set. When she was little, she loved to put the tracks in a circle and watch that little train go round and round for what seemed like hours. But when she was older, she learned to use a very important track piece that had a switch on it. She found out she could make all sorts of different track layouts and that the train would go a different way if only she would flip the switch. If not, it was doomed to go round and round and round and would miss out on so much of the journey. Ladies, we have a switch in our mind that was factory-installed at birth. We can flip the switch and allow our thoughts to go down the paths of praise, worship, faith, and trust or we can keep going round and round the negative circle. But the trick is, no one can flip the switch but us.

LESSONS FROM ELIJAH

We all know the story of Elijah sitting under the juniper tree. He had had a great victory on Mt. Carmel, and then Queen Jezebel basically put a hit out on him. He was thinking nationwide revival. He may have even been thinking the fire that came down from heaven would kill that wicked king and queen along with the sacrifice. When it didn't and the problem went from bad to worse, we see discouragement set in as he begged God to end his life. This story, which we can all identify with, has some wonderful truths that will help us combat discouragement.

1. God cares for us physically. 1 Kings 19:5 shows God making sure Elijah's physical needs are met. Discouragement often rides piggyback on a very legitimate physical need. Perhaps it is sickness

and pain or maybe a very real basic physical need that must be met. Whatever it may be, we see that God sees it and cares about it. He knew this man was tired and hungry. So, He provided rest and nourishment. These needs weren't too small or too bothersome for God to see to them. The same is true for your physical needs.

2. God will see to our safety. 1 Kings 19:8 God kept Elijah safe from the evil Jezebel's plans.

3. God spoke to Elijah while he was discouraged. 1 Kings 19:11–13. He may not have looked or sounded like Elijah thought He would, but show up and speak up He did.

4. God gave Elijah a purpose and a mission in 1 Kings 19:15–16. Go anoint Jehu king. In doing so, He let him know that Ahab and Jezebel wouldn't be on the throne forever. There would be an end to their evil reign.

5. God gave Elijah a companion named Elisha that stuck with him to the end. 1 Kings 19:18.

Discouraging seasons are always seasons filled with questions. What if? Why not? How could? Why me? I am not going to tell you that you shouldn't ask questions during your discouraging time. Questions abound during those seasons. It is just the nature of the beast. How about instead of asking the wrong questions or trying not to ask questions, we just simply switch the question? Instead of 'what if' how about we ask 'what now'? We may not ever be able to answer our 'what if,' but we can answer the 'what now.'

Someone who changed the question from 'what if' to 'what now' was a lady by the name of Ruth. As she stood with her toes in the dirt by her young husband's grave, she answered that exact question. Her 'what now' was answered with 'go to Bethlehem.' That was her answer, her next thing, and that's just what she did. We all know how that act of obedience worked out for her. Maybe, just maybe, God has a Boaz blessing for us, if we would only switch the question from 'what if' to 'what now.'

Each discouraging season gives us a gift. I know, I know. It doesn't feel like it. But it is the truth. We have the gift of CHOICE. What will we do with our 'what now'? Below I will list some options for that answer:

1. Allow despair to lead you to prayer. Instead of allowing it to put a wedge between you and God, allow it to drive you to God. Instead of it making you hide in the closet, go to your prayer closet and pray those head to toe prayers. God is wanting to draw you to Him. He is your safe place. Go to Him, get honest with Him, and pour it all out to Him.

2. Read God's Word. What does God say about what you are going through? Dive in. Look up. Search the Scripture using key words, commentaries, and devotional books by trusted authors. Learn. Grow. Become what He wants you to through this. Don't waste this time. Ask yourself: What is God trying to teach me? What is He wanting to change in me? What do I need to work on?

3. Commit to the plans of God. The biggest gold strike in the history of the United States happened when a miner gave up after digging in his mine for over a year. In disgust and defeat, he sold it, packed up, and moved back east. The new owner dug just two more inches and hit the largest gold strike on record in the US! Don't quit; don't give up. You could be just two inches from victory.

4. Embrace, accept, and believe who you are in Christ. Discouraging seasons are famous for Satan-led field trips to the fun house. Only it isn't so fun. What do I mean by that? Remember those old, fun house mirrors? They were distorted in all sorts of ways. You stepped in front of one and you were tall and really skinny. A different one

made you look short and fat. Then there were the wavy ones that made you look like you were all wavy. Were those mirrors reality? Did you really look like that? The answer is obviously 'no.' But the spiritual parallel is striking. Satan places a distorted mirror in front of us during discouraging seasons. He causes us to see ourselves as worthless or somehow faulty. We see a reflection that is unloved, unwanted, unimportant, and invisible. He causes us to see our situations in those same distorted mirrors. We look at them and see hopeless, helpless, and never-ending. But in reality, if we would view ourselves through the clear mirror of God's Word, we would see something much different. We would see a woman worth dying for. We would see someone loved greatly, who is cherished and never ever invisible or unimportant. We would see our situation as having a purpose and God as having a plan. We would see an expected end and somehow God working good out of it all. Discouraging seasons demand declarations of truth about who you are in Christ. You will find these truths all throughout scripture. Write them down and declare them to yourself while you look in the mirror. Do this as many times as needed in your discouraging season.

5. Praise Him anyway. As the old timers used to say, 'Sometimes you just have to praise God on credit.' What does this mean? It is simply praising God in the meantime for what He will do to bring you through to the other side. This kind of praising is done *before* the answer is given, *before* the relief is felt, and *before* the breakthrough is reached.

6. Get busy. In our hard time, we are tasked with a mission. This mission is to 'make a ministry.' *In* your difficulty and discouragement, a sure-fire way to help yourself to get up and *out* of that difficulty is to deliberately make the choice to help others who are in their own hard season of life. Making the choice to make it about others

will go a very long way in getting your eyes off of yourself and your difficulty. Hard times are very conducive to it being 'all about me.' Turning our eyes inward is a guaranteed way to make discouragement last longer. Forcing yourself to look outward will take your focus off of your own woes and onto helping others through theirs. Someone in the Bible who did this is old Anna. She was a widow of eighty-four years! Can you imagine eighty-four years of lonely, hard, sad, and difficult? That's an awfully long time! What did she do with those eighty-four long years? She ministered with fastings and prayers at the Temple. That's what. She was at the Temple so much that they actually let her live there! She made a ministry and if she can, so can we.

RESPONDING TO DISCOURAGEMENT

1. Call out to God. When Nehemiah was faced with so many discouraging circumstances while building the wall, he took that despair straight to God (Nehemiah 4:9). He didn't go to the people. They couldn't fix it. He didn't go to the pop psychology of the day either. They had no real answer. He didn't go to himself to try to find a fix to the problem. He told God on the enemy. He poured out all the worries, fears, and frustrations to the only One who could fix it. Here's a question we need to ask ourselves: Is God our first resort or our last-ditch effort after we have tried everything else? And another on we need to ask ourselves: Do we pick up the phone and start texting when the bottom drops out or do we hit our knees immediately upon the news we dreaded to hear?

2. Keep at it. Nehemiah did not stop working to go down and talk about the issue with his enemies. That was just what they wanted him to do in Nehemiah 6:3. But not Nehemiah, oh no. He just kept on building and saw the distraction for what it was.

3. Fix your focus. Nehemiah did not sit and stare at one spot on the wall. That little spot wouldn't give much encouragement. It wouldn't seem to make much of a difference. *But* if he took a step back and looked at all they had done, this would help him to see that all those little things add up to a big task accomplished. Sometimes we just need to take a step back and see what all God has done and how far we have come to get a proper perspective.

4. Live in the reality of God's promises. Make sure you are in God's word *daily*. This will be the very first thing Satan will try to separate you from. We must never allow him to separate us from our strength. Get into His word and read smart. That means go to where your help will be found. Look up key words online or in a concordance. Words like help, hope, strength, healing, friend, peace, rest, and refuge. Write them out on index cards and post them everywhere. Memorize them. Read stories in the Bible with which you can identify. See how God related to that person and how He moved in their situation. Choose a Bible study on a topic that will encourage you.. However you do it, just do it. Faithfully.

Making It Personal

Answer the following questions in your journal:

1. Look back at the section "Warning: Discouragement Ahead." Which of those points did you need to heed the most? Why?

2. Write out Jeremiah 29:11. How can this verse help in discouraging seasons?

3. How can Elijah's story offer encouragement to you today?

4. Have you allowed this time to lead you to God or push you away from God? What can you do to make sure you are sticking and staying close to the Savior through your discouragement?

5. How can 'make a ministry' be words to live by in a discouraging season? How would this help you in your time of discouragement? Write out a plan of action for making a ministry. Some ideas could be:volunteering in a ministry at church, reaching out to a person who could use some encouragement or a friend, offer an act of service for someone else in need, or make a prayer list of names and situations that you could earnestly pray for daily.

CHAPTER NINE

Sadness and Hurt

Sadness – "affected with or expression of grief or unhappiness: downcast, causing or associated with grief or unhappiness"

Hurt – "mental pain or distress"

The high school girls' locker room can be a vicious place. On an unsuspecting day in the middle of my sophomore year, I found out just how vicious and hurtful this place can be. Let me give you the background. My parents wanted my sisters and me to dress up one day a week and wear a nice dress to the public school that we attended in our small town. Of course, I hated it. None of my friends had to do this. So, for one hated day per week, I was different, and, for a teenage girl, being different is a fate worse than death. Like a sore thumb, I stuck out as I maneuvered the hallways in my dress and heels while everyone else wore cool high tops, gummy bracelets, and acid-washed mom jeans. It was on one of those fateful dress-up days that I happened to have PE class. The dress I had chosen for that day was baby blue with a large over-the-shoulder collar that tied in the front. The look was completed with big, bulky shoulder pads. Ahhh, the 80s! There's nothing quite like it in fashion history. Anyway, back to my story. These dresses were all the rage and I just had to have one. Unfortunately, they didn't have my size, but that didn't stop me, determined teenager that I was. I just got a size larger and would make it work. I got dressed that morning thinking at least I had a cool dress to wear, even if it was a dress. That day in the locker room, one of the 'cool' girls happened to see the size on the label of my dress while it was lying on the bench. And so, as we all trooped back in the locker room to change back into our clothes, she decided everyone in the locker room needed to know the size of my dress. She began to chant it out and ask if everyone knew what the number meant. Some joined in and laughed, some looked at me with pity, while others were completely clueless. Sadly, I was not. I knew exactly what she was talking about. It didn't matter that it was a size too big. It didn't matter that she was being spiteful and mean. It didn't matter that next week someone else would be the butt of her cruel jokes. All that mattered was the hurt that sliced so deep in my heart that it took my breath. The laughter of people, who I had thought were friends, came at me like arrows. To this day, all these years later, I can still feel the shame and the pain of that one moment in time. This painful story has been the hardest for me to share with you. That hurt caused a lot of damage. It caused me to distance myself from other girls because they might hurt me again. It caused me to have trust issues that, if I am honest, I still deal with even today. What if someone sees another 'label' in my life? What if they catch a glimpse into something that was supposed to be private and they broadcast it to the whole locker room again? Opening up and having close friends that I can totally be myself with has been a challenge since that painful moment in time. Hurt is like that, isn't it? But if I can open up to you and share a painful hurt from my past and the baggage it has caused, perhaps you can open up right alongside me and we can find healing for our hurts together.

BEFORE WE BEGIN

Before we begin this chapter on the tangled emotions of sadness and hurt, I want to add a little disclaimer. You can be sad and still be right with God. You can be hurt and not in sin. These emotions were created by God and experienced by God. We see in Scripture that certain things 'grieve' the Holy Spirit. We see Jesus Himself crying, lamenting, being hurt, let down, and dealing with sorrow from start to finish in His ministry on this earth.

So, first things first. Stop thinking that sadness is sin or somehow unspiritual, and that experiencing hurt somehow makes you less of a Christian. You don't need more faith to heal from these things. You don't need to avoid them or stuff them or act like they don't exist. You just need the God of them. That's all. So, give yourself permission to be human, to experience these unpleasant emotions, and to embrace them as being part of this thing called life.

OUCH!

Many times, when in the middle of hurt or sadness, we find ourselves wondering, *Is there no help? Is there no relief? Will I ever find healing or help?* That question, or one just like it, was asked in the book of Jeremiah. Verse 22 of Chapter 8 asks this question: "Is there no balm in Gilead; is there no physician there? Why then is not the health of the daughter of my people recovered?" I thought of this verse the other day when I was dishing something out of a Crockpot. Some of the sauce sloshed over onto my finger and an immediate blister appeared. That was an incredibly painful burn. It was on my right pointer finger, so you can imagine how it bothered me the rest of the week. Everything I touched seemed to hit it. Putting it in water made it sting like mad. I found myself wondering, *Is there no balm in the world that can ease a minor, but very painful, burn?* After researching a little on the internet, I discovered that there was one thing I could put on it that would ease the discomfort. Lavender essential oil would help, according to Google. Sure enough, it did. That was my balm. It didn't make it disappear. It didn't make the burn never happen. But it did ease the discomfort that was a result of that burn. Now, if I look at that finger, there is a small red place that marks the spot where I was hurt. If I hit it, it doesn't hurt anymore. The blister is completely gone now, and only the memory of it remains. The hurt is healed. It didn't happen overnight, but at the very moment I got burned, my body began the process we call healing.

In order to be healed, we must learn three things: 1) How to apply the balm of Gilead; 2) How to follow the Great Physician's instructions; and 3) How to give His medicine time to work. Jeremiah 17:14 says, "Heal me, O LORD, and I shall be healed...."

THE WHO OF OUR HURT

One of the names of the Lord is Jehovah-Rapha, which means 'the Lord who heals.' The first time that this name is recorded in Scripture is when He healed the bitter waters in Exodus Chapter 15. Do you have a bitter hurt, past, situation, devastation, physical ailment, relational situation, or financial situation that needs to be healed? If so, you have come to the right Jehovah.

Isaiah 61:1–4 says, "The Spirit of the Lord GOD is upon me; because the LORD hath anointed me to preach good tidings unto the meek; he hath sent me to bind up the brokenhearted, to proclaim liberty to the captives, and the opening of the prison to them that are bound. To proclaim the acceptable year of the LORD, and the day of vengeance of our God; to comfort all that mourn: To appoint unto them that mourn in Zion, to give unto them beauty for ashes, the oil of joy for mourning, the garment of praise for the spirit of heaviness, that they might be called the trees of righteousness, the planting of the LORD, that he might be glorified."

Are you not only brokenhearted but also held captive to that hurt? Are you bound up in your sorrow? Are you in mourning? Is your spirit heavy? Are you surrounded by ruin? If so, then these verses are about to become your balm. Look at the promises contained within those precious words! Look what He has in store for you. Divine reversals. God can turn it all around. He can bring joy out of sorrow. Peace out of chaos. Hope out of hopelessness. Dreams, hopes, and plans can come out of the ashes of ruin and despair. That's our God. That's our balm.

Psalm 147:3 says, "He healeth the broken in heart, and bindeth up their wounds." This verse is a promise. For YOU. For that hurt. For that pain. For that grief. For that great sadness that weighs you down. Yes, even that one. But you have to go to Him for that healing. Deliberately and on purpose. You have to CHOOSE Him as your source of healing. We can go to a million other things, but they will never truly heal. They may mask the pain, distract from the pain, or offer a temporary relief that wears off over time. But true healing can only come from our Jehovah-Rapha.

2 Chronicles 15:4 says, "But when they in their trouble did turn unto the LORD God of Israel, and sought him, he was found of them." Where are we turning for our help in our times of sorrow? Are we turning to substance abuse, busyness, distractions, pop psychology, self-help, another person, or a desperate hope that our circumstance will change?

Psalm 62:8 says, "Trust in him at all times; ye people, pour out your heart before him: God is a refuge for us. Selah." Are we looking at God as our safe place? Are we trusting in Him even in our 'all times'? If we are, then we will have no problems pouring out our heart before Him. Why? Because He is our safe haven, our shelter, our hope, our peace, our rest, our refuge, and yes, our healing.

THE WHAT IN OUR HEALING

We have seen WHO the balm is, now, let's look at WHAT the balm is. Psalm 107:20 tells us the answer: "He sent his word, and healed them, and delivered them from their destructions." His word is the balm that we can hold in our hands. We can see it, hear it, touch it, and apply it. Your healing will be found in the person of God and in the Word of God. But until you run into these, you will never realize it. Proverbs 18:10 says, "The name of the LORD is a strong tower; the righteous runneth into it and is safe." Where are you running to in your time of grief and sorrow? I think sometimes we are like the gerbil on the wheel. We are running our little legs off but getting nowhere fast. Pain and suffering are always meant to cause us to run *to* Him. But many times, we find ourselves running *away* from Him, and toward something or someone else, or perhaps, we just sit down in our hurt, in our hard, in our hopelessness and we refuse to move.

This reminds me of a children's book I absolutely loved as a little girl. It was called *Small Pig*. This little pig was raised on a farm, and the farmer's wife began to spring clean one day. She got a little carried away and vacuumed up the poor little pig's mud. He ran away in search of some cool, comforting mud. He ran all the way to the big city, where he found some cool wet cement in a sidewalk. He mistakenly thought it was a puddle of the wonderful mud he was in search of. So, he sat down and sank down into the cool, wet 'mud.' At first, it felt great but then it began to hardened and eventually entrapped the poor little pig. It ended up taking a jackhammer to release the pig from what held him captive. Sitting in our hurt is very much like sitting in cement. It won't take long until we are stuck. Thankfully, God's Word is the needed jackhammer that will release us from a hardened hurt.

During seasons of hurt, we need to be in the Word more than ever. We need to have a daily time of reading God's Word. We need to look up verses that deal with our situation, memorize them, post them all around us. We need to search it like never before, and then we must APPLY it. The balm of the Word will do us no good if we do not make practical application into our lives, habits, thoughts, actions, words, and deeds.

THE WHERE OF OUR HEALING

Ok, so *who* is our healing? Jehovah-Rapha. *What* is our healing? The Word of God. Now for the WHERE of our healing. The location of our balm is Calvary. But you are probably thinking, *That is where I went to get saved, not where I go to get healed from sorrow.* Look at Isaiah 53:3–5: "He is despised and rejected of men; a man of sorrows, and acquainted with grief: and we hid as it were our faces from him; he was despised, and we esteemed him not. Surely he hath borne our griefs, and carried our sorrows: yet we did esteem him stricken, smitten of God, and afflicted. But he was wounded for our transgressions, he was bruised for our iniquities: the chastisement of our peace was upon him; and with his stripes we are healed."

Now, let's unpack those verses for a minute, shall we? Let's start where you are most familiar. We have all heard many times that He was wounded for our transgressions and bruised for our iniquities. We know Jesus died for our sins. We know that we do not have to carry around our sins after we are saved. He died so that we could be FREE from our many iniquities. That was the whole reason why He died—so that He could REDEEM our sins. Yes. Absolutely. You are right. But notice that He also 'hath borne our *griefs*, and carried our *sorrows*.' Did you see that? Not only did He take our sins to that cross but He also took our sorrows and our griefs! He carried our sorrows up that hill. Our griefs were also nailed on that cross, along with our sins. Hmmm. That changes things, doesn't it? If, after we are saved, we do not have to carry our sins, then the same is true for our sorrows! He died to *redeem* them. We no longer have to carry them. So, why are we? That sorrow that you are carrying around has already been carried up Calvary's hill. He 'bore' it already. We can put it down. We no longer have to live life with that weight on us!

I know what you're thinking. *But how can that awful hurt be redeemed?* You didn't know I could read minds, did you? That terrible hurt is redeemed the very same way our terrible sin is. It is redeemed through His precious blood that He shed on Calvary, that's our how. If His blood can wash away all sins' stains, then it can wash away every sorrow's pain as well. The how of this is accomplished in a process. This process is called 'working together' in Romans 8:28. "And we know that all things work together for good to them that love God, to them who are the called according to his purpose." This working together is the process of healing and redeeming our hurts.

It is sort of like baking. The ingredients aren't good on their own, but when added together, worked together, and mixed together, you have something wonderful, something sweet, and something 'oh so good' in the end. Baking is a process that takes time, and a certain order of steps, and it also takes heat. Trying to eat one of the ingredients by itself won't work. I never saw a person yet who liked to eat flour. Not one. Why? Because by itself it isn't good. But added with eggs, sugar, oil, and vanilla, we can have something really good. They work together. So it is with our 'all things' when they are placed in the hand of the Master. The end result will be a redeemed hurt that becomes something awfully sweet and wonderful in our life. But, in order to see a hurt redeemed, we must cooperate with His process.

THE WHY OF OUR HURT

When silver is refined, it is first crushed in the crucible. Before this refining process, it is hard, unyielding, and unbending. After the crushing, the master places the crushed silver in the fire. This fire is not designed to destroy the silver but rather to refine it. The refining fire is the perfect temperature. It isn't too hot because that would destroy the silver. It is not too cool because then it wouldn't accomplish the desired purpose. The silversmith keeps a close eye on the temperature of the fire at all times. While the silver is in the fire, its impurities rise to the top. The master craftsman then carefully scrapes them off. Then he places the silver in an even hotter fire. Why? He knows that even more impurities are lurking under the surface. The higher temperature goes deeper in the silver to reveal the more hidden impurities. As always, he watches the temperature closely to make sure that it doesn't harm the silver. Not once does the master leave the side of the silver during this process. He keeps checking and rechecking until it is ready. He knows just when to take the silver out of the fire by how clearly he can see his reflection in it. If it is cloudy, it needs more time in the fire. If, however, he can see his reflection clearly, it is time to remove it from the fire. The fire has served its purpose and the silver is refined. It now reflects the master perfectly. Ladies, this is the WHY of our hurts.

1 Peter 1:6–8: "Wherein ye greatly rejoice though now for a season, if need be, ye are in heaviness through manifold temptations: That the

trial of your faith, being much more precious than of gold that perisheth, though it be tried with fire, might be found unto praise and honour and glory at the appearing of Jesus Christ." Job 23:10: "But he knoweth the way that I take: when he hath tried me, I shall come forth as gold."

THE HOW OF OUR HURT

In Scripture, there are two examples of ladies that dealt with deep hurt and did it well. The first one I want to look at is found in 2 Kings 5:1–3. This little girl is known as Naaman's little maid. She was a young girl that was taken captive by Naaman. He marched in with all his troops, defeated her homeland, and took her to be his wife's maidservant. She was removed from all she held dear. Her normal had been shattered and her life was turned upside down. Over time, she realized that her captor was being held captive by the angry disease of leprosy. As time passed, she allowed compassion to be born in her life and she decided to live out Jude 1:22: "And of some have compassion making a difference." She spoke just twenty words in Verse 3, and this man's life was changed forever. She chose, even in her pain, to have compassion and to make a difference. She could have wished him evil; after all, it was all his fault that she was in her predicament. But she didn't. She did not allow herself to turn inward. She didn't allow herself to grow selfish and self-centered. She didn't hate the one who had caused a hateful situation in her life. Instead, she turned outward and had compassion on another's pain. This, ladies, will be key to your victory in your pain. Reaching out and helping others, whether it is by your words, actions, or prayers, is a must if you want to reach healing. I am reminded of a song entitled, "Everybody's Going Through Something." Such true words penned by the songwriter! *In your hurt, look out, reach out, help out, and you will eventually get out of the prison of that hurt.* Through the help of this concept, I have been able to do that with my locker-room issue. I have thought about that girl and what she must have been facing or going through that day. You see, hurt people turn around and hurt people. Perhaps she had been made fun of the day before. Or maybe she had a hidden label herself and to take attention away from it, she thought it necessary to shine the light on someone else's label. Maybe she just found out she was pregnant. Maybe her parents were in the middle of a nasty divorce. Or maybe she was just trying to navigate the brutal waters of a high school girl's locker room the best she could. Humanizing the one who hurt us can help us to extend grace. To that girl, wherever she is, I am sorry for what you went through that made you feel it was necessary to hurt another person. No one should have to endure label shaming. Whatever your hurt was, I truly hope it has been redeemed, as mine now has.

We have already mentioned how Anna made a ministry, but I want to go a little deeper in her story that is found in Luke 2:36–38. When we read about her in the pages of Scripture, we see that she was a little old widow who lived in the temple, serving day and night. The Bible gives us some details that can assist us in painting a pretty detailed picture of this little lady. First of all, she had been married, but only for seven short years before she buried her husband, the love of her life. Then for eighty-four years she had been living the lonely life of a widow. That's eighty-four years of hard. Eighty-four years of lonely. Eighty-four years of tears and fears. That's a long time! Interestingly, we see that God's Word calls her a prophetess. That word isn't used much in Scripture and only this one time in the New Testament. It means 'an inspired woman.' Wow. That says volumes. She was inspired, not bitter. She was inspired, not hateful. She was inspired, not vengeful. We also find out that she lived at the temple and served around the clock with fastings and prayers. This was how Anna beat it. She beat the hurt by praying. She found her filling and her healing in prayer and in service to God. She gave of herself when it was the hardest to give. She gave when she had every excuse not to. When everything in her said take, she gave instead. When everything in her said hate, she loved. When everything in her said sit, she served. She made a ministry. In the hard. In the hurt. In the sorrow. In the lonely. In the difficult. She served. Can't you just see her crying with the ladies that came to the temple, praying with them, hugging them, and telling them about how they could find healing? Girls, this is it. These ladies give us the HOW of our hurt.

Want out of your hurt faster? Start getting out of yourself. That is one of the most effective 'hows' there is. Serve. Do. Have compassion. Reach out. Help. Bring hope to another who is in pain. Fight the pull to turn inward and become self-absorbed. I know that isn't an answer you want to hear in your pain, but it is a mighty effective one. Ask God to give you compassion to make a difference and then look for ways to make a ministry out of that compassion and you will watch God fill and heal you. You will become a miracle in the making.

THE FACTS IN OUR HURT

We have now looked at the *who, what, where, why,* and *how* of our hurts. Now let's look at the God of our hurts. Please read Psalm 139:1–24. No, really. Go read that chapter. Then, let's dive into the beautiful facts presented in the chapter.

> Verses 1–10: God knows me. He knows where I am. He sees me and understands my thoughts and emotions. He is with me, and gets me. He hears everything I think and say. He is before me and behind me. There is no place I can go or thing that I can go through that can separate me from God. He will never leave me.

> Verses 11–12: Even when I am surrounded by darkness, He can see me and the way that I should take. My confusion, my darkness, and my unrest are not causing God any confusion, darkness, or unrest.

> Verses 13–16: I am preplanned and was designed to be the way that I am on purpose. I am not a mistake. I am

imperfect, but I am loved, accepted, chosen, and cherished just as I am.

Verses 17–18: I am not forgotten. He thinks about me more than I can even count. In fact, He thinks about me more than the grains of sand on the whole earth put together. I am never alone. I am never forsaken.

Verse 19–22: God will right all wrongs and heal all hurts.

Verse 23–24: I must cooperate with God on this journey toward healing. He will lead me toward healing, but I must choose to follow.

These facts remain. No matter the hurtful season we are in. This must be what we go back to and the balm that we apply daily to our hurts. Even when. Even then. And as Psalm 139:10 says, 'even there.'

A QUESTION IN YOUR HURT

In John 5:6–7, we see a fascinating exchange between Jesus and a man who had been living in his hurt and sadness for thirty-eight years. The setting was by the side of the pool of Bethesda. The man asked to be carried there every day because he wanted to be healed. Scripture tells us that an angel would trouble the water and the first one in would be healed. But when Jesus showed up that day, the man wasn't healed; he was lying on his mat, unable to get to his healing. Someone else always beat him to it.

Jesus walked by, took one look at him, and asked him a question that He has asked to countless hurt people down through the ages. The question was this: "Wilt thou be made whole?" Of course, he wanted to be healed. He wouldn't be there if he didn't. The man answered with a reasonable excuse. "Sir, I have no man, when the water is troubled, to put me into the pool: but while I am coming, another steppeth down before me." Jesus then said, "Rise, take up thy bed, and walk."

This curious exchange by the pool that day speaks volumes to us in our hurts today. First of all, Jesus is asking us the same question. "Wilt thou be made whole?" Well, will you? Do you want to be healed of your hurt or do you want to wallow on the bed surrounded by excuses for a little while longer? Hmmm. Do you want to hide behind it for a bit longer or do you want to step out from behind it and engage in life again? Hmmm. Do you want to let it keep you down or are you ready to rise? Hmmm. Are you ready to stand up in faith and follow God's commands and directions, or do you want to keep blaming others for your situation? Hmmm. Maybe this is hitting a little close to home. No wonder Jesus asked him this question, which on the surface seems to have an obvious answer. Maybe there was more that was keeping him on that bed than his sickness. And maybe there is more that is keeping us in our hurt than meets the eye.

Are you ready to be made whole? Are you ready for healing? Are you ready to rise up and move on? Well, are you? Be honest. Be brutally honest. Are you ready to do what you need to do in order to get to your healing? If so, then what is stopping you? Rise up. Roll up that bed filled with excuses and reasons to stay down that you have been laying on for so long. Stand in power on the authority of God's Word. Then, and only then, can you move forward through the power of God. If this man could do it, so can you. Jesus had the authority over what was keeping this man down, and He has authority over what is keeping you down, as well.

Let's break this down a little further. What is WHOLE? Whole isn't wallowing. Whole isn't reliving, rethinking, revisiting, or rehashing the hurt. Oh, (gulp) that's what whole means? Well, that might be a different story, huh? Whole isn't getting people on your side and turning them against the person who hurt you. Whole isn't staying in the same spot for thirty-eight years. Whole isn't hiding behind excuses or blaming other people.

That's what whole isn't. Now, let's look at what whole is. By definition, whole is 'unimpaired, unbroken, uninjured. Sound. Not hurt. Restored.' Wilt thou be made whole? Is that really what you want? Are you ready to live unimpaired? Rolling up the mat meant he wouldn't return to it. He carried what had carried him. He now had power over what had had power over him. Going back wasn't an option.

Rising up took faith. He had to believe he could through the power of the spoken word of Jesus. The same is true for us. God's Word has said we can rise up. It has said we can do all things through Christ which strengthens us. So, will we believe that as truth and let that belief color our actions, or will we choose to continue living bound up to our hurt?

Notice in Verse 9 it says that he was immediately made whole and then he took up his bed. The healing happened when he believed it actually could happen. The belief was key. God has healing for you, dear one. He has placed the power in you to rise up. He has placed the power in you to overpower what has held you down for so long. But you must believe. You must realize the power of the spoken word of God when He calls you to rise up. And then you must obey and walk in that obedience through the power of God toward your victory.

So, I will ask you the same question that was asked that day by the pool so long ago. Will you be made whole? No matter the mat you are lying on, the hurt that has you there, how long you have been there, or the excuses you have for not being able to find healing yet. Jesus is right there in front of you and He is asking you, "Wilt thou be made whole?" Well, what do you say? Are you ready? Whole sure does sound good right about now, doesn't it?

Making It Personal

Answer the following questions in your journal:

1. What is the name of God that shows Him as healer?

2. Have you gone to Him expecting Him to heal and redeem your hurt?

3. Write out the verses in Isaiah that show that Jesus died to redeem our sorrows.

4. Write out your hurt.

5. Why does this hurt so badly?

6. How have you been dealing with your hurt before you read this chapter?

7. What has this chapter taught you to do with your hurt?

8. What steps do you need to take now in order to go to 'the God who heals'?

9. Which portion of this chapter did you need to hear the most?

10. What is your next thing, your 'now what' that you need to do?

CHAPTER TEN

Grief

Grief – "deep sorrow, especially that caused by someone's death"

ou think you are prepared for it. You expect it. You know it is coming. Then when it comes, it is so much harder than you thought it would be. I remember getting my dad's diagnosis of terminal brain cancer in 2017. He had been in poor health for a while and had had some episodes that just didn't make sense. When we received his diagnosis, the logical and efficient part of me reasoned that it seemed like the next step in the progression of events that had led us to that moment. As we walked through the next six weeks, the journey became excruciatingly difficult. After about a two-to-three-week period, when he seemed to be just fine, his health began to decline rapidly as the tumor wreaked havoc on much of his physical and mental abilities. But it was the next step, I told myself. This was how my dad would exit this life and enter into heaven, where there is no pain, no suffering, no diabetes, no strokes, and no cancer. Yes, it was for the best. In my family, I have three older sisters and we each processed this difficult journey differently and in accordance with our very different personalities. My oldest sister is more emotional and cried a lot while feeling like her world was falling apart. My practical and medical sister was all business in her approach while scheduling appointments and discussing medicine with doctors and nurses. My sentimental sister was more withdrawn and quiet while she processed the hard more privately.

And then there was me. All logic, facts, lists, timelines, and spiritual answers. I approached everything with a 'check it off the list,' problem-solving, reasoning, and cause and effect approach, even on those incredibly difficult days. I didn't have time to cry. I didn't have time to hurt. I had to figure out what to do and how to make it easier and more doable for us all. I was in my 'manage mode.' This mode was in full swing even after my dad passed away. After all, there were a million and one details to attend to, a eulogy to write, and a funeral to plan. Manage. Check off the list. Organize. Clean up. Get it done. It wasn't until the bagpipes played their haunting rendition of "Amazing Grace" and the echoes on the mountain-side graveyard faded away that the finality of it all hit me. There was no more doing. No more checklists. No more organizing. Now it was time for the feeling part. This was certainly new emotional territory for me. When I got back home and life got back to 'normal,' I had a very hard time getting back to normal along with it. I was numb. I couldn't cry. I couldn't feel anything. Not joy, sadness, relief, peace, or hope. It was like I was in a fog. Concentrating was a challenge, as was completing multistep tasks, and as for multitasking, forget it.. Finally, over time, I began to process all that had happened over the traumatic six-week period. The tears finally came as I allowed myself to feel the sadness and experience the hurt. Some days were harder than others. I found much comfort as I journaled and prayed. Tears eventually found their way down my cheeks as I finally allowed memories to wash over me. Time marched on, as it always does, and the tears became less. I began to find myself smiling more as certain memories of my dad replayed in my mind. His laugh, his funny little dance he would do, his love for the Lord, and his sunny outlook on life. As I traveled through the journey of sadness, sorrow, loss, and grief, I learned a lot. I learned that everyone grieves differently. And that is OK. You can grieve and still be alright. You can go back to living and still love that person. You can process grief at your own pace and still honor their memory. You can have really bad days and still be a good Christian. You can completely believe in the reality of heaven and still miss that person terribly. I guess you could say, that I learned the reality of the power of 'and' that I had written about before I had gone through my time of loss. Grief is filled with 'ands.' Our journey in this chapter will be filled with this very important word called 'and.' I hope that learning to embrace this little three-letter wonder will help you as much as it did me.

FIRST THINGS FIRST

First of all, I want to say I am so sorry for your loss. If you are reading this chapter, it is because you need it. Your loss is real and your pain is overwhelming. What this chapter offers are tips and truths that will help you through this process we call grief. But in no way are the words in these pages telling you to 'get over it' or to 'just move on.' The dignity of the love you had for that person demands respect. It demands to be recognized. I know and I have learned that myself in my own personal walk through grief. Once again, these pages are not diminishing that loss or belittling that pain. They are written to be life preservers in a raging sea that threatens to swallow you whole. Read them as you wipe the tears and even as you may face feelings of wanting to throw this book across the room. I understand. Grief is hard. Grief is awful. And grief is awful hard. It can also be consuming. I encourage you to read small sections of this chapter at a time. Journal about what you read. Pray about what you read. Then reread that section. Journal about something else you learn or some other question you may have. Then head onto the next section. Ingest small portions at a time and allow the truths to comfort and challenge you at the same time. Please know that no one is fussing at you for being sad. Another truth to tuck away is that to 'get through' to the other side of grief in no way dishonors the memory of the one you loved so much. It is just a way to put into words the actual journey through the deepest and most intense part of loss. Dear one, please know that there are so many women that are battling the same intense pain you are and reading these very same pages. Please know you are not alone. Please know that this author has prayed for you. Each word of this chapter has been prayed over. Your heart and your hurt have been prayed over. Know that and let that fact walk through these pages with you. To heal is not to forget. To heal is not to leave behind. To heal is not to negate your love for that person or their importance to you. Now that we have that nailed down, we can proceed.

THE PROCESS OF GRIEF

Psalm 6:2–3, 6 says, "Have mercy upon me, O LORD: for I am weak: O LORD, heal me; for my bones are vexed. My soul is also sore vexed: but thou, O LORD, how long? I am weary with my groaning; all the night make I my bed to swim; I water my couch with my tears. Mine eye is consumed because of grief; it waxeth old because of all mine enemies."

That's a pretty accurate picture of grief, isn't it? Grief makes you groan. It ages you. It hurts. It won't go away. It affects you physically and drains the life out of you. It is absolutely exhausting. If you spend any time at all studying or learning about grief, you will find one word that pops up in article after article and book after book. That word is 'process.' Don't you just hate that word? That word means time. It means steps. It means slowly and methodically. It means this won't have a quick fix or a shortcut that you can take to get to your destination faster. No wonder the psalmists ask, "O LORD, how long?" While everyone grieves differently according to the situation and their personality, there are some things that just seem to come with the territory of grieving. These will be pit stops for some, while others may unpack and stay much longer. Here are some of the steps that you can expect to experience on your journey through grief.

1. Depression. Expect to feel a deep sorrow and sadness that won't go away. This will manifest itself in feelings of sluggishness, low energy, fatigue, helplessness, trouble sleeping, difficulty making decisions, an overall numbness, or even a disconnect with life. It has been described by many as a feeling of living in a 'fog.'

2. Feeling like you have lost your mind. You will experience difficulty concentrating or managing your time, or you may become forgetful. You may forget how to get to certain places or have difficulty recalling facts. Things that you used to do easily may become very challenging for you.

3. Feelings of denial. This happens mostly at the beginning stages of grief. It is too much to handle, too much to think about, so you may feel the urge to put your head in the sand. Some may even deny that their loved one is dead. They may deny that they need to deal with certain issues or decisions that need to be made. It is important to note that this is a coping mechanism that is natural and normal but should not be allowed to continue for a long period of time. Healing will not happen when one gets stuck in this stage of the process.

4. Physical problems. Your body is 'groaning' under the grief. Grief has been called the most intense stress the human body can weather. We all know that stress can wreak havoc on the human body and mind. Therefore, it is easy to see why grief is so hard on a body. Expect physical issues to crop up during a season of grief. It will take a toll on you. Take care of yourself, exercise, eat right, and get the needed amount of sleep. If something comes up, go to the doctor and take the necessary medication. Head outside and get some sunshine. Take a walk. Do what you know you need to do.

5. Relief. Some mourners actually have feelings of relief, especially if your loved one went through a long and painful process of sickness before death. Prolonged illness and care of a loved one is incredibly difficult and draining. It is completely natural and normal to feel a sense of relief when they are finally at rest and feeling no more pain or suffering. This does not mean that you do not love them or miss them and should not be something to feel guilty over.

6. One big ball of tangled emotions. This comes with the territory of grief. If you have ever injured a foot or a toe, you will understand this illustration. Once the toe or foot is injured, it is like a target is now on the injured body part. You seem to stub it often or drop things on it, or people seem to step on it or bump into it

often. Why? It is sensitive and 'out there' for the hurting. This is the way it is with grief. Your emotions are injured and inflamed. It is like you are walking around with a target on your back. You will be easily hurt, offended, angry, and every other emotion out there. People will very easily 'bump into you' when you are grieving. Expect to feel every emotion all at once. Many people explain it as feeling like you are in a constantly agitated state.

7. Spiritual dryness. Expect to feel spiritually dead. Nothing will stir you or comfort you or bring you hope as it once did. You may wonder where God is or why you can't feel or hear Him. You will wonder where all this grace and mercy and the promised help and miracles are. You may even feel like all the promises in the Bible are lies because you aren't experiencing any of them. Reading your Bible and praying fall flat and feel useless. For most people who are grieving, going to church becomes an excruciating event. All the people, the smiles, the happy couples and families are stark reminders of their loss. Then there are the hugs and the people who ask how you are doing. It seems just too much to handle. Many say the overwhelming feeling of loneliness is more pronounced at church. Expecting this, and realizing that you are not a terrible Christian because you have these feelings, can help you push through this stage and get to the other side.

8. Grief storms. Expect them. They will come. You will be doing ok and making progress when, out of nowhere, you will be sucker punched right in the gut. You won't be able to breathe, you will get a case of the ugly cries, and you will be a real mess for a while. There will be no explanation, no reason for the trigger, and no way to skirt around it. Grief storms are simply part of the process and can even happen years after the death of your loved one.

Giving yourself permission to grieve is of utmost importance. It has been said that the amount of grief you feel at the loss of a person is in direct proportion to the amount of love you had for that person. Great love = great grief. If this is true, then there must be a season of great grief when we lose someone we loved greatly. We won't just get over it and get past it and move on quickly, no matter how much we want to.

Another thing we can expect is for some well-meaning people to say some really not well-thought-out things. It is OK. They really do mean well. They just cannot understand what you are going through. Expect it and be willing to extend them some grace. The truth is, your grief scares them to death. It causes them to stare their worst fear in the face, and that makes people say some pretty ignorant things. People will tell you to be brave or to be strong. The truth is, when you are grieving, it isn't time to be strong or to be brave. It is simply time to be human. When we grieve, it is time for us to be weak and for Christ to be strong.

It is important to understand that all the above are 'issues' that stem from the death of your loved one. It is also important to understand that none of those 'issues' are your responsibility to solve or to fix. There is someone responsible for them, however. Psalm 68:20 says, "He that is our God is the God of salvation; and unto GOD the Lord belong the issues from death." Don't you just love that? He's the responsible party for all these endless issues that stem from grief. The 'how long' belongs to God. The physical issues that crop up belong to God. The numbness, fog, depression, sorrow, pain, grief storms, financial worries, stress, and thoughtless people all belong to God. The same God of your salvation is God of your grief and all that comes with it. That, ladies, is some powerful comfort.

SO, NOW WHAT?

In life, we do not get to choose our 'what is.' We do not get to pick our circumstances and our situations. If we had the power to choose our 'what is' not a one of us would ever choose to go through grief. We would never choose to lose a loved one. We would not choose cancer, prolonged illness, funeral homes, caskets, pall bearers, and sitting across from an empty chair at breakfast. We just wouldn't. But grief does give us a gift of choice. We do get to choose our 'now what.'

Let's go back and visit Ruth at the graveside after the mourners turn and walk away. She had had hopes and dreams, and now they all lie in the ground with her cold, dead husband. She wasn't prepared for this. She hadn't expected this. She didn't want this and yet, here it was in all its horrible glory. Naomi told her to go home, to turn her back on God and call it quits. Remember, we said people will say some pretty dumb things to you while you are grieving. This was one of them. But we must remember that Naomi had buried a husband and two sons, so let's cut her some slack here. Her pain must have been so incredibly intense. You will find that you will say some pretty dumb things while you are in the process of grief too. While standing there with her toes in the dirt of that grave, Ruth finds herself faced with a choice. The choice of what to do with her 'now what.' What was to be her 'what next'? We all know what Ruth did and how that one decision forever changed the course of her life. Hers was such a powerful 'now what.'

Your 'now what' is no different. You, yes you, standing there with your toes in the dirt of your loved one's grave. You have the same gift in your grief. You have the same opportunity to choose. What will you do next? When Ruth chose to follow Jehovah and leave everything she knew and held dear, she didn't see Boaz. All she could see was loss and hurt and the unknown. Yet, she made that life-changing choice to step out in faith and follow God into the unknown. What choice are you making? What steps are you taking? What are you doing with your 'now what'?

Here are some tips for when you are facing a 'now what':

1. Do the next thing. Just the next thing. Don't think about down the road or around the bend or ten years from now. Just do the next thing. That may be just getting out of bed, fixing breakfast, or

going to the bank. Make a list for each day and then walk through each thing one at a time. Mark them off when they are done and then write another list for the next day. This will help you when you are in that 'fog' we talked about.

2. If possible, wait awhile before making a big decision. You aren't thinking clearly right now. Avoid making life-changing decisions for a while, if at all possible. Most counselors agree that this isn't the time to decide to move, quit your job, or change careers. Proceed prayerfully and carefully when making decisions while grieving.

3. Let yourself grieve. Don't deny it, stuff it, or try to rush through it. This will only prolong it. Lean into it and invite it in for tea. It will stay awhile, but it won't stay forever. Matthew 5:4 says, "Blessed are they that mourn: for they shall be comforted." In order to receive that promised comfort, we must allow ourselves to mourn.

4. Make a conscious, determined, deliberate, purposeful decision to move *toward* GOD. Just as Ruth took the first step toward Bethlehem and away from Moab, we must take one step at a time toward God and away from the hatred, bitterness, anger, hopelessness, despair, and all the lies that Satan can and will dish up. The world will offer all sorts of unhealthy ways to manage and cope with grief. These unhealthy coping mechanisms can be things like: alcohol, drugs, sex, toxic relationships, working too much, turning your back on God, and withdrawing or walking away from friends and family. Taking the deliberate and purposeful steps toward God will include trusting His character, relying on His strength and healing, walking in His promises, reading His Word daily, pouring out your heart in prayer, holding onto His hand, living in His strength, standing on truth, pushing through hard and staying in church, and choosing to believe in His love and His heart even when it hurts.

BUT SERIOUSLY, HOW LONG?

Everyone who has ever walked the valley of the shadow of death comes to a point when they just want to get to the other side. Grief seems to last forever, and honestly, it is something that doesn't ever really go away. Why? Because that person doesn't ever come back. The grief you feel over the loss of that person is also the grief you feel over the loss of that person's presence in your life. You no longer see their face, hear their laugh, have that conversation, receive their advice, enjoy their companionship, and a million other things. Because none of that comes back, we can expect the grief to stay with us. That's the bad news. The good news, however, is that the intensity of the grief won't always be so sharp. You will get through and that will get better. Grief is sort of like a scar. The wound, when open and gaping, causes immense pain, but over time and with healing, the wound heals and becomes a scar. It is a constant reminder, but the sharp pain has faded over time. Some scars or injuries can still cause pain or aches even years later. Many people testify of a broken bone or a dislocated joint or even an incision that still has an ache with the change of weather or has a shooting pain every once in a while for no reason. That's what healing from grief looks like.

Many who have gone through grief describe it as a darkness that engulfs you, surrounds you, and even gets in you. While that may be true, there is an even greater truth found in Psalm 18:28: "For thou wilt light my candle: the LORD my God will enlighten my darkness." This verse does not say God would take away the darkness. It says He would light your candle *in* the darkness. That's our hope, and that is why we can know our grief is different from those who do not know Christ. 1 Thessalonians 4:13–18 says, "But I would not have you to be ignorant, brethren, concerning them which are asleep, that ye sorrow not, even as others which have no hope." Our sorrow is not a hopeless sorrow. Our sorrow has hope, and hope makes all the difference. Heaven gives us hope. The reality of our loved one being with Jesus, free from pain and suffering and filled with joy and peace, gives us hope. We have the hope of heaven and the reality that we will see them again someday. Not only does God give us a heavenly hope but He gives us an earthly one as well. God will enlighten our darkness here on this earth. On the hard days, I challenge you to light a candle. Every time you look at it, quote Psalm 18:28. HOPE in the Lord and realize you will never ever be hopeless.

Not only are you grieving the loss of the person and their presence in your life but you are also grieving your normal—life as it used to be. Quite honestly, we need to order two headstones when a loved one dies. One for our loved one and one for our normal. Letting go of your old normal will cause a grief all on its own. But letting go will be key to moving on. Having the unrealistic expectation that the old normal will return will only prolong the pain you are feeling. Raging at the new normal will only bring with it more complications and setbacks. Ruth walked away from her old normal and embraced a new one. For sure, it was a vastly different normal than her old one. It included a new country, a new language, new customs, along with gleaning for her meals and trying to provide for her widowed mother-in-law. Yet, embrace it she did. How different would her story have been if she raged at her new normal and demanded her old one back? Your story can be different *and* good. Your normal can be new *and* blessed. Your life can take on a whole new direction *and* still be one that is fulfilled and satisfying. There's that power of 'and' that we talked about earlier.

HEALTHY WAYS OF FINDING COMFORT

Comfort, like grief, is highly individualized. What brings comfort to one does nothing for another. In the introduction to this chapter, I mentioned how my sisters and I all grieved differently. Each of us also found comfort differently. And that was, and still is, OK. God is the God of *all* comfort, but we must realize that we *need* comforting. Women are notorious for feeling the pressure to be strong for the kids or the family or the coworkers or, or, or…. We feel if we start to cry, we may never stop. We just have to keep going and going and going. If you are tempted to take the Energizer Bunny approach in grief, it will just cause you to crash and burn later on. Take the time to be broken and realize you need some comforting. Then be open to receiving the comfort. For some of us, asking for help or appearing weak is the absolute worst thing we can imagine, but giving ourselves permission to be human in this very difficult time is of utmost importance. We also need to understand that we will need to take some steps in order to find the healthy choices that will give us healthy comfort. They won't always just drop into our laps. There will be some things that we will need to do in order to receive some of the healthy comfort that is available. With all that being said, here are some healthy ways to find comfort and healing.

1. Listen to Christian music. I remember when my dad and mom had made the terribly difficult decision for my dad to be transported to a hospice facility. His care was getting so intense that it was taking three adults just to maneuver him around the house. After the last arrangement was made, I had to watch my parents say goodbye to each other in a thousand different ways. I was cleaning out my mom's refrigerator (remember, I am a doer.) Someone had turned on some music and it was Patsy Cline singing some terribly sad song from long ago. It was an excruciating span of time. Finally, I stood up and changed the music to gospel songs about heaven. The entire atmosphere of the house changed. It was a tremendous testimony of the power of music and one I won't soon forget.

2. Get outside. Breathe fresh air, feel the sun on your face, maybe even walk barefoot in the grass and listen to the birds sing. Schedule some time to take daily walks, have your lunch break outside, walk the dog, or do some yard work. Take weekend hikes or go camping. Nature has its own healing properties, but one must go outside to tap into them.

3. Get a pet. Many people testify to this really helping to fill the void and provide companionship. Pets give unconditional love and make much better listeners than people who actually talk back!

4. Journal. Journaling is an incredibly healthy way to get what is going on *in* you *out*. There is a no judgment zone on that paper, and you can be brutally honest as those words spill across the page. You can journal about an important something or about nothing at all. Still skeptical? Try it for a two-week period and see just how much it helps.

5. Look at scrapbooks, photos, and memorabilia. Don't give into the temptation to put away photos and never ever look at them. Display them and walk down memory lane. Many find great comfort just seeing their loved one's face and their smile from long ago.

6. If you are creative, find an artistic outlet that allows you to express yourself in some way. Take a class and pick up that artistic hobby you always wanted to pursue but never had the time to.

7. Reread the many sympathy cards you got after the death of your loved one. Seeing how others loved them and reading their kind words can wash over that raw hurt and bring comfort on those bad days.

8. Serve others. Many of the suggestions thus far can be personalized. One may help you while it does nothing for someone else. For example, you may not be artistic in any way or you may hate pets, so those suggestions are ones you skip right over. But this suggestions is one for everyone. This one has proven to work for all who try it. This one is found in the Bible over and over again. This one is 100% effective. It is absolutely vital that you get outside of yourself in order to heal. Focusing on the needs of others will serve in

meeting your own need during grief. Ask God to reveal a need that is around you. Open your eyes and heart and be willing to see the need He will show you. Then take whatever action needed in order to help someone else.

9. Read the book of Psalms. The psalmists are notoriously honest and real. They lay open their hurt, despair, and grief over and over again. On many days, it will seem like the psalmist read your mind as they put pen to paper.

10. Run *to* God and not *away* from Him. Lean into Him, hold onto Him, sing to Him, read His word, and get to know Him in ways you never had to before.

11. Have a consistent Bible-reading and prayer time each and every day. This may be very hard at first, as you may 'feel' nothing. But push through and keep at it. You may need to just go through the motions for a time, but it won't always be that way.

12. Continue going to church. This, as well, will be very hard at first. But pushing through hard is the stuff grief is made of. Keep at it and hang in there. Sit in a different seat and ask someone to sit with you or ask if you can sit with someone you know. Your church is a family and many would be glad to sit with you. It is important that you do not give into hard and that you push through and keep going to church. Satan wouldn't fight so hard to keep you from it if it wasn't important.

13. Join a Bible-based grief group, such as GriefShare. Sharing the hurt with others who are going through similar hardships can be very healing.

14. Read biblical books on grief. Understanding what you are going through can really help you go through it well.

Remember that some of these will speak to you and some won't. For some, they will work, and others will need something else. But numbers 8–12 will help *everyone*. The truth is, we are all different and will receive comfort in different ways. That is ok. Never try to force your way of comfort on someone else that is grieving along with you. Give them space to mourn and to receive comfort for themselves. Give yourself space to do the same.

Just as there are healthy ways to receive comfort, there are also unhealthy ways to do the same. We will call those 'counterfeit comfort.' These counterfeit comforts seek to *numb* the grief and not *heal* it. There is a huge difference. Here is a list of counterfeit comforts that will be readily available to you:

1. Food. Either eating too much or not enough. Food cannot bring comfort. It was designed to provide nutrition, not comfort.

2. Shopping. Whether online or in the store, purchasing things will not bring you healing. It will only bring you debt.

3. Working too much. While this may distract you, it won't heal you. This tactic will exhaust you and will distance you from those who need you, and those who you need, during this time.

4. Sleeping a lot. Using sleep as a form of escape won't do you any good. This tactic isolates you and cuts you off from others and from the help that is real and readily available to you. When you wake up, the pain will still be there and you will find that you sink even lower in the despair you were trying to avoid to begin with.

5. Hiding behind devices. Whether it is watching TV for hours or scrolling on your phone, this tactic will do you no good at all. It is

an unhealthy form of escape that will rob you of time that could be better spent.

6. Prescription medications. While there is nothing wrong with taking a medication that your body needs in order to heal, many come to abuse this during grief. No pill can take away the hurt that the loss of your loved one brings with it.

7. Alcohol and drugs. Grief has created many an addict and an alcoholic. Be aware that you will be vulnerable to these during this time, even if you have never ever been tempted in this area before. The desire to numb the pain is a strong one and alcohol and drugs will provide that numbness. But, just as with a surgical procedure, the numbness won't last and the pain will soon set in again. Only this time, you will have an addiction to deal with along with the grief and sorrow.

8. Unhealthy relationships. Clinging to another can be a strong pull during grief. 'Give me someone, anyone, to fill the void' can become our mantra. The problem with this is that that person cannot fix you. They cannot replace the one you lost. They are not built to sustain the responsibility you have placed on them, and the relationship will crumble under the pressure.

9. Illicit relationships, sex, pornography. Running to this type of counterfeit comfort will bring even more pain and destruction with it. Sure, it looks good and feels good for a moment, but the consequences will not be worth it. Think cheese on a mouse trap. Ask the dead mouse if the bite was worth the price.

Avoiding these counterfeit comforts will be a daily decision as one or more of them will present themselves to you along the way in your journey through grief. Psalm 77:2 says, "In the day of my trouble I sought the Lord."

In this day of your trouble, what are you seeking? Let's put it in a 'fill in the blank' form. "In the day of my trouble I sought _____.' What goes in your blank? Anything other than the Lord won't work. Strive to make sure the Lord goes in that blank each and every day.

FACT VS FICTION

While traveling through grief, you will come across a whole boatload of lies. Satan will practically pave the way with them. You will find yourself having thoughts like *No one loves me; No one cares; I am all alone; Why should I continue living? Life isn't worth living. It is hopeless; I have nothing to live for; It will never get better.* This list could go on and on. These may *feel* true, but they simply are *not* true. They may look like facts, but they are, in reality, fiction. It would be nice if at the funeral home, they equipped each grieving person with a special lie-detector kit. It should be included in the package deal, in my opinion. You could take it home and hook it up, and whenever you had a thought or an emotion that was based on a lie, it would beep. Wouldn't that be nice? Truthfully, we have one already auto-installed when we get saved. The Holy Spirit inside of you is the best lie detector known to man. The problem is, we don't listen to the quiet little 'beep' that He gives us when a lie flits through our mind or is presented to us through a circumstance or through society. We fill our minds with the lies from the world and fail to read and heed life's greatest instruction manual, which is the Bible. Below you will find a list of lies and the truths that refute them. The lies may be so intense for a season that you need to surround yourself with the truth. Look up verses that speak truth to counter the lies you are dealing with personally and write them on index cards or Post-it notes and literally surround yourself with them—in your purse, in your car, on your desk, on the refrigerator, and by your bed. Hold onto those truths for dear life and you won't go under. That's a promise.

Lies	Truths
I am alone.	A child of God is never alone. Hebrews 13:5
I have no hope.	I always have hope. Romans 15:13
No one cares.	God cares. Luke 12:7
No one loves me.	God loves me. Romans 8:35–39
Life isn't worth living.	God has a plan for me. Jeremiah 29:11
This will never get better.	This has an end. Jeremiah 29:11

I could write lots more, but that would be doing your homework for you. Your assignment is to write out the lies that you are struggling with and then search your Bible for the truths that refute them. You can use your phone and search out: "verses about_____." You can also use the concordance in the back of your Bible.

Luke 1:1 says, "Forasmuch as many have taken in hand to set forth in order a declaration of those things which are most surely believed among us." According to this verse, we are going to have to take these lies in hand and put them in their place. Then we are going to need to declare those things that are surely believed by the children of God. This has to be done individually and it must be done personally. Now I need to warn you that you will have to *choose* to do this while those loud lies are screaming at you and trying hard to bully you into believing them.

Here are some biblical truths about grief that we will find in the pages of Scripture:

1. God uses suffering to help us grow. Grief is never ever wasted with God.

2. Peace and pain can coexist in the child of God's life.

3. Time doesn't heal. God heals over time with our cooperation.

4. You reap what you sow. If you sow pushing people away in your grief, you will reap loneliness. If you sow anger, you will reap bitterness. If you sow obedience and make sure you move toward the Lord, you will reap healing and help.

5. Grief reveals the uncomfortable truth that life isn't under our control. We were never in control, even when things were good and normal. God has been, and always will be, in control. God is sovereign and has a providential plan for our lives.

6. God's identity remains firmly intact, even in my grief. He is God. He is good. He is right. He is holy. He is love. He is kind. He is merciful.

7. God will work everything out in you, around you, and for you.

COME OUT WITH YOUR HANDS UP!

\Remember in the old police shows where the cops would say, "You are surrounded. Come out with your hands up"? Why did they say that? They said that to let the criminal know there was no way out. They were giving them the truth about their reality—the police had the power and the control, and it was time for the criminal to surrender. That word, 'surrender,' will be key to your grief journey. You will need to come out with your hands up because you are surrounded by the sovereignty, identity, and ability of God. He's got you completely surrounded. It is time to lay down the weapons of your control, your plans, your agenda, your anger, the many unanswered questions, and all the 'what ifs' and 'if onlys' and come out with your hands up. There have been times in my seasons of intense struggle that I have literally put my hands up in my prayer time. Try it sometime. It is a great physical reminder of our need and our decision to surrender.

Here are some things you will need to surrender along the way on your journey through grief:

1. Your hopes, dreams, plans, and ideas of how things would be or how you thought they should be. The death that you are facing took all of these in the grave with them. To walk around holding onto them is useless and wastes precious energy that you simply do not have right now. Surrendering these to the God who loves you and gave Himself for you is the only way forward. Realizing that God has a good plan for you and that He isn't out to 'get you' will help you to release and surrender. God is your safe place. He always has been. In the movies, when the criminals surrender, they get handcuffs and jail time. For Christians, when we surrender, we get peace, rest, joy, and hope. We get help and we get the will of God realized in our lives. Not a bad deal.

2. Your expectations of what grief will be like. Many Christians think their faith in God is somehow supposed to make grief easier or quicker. This isn't the case. Grief is awful for everyone. It hurts. A lot. But the faith we have in God gives us grief with hope. It is hurtful, but it isn't hopeless. Our faith doesn't take us out of grief, but it will sustain us in grief.

3. Getting your 'why' answered. God has a history of allowing things, incorporating things, and using things His children simply do not like or enjoy. Raging and demanding answers won't bring healing. Surrounding yourself with question marks will only cause you to be imprisoned by them. *He* is the answer you are seeking. Look for the *who*, not the *why*. Instead of why, ask *how*. 'God, how can I get through this?' He will answer that question. Ask, 'What, God, do you want me to learn through this?' That's another one He will answer. It isn't wrong to question God, but by simply adjusting the questions, you will finally get the answers that will bring true healing.

4. Your desire to get better fast. There is no rushing through grief. Back when I was in college, I took several courses in summer school when I went back home. I did this to speed things up a bit. I deliberately chose some of the notoriously hard courses. Why? I figured harder for a shorter period of time was better than harder for a longer stretch of time. Now, if you have taken college summer courses, you understand there is absolutely no way you can teach or learn all that material in a four-week span. The reading assignments were ridiculously long, and the tests came at you in warp speed. I passed those crazy-hard classes because for a summer course, the educators always adjust their expectations. The professor tells you what you need to focus on as you try your best to digest immense amounts of information in a short amount of time. Not surprisingly, I did not learn very much from those courses at all. Not like I did the ones that took more time and were taught slowly and gave me bite-size amounts that I could retain. The principle is the same with grief. You cannot choose to take 'summer school grief.' I wish you could. I wish I could. But it simply isn't an option. You have been signed up for the full semester class. It will be long and it will be hard, but you will learn and you will grow over this lengthy and time-consuming course.

5. Depending on anything other than God for a fix to your broken-ness. Other things and people can come alongside you and assist, but they most certainly cannot fix you. Jeremiah 2:13 says, "For my people have committed two evils; they have forsaken me the foun-tain of living waters, and hewed them out cisterns, broken cisterns, that can hold no water." Depending on someone or something else, other than God, to get you through grief is like pouring water in a container with a hole in the bottom. They just can't hold water. They can't hold you. They can't fill you or fix you. Only God can.

This season of grief is one of the hardest ones you will ever go through. It is like the children's book I used to read to my kids, called *Bear Hunt*. In that story, a group of children were hunting an imaginary bear and had all sorts of obstacles in their way. It was written in a sing-song repetitive way, and over and over again you would read the phrase, "We can't go over it, we can't go under it, we got to go through it." Grief isn't a cute little kid's book, but man, is this phrase accurate or what! We can't go over grief, we can't go under grief, we've got to go through grief. And through it we go, hand in hand with the One who loves us more than life itself. At least if we 'got to go through it,' we get to do it with the One who loved us so much He died for us. He walked through the worst kind of grief imaginable so that He would be able to walk with us in ours. What a God!

Making It Personal

Answer the following questions in your journal:

1. Write out the lies that you have been battling and the truths from Scripture that refute them.

2. Describe your loved one. Write about their personality, how you met, your ups and down, what you loved about them, what drove you crazy about them, and what you miss about them.

3. What has been the hardest part about grief so far?

4. What has been one surprising aspect about grief that you weren't expecting?

5. How did Ruth's response in her grief speak to you?

6. What are some of the next steps that you have decided to take as you have read this chapter?

7. Write out a prayer over your journey through the valley of grief.

CHAPTER ELEVEN

Guilt and Shame

*Guilt – "the feeling of having done wrong
or failed in an obligation"*

*Shame – "a painful feeling of humiliation or distress caused
by the consciousness of wrong or foolish behavior"*

No one knows her name, and perhaps it is best that way. She is known simply as 'The Woman Who Was a Sinner.' Most Bible scholars agree that she had been a prostitute. Her life was a wreck and in ruins when she met Jesus for the first time. She had made one bad choice after another. The things she had done for money were downright shameful. She was unloved, unwanted, and unaccepted by polite society. Proper ladies shunned her and men refused to look into her eyes. Her family had long since disowned her, those she had actually known, that is. Let's just say her family wasn't ever going to win any awards for family of the year. She had no memories of ever having any worth or value, no laughing childhood days of being carefree and innocent. There was no use dwelling on it, but she did, a lot. Whenever she looked into the mirror, she hated the woman who looked back at her. Her eyes were sunken in and dark circles were prominent and ugly. Her body was a walking testament to hard living.

Her health gone, her youth robbed, and her mind rotted with the cesspool she had lived in for years. Shame was her constant companion. She wore it like a heavy cloak. Oh, she understood the proper women shunning her. If she could, she would shun herself. Why did God ever make her to begin with? She had never been as good as those happy, beautiful little girls whose daddies loved them and whose mamas took care of them. She had seen them playing in the street. She had longed to go to them, even as a child, and join in the carefree fun. But, even then, she knew something was wrong with her. She was damaged goods. The only person who made her feel worth something was that Teacher named, Jesus. He was so different from the Pharisees. They condemned her. They hated her. They were disgusted by her. They looked down their noses at her and made her feel like yesterday's garbage. But Jesus was different. He had not only looked at her but also actually looked her in the eyes, and in the soul, she felt like. His teaching was so real and so life changing. He made God sound so accessible and so loving. As a result, she began to follow along, at a distance of course, anytime she could. She hung on His every word. He preached repentance, peace, hope, rest, and forgiveness. For the first time in her life, she felt the stirrings of hope. Jesus made her feel like peace was possible, rest was within reach, and forgiveness wasn't so far away. Then, one night, after yet another lesson from the Master, she had dared to slip to her knees by her bed. She begged God to cleanse her and make her whole. She confessed her sins and her many bad choices. She named them all. She held nothing back, because if He was God, He knew it anyway, right? After what seemed like an eternity on her knees, she stood on wobbly legs, spent and exhausted. She looked out the window up to the brilliant star-studded sky and smiled. She had asked Him to be HER God, to forgive her of her many sins, and to save her from the hellish existence she had been living. 'Deliver' had been the word she had used. And that is just what she felt—delivered. She stepped outside and lifted her face to the sky. More tears, but happy ones this time. It was almost as if she could reach out and touch the stars. Never had she ever felt so clean and so worthwhile. She fell asleep with a smile on her face, and with no one else in her bed, for the first time in a long, long while.

The next day, she heard that Jesus was going to Simon's house for dinner. Simon. She couldn't stand that Pharisee. They were all bad, but he was the worst. His pompous and holier-than-thou attitude oozed out of him. Could she go to that house—his house? Did she dare? She drew herself up to her full height and lifted her chin. She had as much right to an audience with Jesus as Simon the Pharisee. After all, she was a believer now! The gratefulness in her heart bubbled up and over as she dressed simply and modestly. She wore no makeup on her face and no gaudy jewelry. She had spent the day cleaning out her old life, and all the evidence of it, from her home. She picked up her costly alabaster box, the one that contained the precious ointment within. It was her nest egg. She had scrimped and saved for a long time for this little beauty. But now, all she wanted to do was give it away to the one Person who had ever shown her love. Out the door she went and straight into the house crowded with Pharisees and religious leaders of the day. The crowd parted like she had the plague. Loud whispers and finger pointing caused her to falter for just a moment. But then Jesus looked at her across the room and a small smile played about His mouth. It was like He had been expecting her, looking for her even. She held His gaze as she inched forward. The whispers grew louder as she fell at His feet. She couldn't contain the tears for a moment longer. This man looked at her like no other man ever did. He looked at her with kindness and love. He looked at her like she was worth something. He made her feel like somebody. He gave her hope and made her think she could be more than the sum total of all her bad mistakes. And so, she bent over His feet and wept. She cried out all the years of tears of the deeply imbedded shame that had been a part of her for as long as she could remember. She cried out all of the self-hate along with all the condemnation from others. That's when she noticed how dirty the feet of Jesus were. What was wrong with Simon? Why hadn't he taken better care of Jesus? She saw her tears splash in the dust and the dirt that covered His feet and she began wiping them with her hair. Next came the ointment. She lavishly poured it all over His feet. Not just a drop or two would do. He had given her forgiveness, worth, value, and acceptance. He had held nothing back from her, so she would hold nothing back from Him.

*That's when Simon's condemnation spewed forth. He said, loud enough for everyone to hear, thar she was a dirty, worthless piece of trash, and that if Jesus was who He claimed to be, He would have known that and would never allow the likes of her to touch Him. That's when Jesus launched into a little side lesson for this hard-hearted Pharisee. You can read it in Luke Chapter 7. He shares a story of two debtors who could not pay their debts. One had a small debt and the other, a huge one. The creditor forgave them both of their debts and they walked away free. Who would love the creditor most? Simon rightly answered the one forgiven the most would love the most. Then Jesus spoke again saying, "Wherefore I say unto thee, Her sins, which are many, **are forgiven**... And then he said unto her, Thy sins **are forgiven**." Then later He said, "thy faith hath saved the; **go in peace**." (Emphasis added.)*

What can we learn from this rather colorful lady? We can learn to start living forgiven. We can learn to accept the forgiveness of God and to go in peace, just like she did. Welcome to the chapter that can make all the difference in your outlook on life and your 'inlook' at yourself.

SETTING THE RECORD STRAIGHT

You may be wondering why I didn't share a personal story from my life that illustrates the chapter's topic. I have done that with every other chapter. Why not this one? The answer is because of all the emotions we will cover, guilt and shame are the most personal. Because of Jesus's sacrifice on Calvary, my guilt and my shame never have to be made public. They are between Him and me, as are yours. To stay true to that fact, those stories—and I have many—will remain private. There are just some things that need to remain between Jesus and me, or between Jesus and you. And, oh my, aren't we so thankful for that!

Now, before we proceed any further, we need to set some things straight. Guilt isn't a bad thing. In fact, it is a very necessary and healthy tool that God uses to keep us close to Him and clean from sin. It is perfectly normal to feel guilty after doing something wrong. So, let's first explore this thing called guilt. To do so, we will take a deep dive into a passage in Scripture that shows us the importance of guilt and responding to it in the right way.

Let me introduce you to a man named David. He is called 'a man after God's own heart.' This fella had had God's touch on his life for a long time. God had protected him against enemy armies and the enemy of a jealous king who chased him for years. He had helped him build a great kingdom and had blessed him in many ways. But this man allowed sin to lead him astray. Instead of chasing after God's own heart, he chased after sexual pleasure. In my devotional series *Women of the Word*, we uncover a little-known truth about Bathsheba. She wasn't a wanton seductress out to lure in unsuspecting kings. Oh no, not at all. You may be thinking, *She was outside naked for Pete's sake! Of course she was a hoochie mama!* But we need to understand her culture. She was bathing outdoors for her ceremonial cleansing after her menstrual cycle. This was the normal custom of the day. She would have been in a secluded courtyard in her backyard in the cover of darkness and in the middle of the night. She was doing nothing wrong. When David saw her, he lusted in his heart and sent his men to go get her. The Bible says they 'took' her and brought her to David for him to do with her as he pleased. After all, he was the king, and the king gets what he wants. Bathsheba had no choice, just as his men had no choice when he sent them to get her. But David's sin wasn't done yet. When Bathsheba realized she was pregnant, she sent a frantic note to David telling him of her predicament. She would be put to death as an adulteress because her husband, Uriah, was gone to battle fighting in David's army. There was no way the baby was his and everyone would know it. David, instead of coming clean, decided to try for a cover-up. He called Uriah home from the front under the guise of asking him how things were going. Uriah gave his report and David told him to go home and enjoy his wife. Uriah surprised David by refusing and sleeping on the palace steps instead. He couldn't bring himself to go home and enjoy the pleasures of being with his beautiful wife while the other troops were roughing it on the battlefront. David, irritated with this man's righteousness, tried again. This time, he got him good and drunk at dinner, hoping he would forget his high standards and go home. Nope. Even drunk, Uriah was more righteous than a stone-cold sober David. Finally, in utter desperation, David sank to the lowest of lows. He wrote Uriah's commanding officer a sealed letter and sent it back to the front with Uriah. Sadly, the man was literally carrying his own death warrant. David had ordered for Uriah to be sent to the hottest part of the battle and then for everyone to back away, leaving him exposed and unprotected. This was nothing but premeditated murder on the part of David. Sin always, always, always begets more sin, with each one being worse than the last. David's plan worked perfectly, and Uriah was no longer a problem. David then sent for Bathsheba and took her for his wife. There! That's that. Sin covered up and no one was the wiser. All done. Right? Wrong.

Bathsheba's whole pregnancy went by, and David did absolutely nothing to right the wrong he had done. Nine months he had felt awful, and nine months he refused to come clean. Everyone knew what he had done. The men on the front, the men who had been sent to take Bathsheba, the men who saw Uriah sleep on the palace steps, the commanding officer who ordered the men to leave Uriah stranded, David's children, and the woman who now carried his baby. They all knew. But they weren't the only ones who knew. The God David served knew. He knew all the juicy details that others just guessed at. And time and again, this God lovingly laid guilt on this man. He tried to draw David to repentance, but the stubborn king refused.

Psalm 32 shows us, in David's own words, just how he felt during those torturous months. Verses 3–4 say, "When I kept silence, my bones waxed old through my roaring all the day long. For day and night thy hand was heavy upon me: my moisture is turned into the drought of summer. Selah." Do you see how David's unconfessed sin brought physical, mental, and emotional misery to him? That is just how God designed guilt to work. Guilt is awful. It feels awful. It is supposed to. The awful is meant to propel you to get things right so that you can experience relief from the terrible side effects of sin. When David refused, God sent a man by the name of Nathan who pointed a bony finger in the face of the king and told him,

"Thou art the man." He boldly shared a story with David that pinpointed exactly what David had done, but he did it in a word picture using a little lamb. It pulled on the heart strings of the king and made him feel righteous indignation at the one who had stolen and killed the little lamb that didn't belong to him in the story. That's when God lowered the boom on the sinful king. David's response? He finally repented, and we see that repentance penned in Psalm 32:5: "I acknowledge my sin unto thee, and mine iniquity have I not hid. I said, I will confess my transgressions unto the LORD; and thou forgavest the iniquity of my sin. Selah." David began the psalm with, "Blessed is he whose transgression is forgiven, whose sin is covered." David could now, once again, be blessed because his sin had been confessed and forgiven. Nothing more was being held back or covered up. He had finally come clean so that God could cleanse him from his sin.

Guilt isn't something to be avoided, as unpleasant as it is. It is something we need to pay close attention to and strive to be very sensitive to. When we first feel the tug of guilt in our heart over something we have done, or not done, said, or not said, thought, or indulged in, we need to get it right immediately. The time to confess and turn away from that sin is the moment you first feel guilt over that sin. Just ask David. He lost nine months of his life living in pure torment and misery, when he could have repented immediately and lived free and forgiven.

Now, it is important to note that David's confession did not remove the consequences of his sin. Bathsheba's baby died, and much later on, David's own son, Amnon, would rape Tamar, David's daughter. Now, where do you think he learned that trick from? We know where. Sadly, consequences are like the sun that comes up every morning. You can count on them coming. What confession does do, however, is cleanse our standing with God. It removes the obstacle that is blocking fellowship and closeness. It removes what has been hindering our prayers from reaching heaven. It removes the guilt. Consequences will have to be reaped; that is the way it is with sin. Satan won't tell you that. He will only show you the fun, the flashy, and the pleasurable. He hides the painful hook with a fat juicy worm, but rest assured, the hook is there and is razor sharp. A few painful experiences with consequences, and we will hopefully learn a lesson or two about our enemy. Keep short sin accounts. By that I mean, pray and confess as soon as you feel the uncomfortable stirrings of guilt.

CONVICTION VS CONDEMNATION

We know by now that for everything that God has, Satan has a counterfeit. Conviction is a tool God uses to draw you to Him and condemnation is a tool Satan uses to keep you from God. The problem is Satan's counterfeit is sometimes really hard to detect. It can look the same, act the same, and feel the same as conviction, only it is not the same at all. Just like the cashiers take out that little brown marker and run it over the one-hundred-dollar bill you give her, we must do the same with condemnation and conviction. We have to distinguish which is which. We need a marker to help us spot the counterfeit. This section will be your marker from now on. It is designed to help you spot the fake. It is now time to draw a line in the sand, distinguishing between what is from God and what is from Satan in the guilt game.

- Conviction is about something you need to confess. Condemnation is about something you have already confessed.

- Conviction says, "I have done something wrong." Condemnation says, "I am something wrong."

- Conviction drives you toward God. Condemnation drives you away from God.

- Conviction offers hope. Condemnation offers no hope.

- Conviction brings you to a point of decision, a moment when you have the power to choose help. Condemnation tells you there is no help.

- Conviction gives you the power to choose. Condemnation says you have no choice.

- Conviction says you can be forgiven for what you have done. Condemnation says you can never be forgiven for what you have done.

- Conviction points to a specific sin. Condemnation is enigmatic and never points to any specific choice or action. It lumps everything together and calls it all bad or shameful.

- Conviction says you failed. Condemnation says you are a failure.

- Conviction brings progress. Condemnation halts progress.

- Conviction brings security. Condemnation brings insecurity.

- Conviction leads to peace. Condemnation robs us of peace.

Romans 8:1 says, "There is therefore now no condemnation to them which are in Christ Jesus...." Did you see that word 'now'? Why is there *now* no condemnation? Because of *who* we are in. We are *now* in Him. We *now* have His righteousness. We are *now* clean. We are *now* His. We are *now* as right with God the Father as God the Son is. That is our reality. That is our truth. Just as the woman we read about in the introduction had a new reality, so do we. I love how she is called the woman who *was* a sinner, not *is* a sinner. All that sinner stuff was now her 'was.' And that is the truth for you too, if you are saved. Jesus told her, "Thy sins ARE forgiven." Present tense. She was forgiven in her right now. She was clean right then and there. Right now, present tense, your sins are forgiven. You are clean.

Before she confessed, there was a great gulf between her and God. After she confessed, there wasn't a power in heaven or on earth that could separate her from the love of God. Romans 8:35–39 tells us, "Who shall separate us from the love of Christ? Shall tribulation, or distress, or persecution, or famine, or nakedness, or peril, or sword? Nay, in all these things we are more than conquerors through him that loved us. For I am persuaded, that neither death, nor life, nor angels, nor principalities, nor powers, nor things present, nor things to come, Nor height, nor depth, nor any other creature, shall be able to separate us from the love of God, which is in Christ Jesus our Lord." There's your truth. Nothing, not even your 'that' can separate you from the love of God. We all have a 'that.' That thing that we did that was so shameful. That sin that haunts us. That decision we would give anything to undo. Nope, not even *that* can separate you from the love of God. This feeling of condemnation that you struggle with is one of your 'these things' that God wants you to conquer. In fact, He has equipped you to do just that. He has made you to be more than a conqueror over it.

When we feel condemned, we need to realize just who is condemning. It isn't God, that's for sure. The Bible calls Satan 'the accuser of the brethren.' He is constantly accusing us before God. When God doesn't listen, and He doesn't, Satan tries another tactic. He comes and accuses us to us. And unfortunately, many times, we do listen. Romans 8:33–34 says, "Who shall lay any thing to the charge of God's elect? It is God that justifieth. Who is he that condemneth? It is Christ that died, yea rather, that is risen again, who is even at the right hand of God, who also maketh intercession for us." According to these verses, there is no one, not even Satan, who can lay any charge against us. Why? God has justified us through the death of His Son on the cross.

Condemnation will make you feel like God is against you. Like you can never please Him or you can never do enough to get Him to accept you. You will view God as angry or as waiting around for you to fail so that He can punish you. You will begin to see God as an angry old man in the sky just waiting to bop you on the head when you mess up. According to these verses, however, that isn't what is happening in heaven at all. In fact, we see Jesus sitting on the right hand of the Father, *praying* for you. Wow! That is certainly a different picture than the one that Satan paints of Him. Earlier in the same chapter, we see the Spirit also making intercession for us. So, we have the Spirit in us praying for us and Jesus in heaven praying for us. Girls, we are so incredibly loved and we are completely clean and justified! And if that weren't enough, we are prayed for by Jesus Himself! Imagine, right now, your name is being called out before the throne. Can't you just hear Him saying something like this:

Father, today I am praying for _____. I sure do love her. She is so very precious to me. But today, she is struggling with condemnation and she doesn't need to. The enemy has lied to her and told her that she has to carry the weight of that sin. But You know I already carried the weight of it all the way up to Calvary. I know that I carried it too. I well remember it. But she doesn't know that. Help her, Father, to realize that, to know that, and to conquer this condemnation. Help her to realize our love for her and her standing in me. I gave her my righteousness and that is all You see when You look at her. Please help her to live in that truth every day. Help her to walk in that truth and to see herself through it. She is so special and important to us. Help her to feel that today and every day. Amen.

What a thought!

Back in the time the New Testament was written, when a prisoner was put in a cell, the charge, or the debt he owed to society, was written on a piece of paper from a ledger. It was then posted up above the cell door. When the debt had been paid, through money or time served, it was marked 'paid in full' as the door was opened and the prisoner released. I say again, "Who can lay anything to the charge of God's elect?" When Jesus marked the ledger sheet 'paid in full' at our salvation, Satan lost his right to write anything else on our ledger sheet. If this is something you struggle with, I encourage you to take a sheet of paper and write 'paid in full' with the date of your salvation underneath it. If you do not remember the date, write the place and any details you do remember about it.

THE FORGIVENESS OF GOD

Conviction brings one to repentance, and that leads one to forgiveness. Condemnation does not. In fact, condemnation makes one feel stuck like they can never ever be forgiven, or that they are unable to move on or get past that sin. To combat that, let's take a moment and look at the forgiveness of God.

When David finally acknowledged and confessed his sin, he was forgiven. The painful consequences were still there, but the sin was completely forgiven in God's eyes. So is yours. If you have felt conviction over a sin in your past and you have confessed it, you are forgiven. The forgiveness of God removes our sins from our account. It stamps 'paid in full' in our ledger. Psalm 103:12 says, "As far as the east is from the west, so far hath he removed our transgressions from us." I'd say, He did a very good job at removing it!

Isaiah 38:17 says, "Behold, for peace I had great bitterness: but thou hast in love to my soul delivered it from the pit of corruption: for thou hast cast all my sins behind thy back." If God can put our sin behind HIS back, then why can't we? Notice it says ALL my sins. Even that one. You know the one. The one that haunts you. The one that keeps you up some nights. Even that one has been removed from you completely. If you have confessed it, it is time to put it behind your back, as He has done.

Now imagine that ledger sheet again. It has your sin debt written on it. Picture it. Now listen to Colossians 2:14: "Blotting out the handwriting of ordinances that was against us, which was contrary to us, and took it out of the way, nailing it to his cross." There you go. If Jesus took it out of the way while going all the way for our salvation, then why on earth does it keep getting in our way?

THE SHAME GAME

Shame gets its power from the silence that surrounds it. We don't speak of shame. The very nature of shame is to suffer in silence. We cannot put our shame out in the open with words. Shame remains in the shadows—always there, always painful, always reminding, constantly reminding. Shame keeps you silent but is never silent itself. It hisses in your ear that you cannot speak about this, but it speaks about nothing else. Shame name-calls. It calls you worthless, useless, unloved, unwanted, tainted, damaged, broken, and hopeless. Shame convinces you that there is something wrong with you that isn't wrong with anyone else. It is never ever quiet. It hounds and hounds with the meanest of accusations. "You aren't good enough. You can't be forgiven enough or clean enough. You aren't smart enough, holy enough, pretty enough, popular enough, talented enough, or worth enough." Ever. Shame isolates. If it can keep you feeling alone, it will keep you defeated. Shame makes you feel like a piece of discarded clothing in the discount pile marked 'irregular.' You are there because you didn't make the cut and couldn't be placed on the regular rack.

Shame distorts our perceptions about ourselves and others, and even our perceptions about God. Shame colors everything. It begins out of our failures but grows as Satan exploits them. Shame creates a fictional gap that is uncrossable between who you long to be and who you really are.

Shame shrivels up and dies when we put words to it and actually speak it aloud. Although shame cannot unhappen, it can be redeemed. That past, that abuse, that choice, and that failure will not ever be undone, but the hold shame has on you most definitely can. Shame can be healed, but it is a step-by-step process that begins with one brave choice followed by lots and lots of other brave choices. Isaiah 50:7 says, "For the Lord GOD will help me; therefore shall I not be confounded; therefore have I set my face like a flint, and I know that I shall not be ashamed." The progression in this verse shows us the steps in the process.

First of all, we must be absolutely convinced that God will help us, no matter what we have done. Then this knowledge of truth leads us to clear thinking. Shame clouds our thinking, but focusing on the truth about us and about God will clear that all up and remove the confounded confusion that has been our normal. That is followed by setting our face like flint. This shows a steely determination on the direction we are going to take. It speaks of our decisions that will be born out of the truth that we are now clearly holding onto. The last step is an assurance that the damaging emotion of shame has been defeated and that we will not let it gain ground again. So, according to this verse, defeating shame will take a firm belief of truth, clear thinking, unwavering determination, and being carefully in control of our emotions.

We know Jesus died on the cross so He could defeat death, hell, and the grave. He went through all that punishment so we wouldn't have to. He bore our sin so that we wouldn't have to keep bearing it. He didn't just bear our sin, however; He also bore our shame so that we wouldn't have to keep bearing it. He carried all my shame on His back so that He could put it behind His back. As a result, it no longer has to remain on my back. Really. It doesn't. Jesus defeated shame just as He defeated your sin and your accuser.

The other day, Anna's Sunday School teacher had given her class an assignment in order to help them realize their freedom from sin. Their assignment was to carry around a black bag with a brick in it. The brick stood for their sin. The teacher had told them they were to take it everywhere with them so that they could see just how hard it was to do life and carry that brick. Simple and easy tasks were no longer simple and easy due to that blasted brick. Now, most kids would be like, "Sure, I will carry this brick around everywhere." But then five minutes after getting home, the brick is tossed to the side and forgotten until the next Sunday, when they were supposed to bring it back for a prize. But if you are my ten-year-old daughter, you take rules and illustrations very seriously and quite literally.

She took her teacher's instructions to heart. That brick went everywhere she did. I cannot tell you how many times I stumbled over that black bag or had it almost dropped on my foot. It came to the dinner table, into the living room, and out by the pool side. I put my foot down or it would have gone into the grocery store with us too! By the end of that week, we were all thoroughly sick of that black bag with a brick in it.

That, ladies, is a perfect picture of shame. Satan stands at the front of the class and assigns us our homework. "Carry this shame around with you everywhere you go. Do not leave it or forget about it or even think that you have the choice to lay it down and walk away." Some of the students in that Sunday School class got up and walked out, leaving their brick in their seat. No way were they going to do that, not even for a piece of candy. Some took it for a little while and then got weary with it. Some actually forgot all about the assignment. But then there is that one. The one that takes it to heart, the one that takes that assignment so seriously, that they literally carry the brick everywhere. I remember looking at Anna on day two of that week as I tried to explain to her that the teacher was trying to show them a truth; she didn't literally mean she *had* to carry that bag everywhere. Anna looked at me, serious as a heart attack, and said, "No, Mom, she said I *was supposed* to carry it *everywhere, so I have to*." Is that you? Are you the one in the class that took Satan literally when he hissed that you have to carry your shame with you everywhere you go? If so, the goal of this chapter is to equip you to be able to lay down that heavy brick of shame and walk away free.

When God looks at you, He doesn't see your black bag or your heavy brick. When He looks at you, He doesn't see your guilt or your shame. When He looks at you, He sees the righteousness of Jesus. 2 Corinthians 5:21 says, "For he hath made him to be sin for us, who knew no sin; that we might be made the righteousness of God in him." You see, He became my sin and my shame, so that I could become the righteousness of God. His righteousness covers all my sin and my shame. It covers all my failures and my faults. I no longer have to worry about them, or carry them, or allow them to rule my thoughts and emotions. I can be free of them.

To be free of sin and shame is to be clean. That's what you are. That's what I am. We are clean. John 15:3 says, "Now ye are clean through the word which I have spoken unto you." There is that *now* again. The same *now* we saw with the woman who was a sinner. I honestly think Jesus may have been thinking of her when he spoke this verse. When He looked at that woman, all He saw was clean. After all, she was dressed in His best! His righteousness was draped all around her. Notice *how* we are clean—through the word which He *spoke* unto us. The same God who *spoke* and there was light—*spoke* and made me clean. If creation had to obey when He spoke, then my sins do too. The same Savior who stepped onto the bow of a boat and *spoke*, causing the powerful storm to cease, can *speak* and calm my storm of shame. The power isn't in me at all; it is in Him and the completed work of Calvary. The power is in the word He has spoken over my life. Picture Him stepping out onto the bow of your heart's boat that has been tossed here and there by the massive waves of guilt and shame. Thunder crashes and rain pelts down, but He stands steady and sure. The boat is rocking, but He is calm and serene. That's when He speaks a word that roars louder than the crashing waves and thunder. His voice is louder than thunder when He shouts the word "CLEAN." Suddenly the waves and wind, the thunder and lightning, all cease. The Creator, the Sin Defeater, the Cross Carrier has spoken. The clouds clear, the sun reappears, and the waves lie down flat and smooth all around your boat. The sun glints off the water and the birds are singing as they fly overhead. The truth sinks in. Clean. You are clean and forgiven in Him, through Him, and to Him. Right now. You are forgiven. Yes you. Now, all that is left is to believe this truth and to daily walk in the reality of it.

Making It Personal

Answer the following questions in your journal:

1. Describe how God uses conviction.

2. Describe how Satan uses condemnation.

3. How can you tell the two apart?

4. Describe a time you felt conviction. What was your response?

5. Describe a time you felt condemnation and shame. What was your response?

6. Read Isaiah 38:17. What does this verse mean for the feeling of shame and condemnation?

7. Read Colossians 2:14. What does this verse say to you about your past sin and the shame that Satan says you have to carry around?

8. Read Romans 8:1 and 8:33–34. What do these verses mean in your own words?

9. What can we never be separated from, according to Romans 8:38–39?

10. Read Isaiah 50:7. Write out a personal declaration based on what you read in that verse.

CHAPTER TWELVE

Bitterness

Bitterness – "anger and disappointment at being treated unfairly; resentment"

Almost everyone has a moment in time when everything in their life changed. That moment is forever frozen in time and will never ever be forgotten. That moment can be recalled with crystal-clear clarity, even down to the minutest of details. For instance, one might remember the outfit they were wearing, a particular sight, sound, or smell from that moment when their world came to a screeching halt. Your moment could have been a phone call, a diagnosis, an accident, a heart-breaking conversation, an admittance of guilt, a shocking discovery, a betrayal, or a terrible realization. Whatever that moment was for you, nothing was the same after it. Unfortunately, that moment doesn't just stay a moment, does it? A hundred million moments come after it, all filled with trauma, grief, hardship, anger, and yes, eventually, bitterness.

My moment came several years ago in our current house that we had just moved into. We had been in that house for just a short while when my husband got a phone call, followed by a visit, that changed our lives forever. We both were totally blindsided by what we found out in that moment and were left reeling. Someone we trusted had committed a horrible crime that shook our family and our church family to the core. I never planned for the police to be called out to my *new house in front of my new neighbors. I never planned for them to sit in my new dining room taking statements about the crime my husband had to call and report. I never planned on standing in my new living room while overhearing the shocking confession this person was making. I never thought I would have to try to explain such horrific things to my too-young-to-know daughter. Fallout was everywhere, and for years afterwards it was as if we went around in a shocked daze putting out fires here and there that resulted from this one terrible choice. Ripples, I call them. Like ripples from a stone thrown into a pond, these nasty outreaches from that one choice just kept coming and coming and coming. How much destruction can one decision cause? It turns out that the answer to that question is, a lot… a whole lot.*

During those awful days, weeks, months, and years, I watched my husband struggle and become withdrawn as he battled living the life of one who bears a load of blame for something he had no control over. I watched the light of child-hood innocence flicker and die in my nine-year-old daughter's eyes as she learned about an ugly reality that she hadn't even known existed. I watched people I loved dearly weep and hurt, while I stood helplessly by. I watched a church limp along during those years after that terrible moment in time. Slowly, ever so slowly, another enemy entered into not only my dining room but also my heart. The enemy's name was bitterness. I remember writing in my journal one day, "I hate _____." I put that person's name in the blank and it felt good to write it. I meant it. They had destroyed people I loved, and their selfishness had wreaked havoc in the lives of innocent people. I hated watching my husband hurt and not being able to help him. I hated what this person had done, and I felt justified in the hating. After all, what they had done had surely been hateful. In my mind, this person was a monster. A terrible monster with no conscience and no heart. They became my boogeyman under the bed, so to speak. But my bitterness, like all bitterness, didn't behave. It didn't stay where I tried to stuff it. It kept popping out all over the place. First of all, it hijacked my emotions. I couldn't cry anymore. I couldn't laugh anymore either. The only emotion I felt was anger and rage. I was consumed with this person getting justice, and whatever punishment they did get would never be enough in my estimation.

Righteous indignation was what I labeled my bitterness, only there was nothing righteous about it.

It wasn't until several years later, when this person's name was mentioned in a casual conversation, that I realized the hold that my bitterness had on me. It was like a punch in the gut when I heard their name. I literally lost my appetite and became nauseous when I simply heard their name spoken aloud. It seemed I had some work to do. I began to research forgiveness, as it was mentioned in Scripture. I journaled and journaled and journaled. I prayed and prayed and prayed. And then I was honest with myself for the first time in a long time. Yes, this person had done something wrong. Horribly wrong. But my bitterness was wrong too. And that one I could control. So, I sat down and wrote the hardest letter of my life. It was an undeserved letter. It was a letter of forgiveness that hadn't even been asked for. This person had never even apologized to me. They had in no way earned my forgiveness. But I knew, if I was ever going to be ok again, this was a letter I had to write anyway. So, I did. I don't know what that letter ever did for that person, but I know what it did for me. It set me free from a prison I had no idea I was in. I noticed after I wrote that letter, the sun shone brighter, the birds sang sweeter, and I found my laugh again. Eventually, I even cried again. After all that time I could finally FEEL again. My prayer time was comforting and precious, and the pages of Scripture had, once again, come alive in my quiet time. What I hadn't realized was that my bitterness was the equivalent of me slowly sipping poison and expecting that the other person would get sick. But that's not what happened at all. I was the one becoming toxic, while the bitterness was stealing all my joy, my peace, and my hope. This would still be going on today, had God not revealed the truth to me in such an eye-opening way. I am so very thankful that He did. You see, forgiving that person had nothing at all to do with them and everything to do with me. The writing of it was never for their healing or so they could go on; it was for my healing so that I could be the one to go on. The thing about bitterness is, like a parasite, it slowly kills its host. It eats away at you from the inside and will eventually ruin your life on the outside.

ALL ROADS LEAD HERE

We have tackled many difficult emotions in the pages of this book, you and I. We have waded through hard and walked through difficult together. But now we arrive at the hardest one of them all. The 'mack daddy' of emotions, if you will. In the story of Job, we learned about all the emotions he fielded all while staying out of sinful territory. But none of that success turned his captivity around. Not successfully walking through terrible grief, not navigating the waters of consuming sadness and sorrow, or dealing with deep disappointment, frustration, and physical pain. The climax of Job's story, the crescendo of his complex musical score, was when he prayed for his so-called 'friends.' You know the ones, the fellas that accused him of lying, cheating, and abusing widows and orphans. The very same ones that said God went easy on him for the terrible, deep, dark sin they were absolutely convinced that he was hiding. Yeah, those guys. Job had handled many awful emotions, but this one was the one that was the hardest, the most agonizing of them all. All of heaven held their breath as God instructed those men to head back to Job, tail tucked between their legs. God Himself had put them in their place and sent them back to Job with hands full of sacrifices. He told them not to say a word and that He would not accept their prayer of repentance; it was Job's prayer alone that He would hear. Can you just picture when they arrived at the ash heap again? Can you see Job tremble as they told him their predicament? Job had the power. He finally had the upper hand on them. He held their forgiveness in his boil-covered hand. He could refuse. He could send them away unforgiven. Without the sacrifice, they would be doomed, cursed to walk in an unforgiven state before God. This sacrifice was the only way they could come clean in God's sight and Job had the power to stop it. Can you just picture the angels straining to see this scene play out? They had been a witness to the heavenly warfare that had gone on in the throne room. All of heaven had been abuzz when Job stood on shaky legs and declared, "Though he slay me, yet will I trust in him." They had smiled and nodded their heads when he stated through gritted teeth, "when he hath tried me, I shall come forth as gold." I bet they even exchanged angelic high fives when he shouted to the heavens, "I know that my redeemer liveth." But when he humbly and powerfully prayed *for* his friends, well, that's the pivot point of the whole story. That was when business picked up, as they say. That was the hinge point, the turning point, of the whole trial. That single action by Job determined the ending of Job's story, where he got back double of everything he lost. Could it be that all of heaven is holding its breath, waiting to see what you will do with your captives? Could the turning point of our captivity be on hold because it is waiting for us to let loose of those we hold captive to our anger and bitterness? Based on Job's trial, the answer is most definitely 'yes.' This chapter will bring you to your pivot point. What you do with it is up to you, as it was up to Job.

Trust me when I say this chapter won't be an easy one, but it could very well be the most important one you read. This chapter in no way belittles the hurt that was done to you. Your hurt is real and your pain is significant. I wish I could sit across from you and look at you when I say, "I am sorry." I am sorry someone hurt you so very deeply. I am sorry that someone you should have been able to trust didn't take care of you, cherish you, or treat you with the love and respect God designed for you to receive. Your hurt matters. It is real and I respect it. Please know that forgiveness is in no way saying that what that person did to you was ok, that you need to just get over it, or that you need to allow them back into your life. Once again, forgiveness isn't about them at all. It is about you. It is about you being ok and you being healed and you moving forward. This chapter is a safe place for you to find healing. It is not a condemning place for you to feel belittled and the need to be defensive. With that groundwork in place, let's begin the chapter that could make all the difference in every chapter from here on out in your life. Welcome to your pivot point. Proceed prayerfully.

UNWELCOME GUESTS

After that one devastating moment in time arrived in your life, you soon discovered that it didn't come alone. It brought some friends with it, some unwelcome guests, if you will. Soon after you encountered your deep hurt, the first unwelcome guest arrived. Its name is cynicism. This guest can turn a usually positive, upbeat person into a harsh, cold, and critical person. It's kind of an extreme makeover gone horribly wrong. This unwanted guest will color your whole outlook on life, the way you view the people in your life, and even which future events will unfold in your life. After cynicism arrives, you will begin to view others with suspicion and will almost wait for them to let you down or hurt you in some way. Not only will it color the way you view the other people in your life but it will also color the way you view God. After all, He could have stopped that hurt from happening, and that thought plagues you. As a result, you will begin to distance yourself from God and from others. You may even completely walk away from people before they have the chance to hurt or walk away from you.

The next unwanted guest that will arrive at your doorstep is bitterness. This guest will convince us that we are the victim, judge, and jury in not only this situation but in all other situations that will arise, as well. As we struggle to play all three roles, our relationships will buckle under the strain placed upon them. We relentlessly pound the judge's gavel over and over and over again in all our situations and relationships. As a result, we remain frozen in the hurt and simply cannot move forward from that devastating moment in time. Bitterness steals our smile, our trust, and our joy while it destroys our relationships with those we love and undermines our fellowship with God.

Another guest that comes knocking is resentment. This guest offers up fantasies of revenge and getting even with the person who wronged us. It pulls out a projector from its bag and replays the painful event over and over again. It has that conversation you wish you could have, along with that thing you should have said, and that tirade you want to say again and again. It relishes in the bad things that happen to the person who wronged us and it wishes for even worse things to happen in their future. Resentment is a silent killer. It kills marriages, relationships, futures, and spiritual victory.

Guest number four comes disguised as our friend. Its name is our 'rights,' and it is loudly applauded by our society and our ego. Our rights will parade and march up and down in the streets of our hearts and minds, carrying picket signs in well-organized protests. The signs read, 'What about me?' or 'It's all about me' or the ever popular 'I want it my way.' The goal of this guest is to preoccupy us with self and self-centered thoughts and desires. Our pride loves this guest and will make it feel right at home.

The next guest to arrive at this unholy party is one entitled 'trust issues.' This guest offers us a magnifying glass as he walks in. This magnifying glass will then cause us to closely inspect everyone around us as we carefully look for flaws or mean motives. We will use it to look for ways they might hurt us or let us down or wrong us in some way. It will cause us to read into things they do or don't do. It will make us hear things they say in a different light and even judge them harshly on things they didn't say. This guest will cause our people to never be able to do enough or say enough or be enough to make us happy.

Another knock at the door reveals rage. Rage comes from unchecked anger that is allowed to fester. It starts out as understandable and even justifiable but is allowed to wander into sinful territory and put down roots. Rage is anger on steroids and is never ever satisfied. The person that wronged you can never pay enough, never apologize enough, or never hurt enough in our eyes. Rage despises. Rage destroys. Rage consumes.

Guest number seven is 'hate.' It is the best friend of rage. They never go anywhere without the other. They feed off one other and they steal the joy out of anyone who invites them in.

Then along comes 'unrealistic expectations.' These are party guests at many occasions, and we are rarely even are aware of their presence. They are very quiet and polite guests that never cause a scene. Unrealistic expectations walk in wearing an appropriate outfit and may even carry a church bulletin. They appear spiritual and have perfect attendance in Sunday

School. But they cause us to judge people on what they *should* have said or what they *should* have done. They create discontent in our life because our reality isn't as we think it *should* be. Watch out for these guests. They sneak in without even so much as a knock at our door.

The next guest is named 'near sighted.' It brings with it a thick pair of glasses that will blur your vision and cause you to only be able to see what is right in front of you, eclipsing everything else. You are blinded to what is out in the future or out beyond the nasty here and now. You focus on only the situation and pain and the hard of the moment you are in. This guest steals your hope.

Last, but certainly not least, is the actual person who hurt you so badly. They are the guest of honor, if truth be told. They are seated at the head of the table and are always the center of attention. All the other guests sing, "For He's the Horrible Old Fellow" and he always gets the first piece of cake. This person holds all the power and will always be the one in the spotlight so long as you withhold forgiveness. This is actually one of Satan's cruelest tricks that he will ever play. Bitterness actually gives the one who hurt you even more power over you. Even if it has been decades since the hurt happened to you. Even if the person is no longer in your life, and even if the person is no longer living. Not only did they hurt you then, but due to the lack of forgiveness in your heart, they can also continue to hurt you every day after that. Satan will tell you a lie saying that hating them hurts that person, when, in reality, it only hurts you.

It is time to stop this terribly destructive party. Now is the time to open up your front door and kick these hateful guests out. They no longer have permission to gather in the home of your heart and the dining room of your mind. Party's over. Time to get rid of them and clean up the mess they left behind. The time has come to move on and heal. If I am not mistaken, I hear a knock at your door now. Standing on that welcome mat is a fella named 'Decision.' He has been waiting for a long time for you to open the door to him. Forgiveness is your choice. You have the power to decide what comes next in your life and who gets to sit at your table. You know I am right. Ladies, it is time to invite some new guests, whose names are 'Hope,' 'Joy,' 'Peace,' 'Rest,' 'Healing,' and 'Deliverance.' Now, that's a party we all want to throw. But, as with all parties, it will take some planning, preparation, and some good old-fashioned hard work in order for it to be a success.

BUT I CAN'T FORGIVE THEM

God knew we could never make it to heaven on our own. So, He made a way. That way is Jesus and His death on the cross. Calvary made a way—the only way—for us to get to heaven. We have to go through the blood Jesus shed on the cross. That's it. There is no other option. We cannot try hard enough, be good enough, or be determined enough. We must be born again in order to be assured that heaven is our home. (If this is not a decision you have ever made in your life, please go to the section in the back of the book, entitled "How to Have a Personal Relationship with Christ." I implore you not to let another day go by before you take care of this most important step.). I know you feel like you simply cannot forgive this person. Not this time. Not this hurt. It is just too hard and too painful. Girls, it may surprise you to know that I completely agree with you. *You* can't forgive them. The truth is, it is too hard, the hurt is too deep, they are just too undeserving of such a sacrifice. But, through Christ, we can. Just as He became the way over an impossibility when it comes to us getting into heaven, He can become the way over the impossibility of forgiving a horrible hurt in our lives.

Picture yourself on one side of a deep ravine or canyon. To get to the other side is impossible. On the side where you stand, it is dark, barren, dry, and desolate. It is the land of Unforgiveness. On the other side of the great divide, the land is green and sunny, flowers grow, and the sky is blue. You want to get there. In fact, you long to be there feeling the sun on your face and the soft grass beneath your feet. But you simply cannot get there. You can't jump it, scale it, or fly across it. You hit your knees in defeat and cry out, "God, I can't do it. I know you want me to, but I simply can't. The ravine is too deep and the canyon too wide. How can I get to the other side where the sun is shining and the birds are singing?" That's when Jesus shows up. In His nail-scarred hand, he is holding a hammer and nails. At His nail-scarred feet, you see stacks of boards. He smiles at you and says, "So, you are finally ready to get over to the other side? It's about time. I have had all the supplies and been standing here, waiting to help you for the longest time. Together we can do it. We can go from here all the way to there. But it will take you cooperating with me. And I warn you, it won't be easy. It will be back-breaking work done completely on your knees. I have the framework in place for you. All you need to do is build the bridge, with my help, one board at a time."

And so, you take Jesus at His word, and board by board, you build a bridge. The planks are in stacks labeled obedience, kindness, selflessness, humility, grace, mercy, healing, faith, prayer, and letting go. The hammer is your determination and the swinging of it is your obedience. The nails are God's Word and His promises. They hold it all together. Jesus wasn't kidding—it is very hard work. The hardest work you have ever done, if truth be told. Your back aches and your knees hurt. The sun beats down relentlessly on you the whole way. Many times, you miss the nail and hit your thumb, which just adds more pain to an already painful situation. But Jesus is with you all the way. He brings you cool water to drink, bandages your sore thumbs, and offers you shade from the relentless sun. You are never ever alone on this very hard and very long journey. Midway you make the mistake of looking down. Fear crashes down on you as you realize you are perilously hanging over a deep, dark canyon. There is no solid ground underneath you and you are neither on the side of Unforgiveness nor on the side of Forgiveness. You are somewhere in the middle, dangling in space. Jesus lays a calming hand on your shoulder, and as soon as you see the nail scars, you know that He has been on this journey before you. You look up into the kindest eyes you have ever seen. You see a sad smile on his face, one filled with understanding. He knows. He understands. He has been at this exact spot before. He has experienced deep hurt and pain. He has navigated being betrayed, mistreated, misused, and abused. He alone truly knows the depth of your pain. And somehow that realization lessens the fear of your precarious position. You take a deep breath and look behind you. You have come so far. You aren't to the other side yet, but goodness, those boards have inched you out further and further from the barren side of the canyon that you started out on. Farther and farther you go, one board of obedience at a time. Jesus never stops encouraging, handing you boards, nails, and sips of water along the way. Slowly, oh so slowly, you see the end in sight. It gives you a surge of energy and you finally reach the plush green grass of the land called Forgiveness. As you step off the bridge, you relish the feel of the soft green grass and welcome the cool breezes. A beautiful river flows, and you can't help but step into the refreshing water and dip your hands into it as it flows past. All those bruised thumbs and sore knees and back are forgotten. Jesus envelopes you in a warm hug, and the biggest smile is on His face. "I knew you could do it. Nice job. Now look back, my child, and see the true miracle." You turn back and expect to see the bridge and the ugly side of the canyon looming behind you. But instead, all you see is the beautiful side of Forgiveness. Gone is the ugly and the hard and the barren. "Welcome home, my child. You made it. Now let's go explore all the goodness and the joy that the land of Forgiveness has to offer."

REASONS WHY WE WON'T FORGIVE

There are a million and one reasons why we choose not to forgive. Trust me, Satan has all kinds of them and will offer them at a moment's notice. I have listed a few of the most popular below. Take a look and see if any of these excuses, or ways of thinking, sound familiar to you:

- I am afraid the hurt will happen again.

- Being mad and holding a grudge gives me a sense of control in an uncontrollable situation.

- This person hasn't truly validated or even acknowledged the wrong they did to me.

- I feel like to forgive means that what happened to me was no big deal.

- The feeling of anger is so strong that I guess I have to wait for it to subside before I can ever forgive.

- My hurt goes too deep to forgive.

- The wrong done to me is unforgivable.

- Forgiveness means that I have to trust them and open myself up to them again.

- Forgiveness means automatic reconciliation.

- There are so many consequences from this hurt. All of those need to be resolved before I can forgive.

- To stuff this anger down is easier than to deal with it.

- The person I need to forgive is no longer in my life or is no longer even alive. That means I don't need to forgive, right?

- It is too soon.

- It is too late.

- To forgive means I need to forget. I can't forget, so I can't forgive.

Go back and circle any and all of the ones that have been present in your way of thinking when it comes to forgiveness.

AN EXERCISE IN FORGIVING

In researching for this chapter, I came across an activity that will visually help you to see how forgiveness works. I adapted the exercise I read about, and I believe the result is one that will be truly helpful for anyone struggling in this area. You can find the original exercise in the book entitled *Forgiving What You Can't Forget*, by Lysa Terkeurst.

First of all, take a stack of 3 x 5 index cards, and on one side write the name of the person and the wrong they did to you. Stick with only one wrong per card. On the back of the card, write out all the consequences that have happened as a result of the wrong done to you. There may need to be several cards for just one person in your life. That's ok. You may even need more than one card to just hold all the consequences for one single hurt. That also is ok. Be honest and include all the consequences that have resulted from the hurt. These cards are safe. They won't repeat anything or tell anyone what you have written. After you are done writing, arrange your cards in a path of sorts. At the end of the path, write the word 'HEALING' in all capitals on a piece of paper. At the beginning of the path, write on cards every name of the guests that have come knocking at your door (cynicism, bitterness, resentment, rights, trust issues, rage, hate, unrealistic expectations, and near sightedness). Scatter them around your starting point.

Now take red construction paper and cut out 4 x 6 rectangles—one for every index card in the path of cards on the floor. When that is done, go to each card on the floor and read aloud both sides. Then place the red card on top and say something like this, "Today I choose to cover this hurt and this person in the blood of Jesus. I will forgive by the power of that blood." Place the red card over the index card. The 4 x 6 red card is larger and covers the smaller 3 x 5 one. It is sufficient to cover the hurt and all the consequences. When you look down now, you do not see the hurt card; only the red card can be seen. Then on to the next one and the next until you reach the end of the path and the word 'HEALING.' This may need to be done several times, and you may need to update the cards along the way. When you feel that the exercise no longer needs to be repeated, you can destroy the cards. Once you feel you have reached the place of healing and can stay there, write out some other words that you have discovered there. Words like joy, peace, rest, hope, help, strength, laughter, restoration, purpose, and renewal, and any others you have discovered at your destination of healing. On the back of those cards, you can even write out a moment of time that you experienced that word, a situation, a feeling, or even a thought process. Keep these cards for future reference when the tug of unforgiveness can be felt again. Reread them and then choose not to give them up for bitterness again. To trade all those cards in is too high of a price to pay.

No, this exercise won't magically make the forgiving happen, but it will provide something visual and tangible that will help to solidify the action in your heart. What if you don't feel like it? Do it anyway. Obey first; your feelings will eventually follow. Never wait on your feelings—they won't cooperate until you rein them in and make them.

A great prayer to pray when trying to forgive is to ask God to 'supernaturally enable' and 'divinely empower' you to do what you cannot do on your own. You could add that to your prayer you pray over those cards. "Today, I ask God to supernaturally enable me and divinely empower me to forgive _____ through the power of the blood of Jesus."

That's a powerful exercise and an even more powerful prayer.

ROCKS AND RIPPLES

Why did I have you include the consequences of the hurt on the back of the card? Because there are so stinking many of them! If it was just the initial hurt that we had to deal with, many of us could probably deal with it.

But those consequences just keep coming, don't they? And when they do, they keep kicking the scab off of the wound from the initial hurt. It is like when you throw a rock into a pond. The initial plunk comes and goes, but the ripples keep going, reaching farther and farther out. The consequences are your ripples. Those ripples are what makes forgiveness such a tough process. They keep the hurt fresh and the pain current. Forgiveness always has, and always will be, a choice. It is choosing to forgive that person for the rock they plunked into your pond *and* for every single consequence that has happened since. Are you starting to see that forgiveness is not just a quick one-and-done decision? I wish it was. Forgiveness is a process, and a long hard one at that. Remember the bridge with all the planks? That's the idea. The bridge was built one board at a time, and forgiveness is built one choice at a time. The ripples can very easily color our reality. That hurt changed everything. I mean everything. The ripples are all the hard and ugly fallout that is now part of our everyday life. For instance, that affair (the hurt) now has caused an expensive divorce lawyer and an ongoing hardship of joint custody and the pain the kids are going through, not to mention having to deal with his new girlfriend on a regular basis. Ripples. They are a constant reminder of the painful plunk that rocked your pond.

HOW DO I KNOW IF I AM BITTER?

Satan isn't stupid. He will camouflage your bitterness so well, you may not even be aware that it is in your heart. So, how do you know if bitterness is really a problem for you? Ask yourself the following questions in order to find out if you have bitterness in your life. Warning: This quiz will be harder to pass than you think!

- Do I have some sort of physical response when I see or hear this person, or if someone even mentions their name? This could be a sick or a sinking feeling in the pit of your stomach, increased heart rate, shortness of breath, sweaty palms, flushed face, etc.

- Do I enjoy when bad things happen to them?

- Do I fantasize about bad things happening to them?

- Do I rehearse what I would like to say to them if I got the opportunity?

- When I talk about them, or the situation, do I embellish my side, hoping to get a sympathetic response from the person I am talking to?

- Do I expect the worst from them?

- Can that person do nothing right in my eyes?

- Do I replay the painful event over and over and over in my mind?

- Do I agonize over what I should have said or done at that painful moment in time?

- Do I feel I have the 'right' to hate them?

I told you it would be harder to pass than you thought. That quiz reveals a problem with bitterness, even if you only answered yes to one of those questions.

This next quiz reveals if you have reached the place of forgiveness toward that person.

- Do I acknowledge the hurt but feel a sense of peace anyway?

- Can I pray for God to bless them? (Remember Job)

- Can I feel ok when they are experiencing good things?

- Can I share my hurt and experience so that others can have hope and help?

- Am I trying to learn and grow from my hurt?

- Am I trying to understand that hurt people hurt people? My offender has hurts and probably hurt me out of their own brokenness. Am I willing to offer grace to them in their brokenness?

- Am I willing to acknowledge that there may be a different perspective to the situation?

- What has God done in and through this situation? Am I even willing to see this and acknowledge it?

- What beauty has come from my ashes?

- Can I look to the future with hope?

Another hard quiz, huh? But an eye-opening one, for sure.

MY HURT, MY CHOICE

One of the most maddening things about being done wrong is that you had no choice in what happened to you. Someone else chose to hurt you. They chose sin. They chose selfishness. You now stand in the rubble and the debris from the explosion of sin they chose to detonate on purpose. Although you may not have had a choice when that person hurt you, you do have a choice now. You have the power of choice. You do have a voice in what happens next. You do get to choose whether you will forgive or whether you will not. It seems like this is a simple black-and-white choice. Choose forgiveness and receive peace, healing, and blessing. Choose bitterness and receive hate, harm, and more hurt. Pretty simple choice, right? Wrong.

Bitterness never comes in unless there is a vacancy. Someone has left you. Your trust has left the building. Your innocence was ripped away from you. Your normal can't be found with the FBI. Vacancies one and all. And so, bitterness sees the VACANCY sign in the window of your heart and knocks at the door. It has quite a lot of baggage but shows up promising that the other person who harmed you will pay. With that promise, you open the door and let it in. At first, you tell it to stay in that empty room that has been vacated. You notice that out of one of the bags, bitterness pulls a can of the blackest paint you have ever seen. Bitterness wastes no time in turning its new home into a very dark and foreboding place. *Oh well*, you shrug, *to each his own*. It isn't bothering you or your other rooms. The next morning you go back to check on bitterness and are horrified to find it is out of its room and painting the room across the hall. You fuss at it and tell it to go back to the room you allowed it to have and go about your busy day. When you come home from work, you notice that the hall-way and the kitchen are now black. "What are you doing?" you scream. But, by now, there is no stopping it. Now you know what was in all those bags. Paint. Lots and lots of dark, ugly, menacing paint. Pretty soon, all the rooms of your heart and mind are as dark as can be.

Bitterness is never ever satisfied. One room won't do. It won't stop until it has all of you and all of your life. The darkness of bitterness spreads like a spilled can of black paint. It colors everything it touches and takes an awfully long time to clean up. Oh, and one day it saunters up to you with a smirk on its face and has the audacity to hand you a bill. The bill is an astronomical amount. Someone has to pay for all that paint. Bitterness snuck in with the promise to make the offender pay, but instead, you your-self are going to have to pay an extraordinary price, much more than you could have ever bargained for. In order to ever get rid of it, you will have to get your own can of pure white paint labeled forgiveness and a paint brush. You will also need to block off a lot of time and effort. The first few brush strokes are hard, and the task overwhelming, as you look at all the rooms it has ruined. But one brushstroke at a time, you notice the rooms lightening and the atmosphere changing. You dip with determination into the bucket of forgiveness over and over and over again. Never once does it run out though. There is always enough to cover the darkness. You get awfully tired in this process, but you are dedicated to finishing the project because you know who will show up with that bucket of black paint again and take away all the progress you have made. No way! You have worked too hard to let that happen.

Finally, you finish up that last room and walk through the house. Sunshine pours in the open windows and the breeze blows the curtains as fresh air circulates once again. My, what a difference in this place! The birds are singing and you find a spring in your step as you walk around and inspect a job well done. It's like the black paint was never there. All you see is clean and white. You sit down and rest. How long has it been since you could truly rest? That's when you notice that you are calm and at peace. You take a deep breath in and slowly let it out. Peace. That was it. That would be the name of the white paint—Peaceful White. You have learned an important truth while doing all that painting: no forgiveness means no peace, and to know forgiveness means that you will know peace.

One of the key ingredients in the can of white paint is compassion. Understanding that hurt people hurt people is key. The person who hurt you so badly has a profound hurt in their life that hasn't been handled properly. Understanding that can help you to offer forgiveness and to lay down the expectation of perfection from your people. It will add that brightness to that white and add an emulsifier to it that will cause it to be easier to spread and help it cover better. I would not suggest you try to paint without it.

You may be wondering if this forgiveness thing is really that important. Well, to answer that question, we will go to the expert—Jesus. In His model prayer, often called The Lord's Prayer, we see that forgiveness is included. Take a look at Matthew 6:9–13. We see that Jesus instructs us to ask for daily bread, daily forgiveness, daily forgiving, daily deliverance, daily protection, and daily leading. Each of these are *needs* that we are instructed to ask for. We need to forgive as bad as we need forgiveness. We need to forgive as bad as we need food. We need to forgive as much as we need God's deliverance, protection, and leadership. I would say that it is quite important, wouldn't you? To show you how important, let's break it down mathematically. Jesus instructs us to ask for six things. Two of those have to do with giving or receiving forgiveness. That means forgiveness carries the most weight out of all those things He modeled in the prayer. It is the most important thing we can ask for.

WHY IS FORGIVING SO IMPORTANT?

I realize this may sound selfish, but you give forgiveness so you can receive forgiveness. Period. Withholding forgiveness blocks you from getting forgiveness. Don't believe me? Read Matthew 18:21–35. Take a moment and put this book down and read those verses. If nothing I have said in this chapter so far has caused you to see the need to forgive the person that wronged you, then please, I beg you, allow these words from the lips of Jesus to sink in. If you don't offer forgiveness, you won't get forgiveness. It is that simple.

We somehow want to hoard the forgiveness of God. We want to approach God with a big bowl and ask Him to give forgiveness. We then slap a lid on that bowl and put it in the cabinet. It is ours, all ours. The problem is that isn't the way forgiveness works at all. Instead, we are to go to God and ask for forgiveness, not with a bowl, but with a colander. You know, the kind that you use in the kitchen to hold the spaghetti and strain out the water. A colander is used to let things flow through it. It is designed to be open at the top so that it can receive something from a higher elevation. It is also designed with lots of smaller openings on the bottom so that it can release what it has been given to a lower elevation. That's a perfect picture of forgiveness. We receive it from on high so that we can release it to others down below. Is that how we are approaching forgiveness? If not, then we are not receiving it at all. If nothing else, this realization can give us the proper motivation to begin building the bridge toward forgiveness.

FORGIVE AND FORGET

We have all heard the saying that we need to 'forgive and forget.' The problem with that is we cannot 'forget' the horrible hurts we have had to endure. So, we think that if forgetting is impossible, then forgiving must be impossible too. Wrong. God doesn't command us to forget. In fact, when God forgives, He doesn't suddenly get a case of divine amnesia. He chooses not to bring it up anymore. He chooses to let it go, to release it, and not to hold it against us anymore. That is entirely possible for me and for you. He isn't expecting us to neurologically forget, but to spiritually and emotionally let it go. There is a big difference. Isaiah 38:17 says, "Behold, for peace I had great bitterness: but thou hast in love to my soul delivered it from the pit of corruption: for thou has cast all my sins behind thy back." He doesn't forget that we sinned. He just chooses to throw them behind His back instead of in our faces. Oh, that we would do the same with the sins of others! We have the choice of where to throw them. We can throw them behind our backs, throw them in the face of the wrong doer, or throw them in the spotlight on the stage of our lives.

Corrie Ten Boom battled with forgiving those who had tortured her in a concentration camp many years earlier. In this battle, she had actually chosen to extend forgiveness to a soldier who had made her life miserable during her time in that camp. That, in itself, was an amazing feat. But, for the life of her, she couldn't forget. This fact kept her up at night and robbed her of much needed sleep. Terrible memories haunted her as they replayed them over and over in an awful horror movie of sorts. The things she had seen and endured just wouldn't be put to rest. This wise woman sought the counsel of an old minster. She approached the man with a barrage of questions. How could she forget? Shouldn't the forgetting come with the forgiving? What was wrong with her? The wise old minister took her up to the bell tower of the church while the bell was being rung. There, in front of her, a man was pulling vigorously on the rope, causing the bell to ring fast and loud. But when the man stopped pulling the rope, the bell's ringing slowed down and got softer and softer, eventually fading away completely. The minister then looked at Corrie and told her to stop tugging the rope, and the bell of her remembering would slowly fade away. The truth dawned on Corrie as I hope it will dawn on you. Will you ever completely forget the hurt? No. Did she? No. But the bell will stop ringing so loud and so fast when we stop tugging the rope so vigorously. We can consciously and deliberately let go of the rope and climb down the steps of the bell tower in our mind. Armed with that powerful visual, Corrie did in fact find peace from even the terrible horrors of a German concentration camp. The same can be true for us, too, if we decide to stop tugging the rope.

Making It Personal

Answer the following questions in your journal:

1. Read Mark 11:25, Matthew 6:15, and Matthew 18:21–35. According to these verses, *why* is forgiving so important?

2. Read Ephesians 4:32 and Colossians 3:13. According to these verses, who is the pattern for how we are to forgive?

3. Describe the difference between the 'bowl' mentality and the 'colander' mentality concerning forgiveness.

4. What does the visual of 'tugging the rope' teach us?

5. What questions on the bitterness quiz did you circle?

6. What is your plan of action to overcome bitterness in your life?

7. Why is it important that you choose to forgive?

8. Complete the index card exercise described in this chapter.

9. Copy the following declarations in your journal, filling in the blanks as you go. Or write out your own forgiveness declaration. Don't forget to sign and date it at the end.

   I, _____, do declare on this date,
   _____, to begin the journey to
   forgive _____

   for_____. I choose to
   do so out of obedience to God. I will take the necessary steps in

order to reach the goal of forgiveness. It will be a process and will require many daily decisions. I will ask God to supernaturally enable me and divinely empower me to complete this process in my life. This is a choice I freely make without the person deserving it or asking for it. This is a choice I make for myself in order for me to be ok and to live in the peace that God has for me. I realize that forgiving this person does not say what they did was ok. It also does not mean I am inviting them back into my life or choosing to trust them again. This choice covers the initial hurt and all the consequences that have developed as a result of their sinful choice. I am choosing to live out this choice by the power of the blood of Jesus. I choose to forgive as Jesus forgives and that choice begins today.

Signed _____

Date _____

CHAPTER THIRTEEN

Insecurity

Insecurity – "uncertainty or anxiety about oneself; lack of confidence; the state of being open to danger or threat; lack of protection. An encompassing feeling of self-doubt and uncertainty about your value or worth which leads to chronic self-consciousness and anxiety"

It all started back in kindergarten. My sisters and I changed schools from a small Christian school to the local public school mid-year. I hadn't been too thrilled with leaving my home and my mom in the first place. But after this life-changing event mid-year, I was even less thrilled. That change completely rocked my little five-year-old world. Everything was different, new, and unfamiliar. If you look at the above definition of insecurity, you will see that what I was experiencing was a feeling of being open to danger or threat. I felt the protection of the familiar was gone. And now, here I was, walking into a big public school, completely vulnerable and unprotected. Everyone knew each other and everyone had already figured out their place in the pecking order of kindergarten. Everyone but me, that is. I remember walking in that room on my first day, which just happened to be a completely normal day for everyone else. But for me, it was a dreaded first and I was going to have to field it alone.

My mom walked me in and I met my teacher, Mrs. Pritchard, who was really sweet. She was short and had even shorter blond hair with a round cherubic face that wore a perpetually patient and cheery smile that is a must for every kindergarten teacher. She patiently cajoled me to come on in and meet the class. I hid behind my mom's legs. Mrs. Pritchard then reached for my hand and lightly pulled at first. That light pull soon turned into a firm tug as I stubbornly refused to budge. I then turned and saw my mom, my world, my stability, my sameness, my comforter, and my shelter just turn and walk away. She left me! She actually left me! And she took every bit of my security with her. I walked into that room on trembling legs. Let me tell you, kindergarten is one of the scariest places on earth, and don't let anyone tell you otherwise.

Everyone was sitting on their little carpet squares, learning about the letters of the alphabet. That day the class was learning all about Mr. H. The teacher pulled out a huge life-size Mr. H balloon. I was terrified and quickly sat down on an empty carpet square as far away from the evil balloon as I could get. I tried to pay attention—honestly, I did—but all I could feel were the stares of the kids sitting around me. One boy was watching me out of boredom while picking his nose, and a little girl was twirling her hair while staring me down and sizing me up. The boy only thought I was worth a three-second long stare before some other distraction came along and claimed his attention. The girl, well, she thought I was worth a little more time and attention. After all, in her eyes, competition had just walked in the door and she needed to know more about this potential threat that had just plopped down on a carpet square near her. I sent her a wobbly smile—it was all I could muster. Even in my state of sheer terror, I realized that this girl could be my savior. She could be my friend, my lifeline. It was worth a shot. My smile got bigger. Looking back, I realize it was probably more of a terrified grimace. Her response? She pointed at me and turned to say something to her bestie seated beside her, who then also turned to stare at me. They both giggled and whispered so much that the teacher called them down. My face burned. What did they find so funny? What was wrong with me? I would never fit in this horrible place with these horrible kids. I was different. I wasn't the same. I was no good. I wasn't even worth more than three seconds' time and attention from the boy and apparently didn't measure up to the girls' scrutiny either. It was going to be a long year.

The next morning started a long string of mornings where my anxiety was so bad that I threw up every day when I got to school. I have vivid memories of poor, sweet little Mrs. Pritchard trying to cajole me in, then having to peel me off of my older sister, who walked me down that ominously long kindergarten hallway. Mrs. Pritchard would try to distract me from my fears and tears by asking what I had brought in my lunchbox that day. Each morning she would take me on her lap and open my lunch box. And each morning I would throw up into it. I can still see my little sandwich in its trusty Ziplock bag hanging on a makeshift clothesline strung across the restroom so it could dry out. I will never know why she kept trying the 'what's for lunch' trick. I guess she figured the lunchbox could at least catch the projectile vomit. That woman earned many a crown in heaven that school year.

Now, all these years later, I have realized that life is a terrifying classroom full of people who have it all together way better than I ever will. These secure and confident people are already well established and comfortable in the pecking order of life, of which they are on top, by the way. They have more fulfilling friendships that I ever could and will always find something worth staring and giggling at when they look at me longer than three seconds. They can manage the front tuck in their jeans without looking nine months pregnant and can even, God bless them, try on bathing suits without having a total meltdown. Yes, the world is a terrifying place that often makes me want to throw up on my PB&J sandwich all over again. Has anyone seen Mrs. Pritchard? I think I feel nauseous.

IN OVER OUR HEADS

Insecurity, in my estimation, can be likened to an ocean—a very deep, dark, turbulent one. As with any ocean, it is fed by many rivers. The rivers that feed our personal vast ocean of insecurity, in no particular order, are society, social media, status, possessions, positions, our past, shame, regret, men, other women, our own distorted way of viewing others, ourselves, and God, along with listening to and believing the lies from the enemy. No wonder it is such a stormy sea for each and every woman who ever breathed a breath on this planet we call home.

Let's unpack a few things on that list, shall we? What we don't get to now, we will visit later on in this chapter. Let's just go ahead and talk about a sensitive topic on that list right out of the gates - men. Why do men feed our insecurity? Well, to be fair, it really isn't their fault. It's us. It's what we are so desperately trying to get from them that is the issue. We are trying to define our womanhood from a person who isn't even a woman and cannot possibly understand our needs or struggles. If a man finds us desirable, affirms us, or gives us praise, love, and attention, then we reason that we are valuable, worthy, and secure. If denied this from the opposite sex, well, you have yourself a raging case of insecurity on the nuclear level. Interestingly, men *hate* being assigned the task of giving us our worth and value. They describe it as being 'needy' or 'clingy.' And nothing, I do mean nothing, will make a guy turn tail and run like when he catches a whiff of a needy girl. No other human on earth can carry the responsibility of assigning us our worth or value.

The next item on our list may have been a surprise to you—then again, it may have been your number one ocean-feeding river—other women. Friends, coworkers, family members, or complete and total strangers, it doesn't really matter *who* they are, so much as *that* they are. Women compete. We size one another up and then we try to one-up each other. On a good day we one up, on a bad day we are one upped. We vie for approval, applause, acceptance, and attention like a pack of wild dogs would over a bone. Don't think you have this particular river? Check and see if any of these symptoms can be found in your heart and life: comparison, competition, criticism, cynicism, and an overall judgmental or critical attitude. Hmm, not so easy to get past that list, is it? Just ask Rachel and Leah or Sarai and Hagar how that particular river fed their ocean of insecurity. I believe we can all see ourselves in those stories, if we are honest.

SOCIETY'S 'SUPPOSED TOS'

Society is one of the biggest influencers for insecurity. Everywhere we look, we see half-naked skinny women who have had tons of plastic surgery and whose photos are altered further still. I remember seeing a well-known model on a talk show once, and the host asked her if she had seen her latest photos from a recent shoot. The model answered that she had not and did not like looking at the pictures of herself from professional shoots. The host was surprised and asked her why, to which she replied that it made her wish that she really looked like that!

We live in a society that sexualizes everything. On a cooking show, recently, a judge commented that a dish wasn't 'sexy' enough. Umm, it's food. Food isn't sexy. Food is food. It is not a sexual object that promotes sexual feelings, yet this *female* judge wanted it to be sexier. See the problem? Models have always been skinny, but now our friends are posting cropped, filtered, sexy pictures, and we feel even less now that someone we know looks like that and fits in that and gets to do that.

Society has also been pushing how women are supposed to 'do it all' and 'be good at it all' and how they can 'have it all.' According to society and social media, I am supposed to have a great, fulfilling career that makes me just want to jump out of bed in the morning. It is supposed to pay me plenty of money so that I can buy whatever I want. I am supposed to have regular girl's night outs or weekend trips to fun and exciting places—all posted about on social media, of course. I am supposed to have the picture-perfect Joanna Gaines home, all without her talent and bank account. I am supposed to have the picture-perfect kids, whom I make lots of time for. We are supposed to have nightly cuddles and days filled with homemade crafts, trips to the pumpkin patch, and days where I teach them how to make butter by shaking a jar. Oh, and I am somehow supposed to teach them how to make homemade applesauce from apples we picked at the orchard two hours away from our house. All very 'postable' photo ops, by the way.

My husband? Well, he is supposed to be like the guy in the Hallmark movies. You know, the big-city-lawyer-turned-small-town-lumberjack? That one. He is supposed to be a hunk who is in touch with his feminine side all while wearing flannel, mind you. He is supposed to always be patient, thoughtful, romantic, and can only have a few and very easily fixable issues. He is supposed to know what to say and when. He is supposed to be incredibly romantic and willing and able to do grand romantic gestures in front of the whole town at the Christmas lighting ceremony. Oh, and he is supposed to love drinking hot chocolate and ice skating hand in hand.

I am supposed to have friends, lots of them, and they all get me and understand me and want to hang out with me. If I don't have those, I cannot be fulfilled, society says. I am also supposed to be sexy and have fulfilling and exciting sex, even after being at the apple orchard all day with the kids. I am also supposed to somehow fit in that stringy lingerie after having given birth to children and no time for exercise. The no time came from the apple-orchard visit, and the not fitting into the lingerie, well, that was the apple pie's fault—you know the one I bought while at the apple orchard.

I am supposed to buy everything organic and non-GMO. Does anyone out there actually know what a 'GMO' is? I guess it is bad, whatever it is, because the stuff with 'GMOs' in them are the affordable stuff and the ones without them are more expensive. I am supposed to read labels and make things from scratch and be a 'foodie' who posts lots of pictures of her homemade gourmet meals that are plated just so.

And my kids? Well, they are supposed to like the leafy green pile of 'yuck' better than anything Chef Boyardee can whip up. My kids aren't supposed to have any issues either. They are supposed to be on the honor roll and good at every sport and have lots of friends that can come over to our house anytime—because our house is supposed to be the 'fun' house with the 'cool' mom.

My mornings are supposed to be filled with cute pj's (that preferably match with my whole family), coffee, and Jesus. All posted about, of course. I am supposed to be the mom that made the organic, made-from-scratch, GMO-free lunches, complete with carrot and celery sticks, the night before. I am supposed to be the mom that gets up right when the alarm goes off—the first time. I am supposed to roll out of bed early and have at least thirty minutes with Jesus—posted about, once again. Then I am supposed to put on the super-cute outfit from that boutique and post a full-length mirror photo of said outfit, all before getting the kids ready and out the door for school by 7:30 am. I am not supposed to be a Lunchable, sweatpants-wearing, 'running ten minutes late,' oversleeping, 'just hope to get ten minutes with Jesus,' 'drank my hot coffee too fast so I burned my mouth and spilled it down the front of my $15 shirt from Walmart' kind of mom. You know the one, the lady who screams at her kids and loses her cool all before she flies into the car rider line tires screeching right before it closes and the bell rings kind of mom? Yeah, we aren't supposed to be her at all.

HOUSTON, WE HAVE A PROBLEM

Now, let's see how big of an issue insecurity really is. Seventy-eight percent of women surveyed said they have so much insecurity that it really bothers them and hinders their quality of life. Forty-three percent described their problem with insecurity as 'huge.' Ninety-seven percent of women admitted that they were unhappy with their body! Over eighty percent said the mirror made them feel bad. Losing weight was considered the number one success for women. Not a happy marriage, not giving birth to a healthy child, nor owning a thriving business. Nope, for almost every woman, losing weight topped her chart of success. The survey found that the more time a woman spent on her appearance, the worse they felt about themselves. Sixty-four percent said social media made them feel worse about themselves, and then admitted they spent over two hours a day on social media! Girls, we need help. We are drowning in a sea of insecurity, and Satan is standing on the shore, enjoying the show.

WHAT DOES INSECURITY LOOK LIKE?

\Insecurity's number one disguise may surprise you. It wears a mask called 'perfectionism.' Show me a perfectionist, and I will show you a woman who is eaten up with insecurity on the inside. She feels strongly that she has to be the best, has to appear to have it all together, and then shames herself when she knows she really doesn't. Her achievements must outdo, her outfits look better, her ability at work must outshine, and her kids must overachieve. Her husband is expected to be more and do more, and her emotions/spirituality/weaknesses must be in check at all times. If not, she is nothing. Her pictures must be filtered, cropped, and photoshopped. Oh, and her life should be 'postable' at all times. She feels intense pressure to be liked and well thought of. She needs affirmation and approval like a plant needs water. This woman *feels* more intensely than others do. She feels rejection, failure, dislike, disapproval, and self-doubt on a more intense scale than her friends. She tends to rate high on the obsessive scale. She obsesses over an unanswered text, then obsesses if she worded that last text wrong. She obsesses over her appearance and wonders if her outfit looked right at that meeting at work. That one small flaw is all she sees. She obsesses over not only her own weaknesses but also the weaknesses of those close to her. She longs for control, and she isn't afraid to manipulate in order to get it. She micromanages the lives of those she loves and justifies it because "it is for their own good." She rarely rests, relaxes, or exhales and enjoys. She is forever moving on to the next thing on her list that needs to be checked off. There is always a project, an improvement, something else to work on, to make better, or to improve. She has an itemized list in her mind that if she could only achieve and mark off those items, then she could relax and be happy. The items vary according to the person, but here are some examples that might top her list:

- Marry a great guy

- Have a great body

- Live in a great house

- Get a great paycheck

- Have a great job

- Live with a great family

- Accomplish something great

- Have great kids

- Be in a great season in life

- Have lived a great past

- Possess a great degree

- Enjoy great friendships

- Experience a great spiritual life.

This woman obsesses over what 'could be' or what 'should be' in her mind and rarely appreciates, accepts, or enjoys her 'what is.'

Did you notice the word 'threat' in the definition of insecurity? An insecure woman is constantly on edge because she perceives a threat – all the time. There is a 'who,' a 'what,' or a 'what if' that looms large on her horizon. It could be jealousy, such as Hagar, Sarai, Leah, and Rachel experienced. Or it could be failure and inadequacy, such as seen in the case of Moses at the burning bush. It could also be comparison and pressure— think Saul when David began to gain popularity.

To be insecure is to be afraid. An insecure woman has the scary music in a horror movie playing on repeat in her mind. Each new day offers up new reasons to jump when a loud noise comes. The basement is continually dark and scary, and the serial killer is constantly on the loose in her life. Insecurity is always, always, always fear-driven and fear-fed. Saul illustrates this beautifully in Scripture. He was *afraid* he would lose the throne. He was *afraid* others liked David better. He was *afraid* he was going to look 'less than' in the eyes of the people.

This insecurity-feeding fear is running rampant in today's society. That's why we took a brief look at it in the chapter on fear. Now, I want to go a little deeper into it this particular fear and how it plays a very important role in our insecurity. This type of fear is now so bad that a 'new' word for it has been defined by Webster's Dictionary. The word is 'FOMO.' It means 'fear of missing out.' In our reality, it means that we live in fear that someone else is doing something we didn't get to do, going somewhere we didn't get to go, experiencing something we didn't get to experience, or were included in something we didn't get included in. Someone else had a better weekend, posted more pictures, and got more likes than you. Someone else had a romantic get away weekend that you didn't get. Someone has more accomplished kids, a better job, more fulfilling friendships and so on and so forth. This intense fear believes something good is going on without them somewhere, and it robs them of enjoying their here and now. Although this word is a newly defined word in the dictionary, it isn't really new in our ways of thinking at all. In fact, the disciples showed it way back when Jesus was on the earth. They argued about who would be the greatest when Jesus set up the earthly kingdom they were sure would come next. In their fear of missing out on what they thought would be the most amazing opportunity, they completely missed the most amazing opportunity they had *right then*. Jesus, the Son of God, was right there in their presence! By not wanting to miss having a powerful future position with Jesus, they failed to appreciate their current position as disciples and followers of that same Jesus while He was right there in their midst. They failed to take it all in when their fear kicked in. They failed to bask in His presence, when in just a little while, He would no longer be in their presence anymore.

How many moments in life do we miss simply because we are afraid of a 'what if' moment that never really comes? In trying to reach for what they thought they deserved, they failed to appreciate what they already undeservingly had at that very moment. Read that again. These fellas missed the point. They already had Him, and they already held a pretty amazing position. And yet they failed to be content. The driving desire for more robbed them of appreciating the special moment they had right then and there. Ladies, what position or next thing are you seeking? What glory, honor, achievement, or perfection throne do you long for, all the while, completely missing the One who truly sits on the throne? Insecurity is a thief and a liar, and it is time we kicked it off the throne of our heart.

SOURCES OF OUR INSECURITY

Not everyone's sources for insecurity are the same, but everyone has sources that feed their own personal insecurities. Let's take a look at each one individually for a few minutes. Some of you will be able to identify your sources immediately, while some will find it more difficult to do so. I encourage you to read through this section thoughtfully and reflect carefully on what you learn. Some of the most common sources of our insecurities are:

1. Instability in the home (past or present): This looks like relational strains, abandonment, abuse, arguments, fear-laden situations, trauma, financial woes, divorce, addictions, physical illnesses—especially prolonged ones—absent parents (emotionally or physically), and lack of affection or affirmation. Any or all of these can lead to an adult that has a deep-rooted fear that no one will care for or take care of them. This fear drives every decision and relationship as we become an adult and even after we have been an adult for years and years. Like an unseen director standing off stage, this fear calls the shots and controls what happens on the stage.

It sabotages relationships, even the good ones. It can also cause a person to cultivate unhealthy relationships, even abusive ones.

2. Significant loss: This is a loss of anything that you felt gave you stability and worth. This could be a hope, a friend, a status, a position, a financial situation, a job, a ministry, or a person. Insecurity results from a broken attachment. We held onto something, giving it significance in our lives, and then we lost it. You are left empty inside, and that emptiness travels from our heart to our minds and our behaviors, coloring every thought and action well into adulthood.

3. Rejection: This one is the fastest path to insecurity, for sure. Rejection is a direct deposit into an account entitled 'Worthless.' As we make the devastating deposit, the teller smiles and gives you a sticker to wear. "Hello, my name is Worthless." We place it tearfully on our chest, right over our heart, and before long that label is seared into our hearts and minds.

4. Dramatic change: Most women flourish in the predictable. We wrap expected around us like a warm sweater on a cold day. We love it. Therefore, we hate its opposite, who's name is change. Security cannot stand on something that keeps shifting. Its tent pegs cannot hold well to a sandy base. Sand keeps shifting, changing, and moving. All it takes is a good stiff wind and the landscape is completely different. When change comes our way, we will react in one of two ways. We will grab onto anything that makes us feel normal and hold onto it for dear life (picture a toddler who doesn't want to leave his mother and go into the church nursery). Or you might react by not wanting to get close to anything all, for fear of losing it (picture that same toddler running from his mother, who is trying to put a jacket on him). Which way you respond is according to your personality and makeup.

5. Personal limitations: A disability, a hang-up, a quirk, an oddity, an unusual physical attribute, or a mental deviation from the 'norm.' Limitations can actually have the power to spur us on to reach an achievement even with the limitation we have. Think Bethany Hamilton. After losing her arm up to the shoulder in a shark attack, this young surfer refused to stop surfing and, despite her new disability, continued being an award-winning surfer. Why? How? She was determined to overcome what had the potential to overcome her. She made a choice and was willing to work incredibly hard to make that goal happen. She fought through what legitimately threw her off balance and found a new balance through much trial and error and immense effort. Limitations, one and all, can either cripple or catapult us. Which one becomes our reality, is completely up to us.

6. Personality and personal choices: Some people are wired to *feel* more deeply than others. The more sensitive you are, the more you will tend to battle insecurity. Choosing unhealthy coping mechanisms will result in insecurities galore. It goes something like this: EVENT + PERSONALITY + GENETIC WIRING + PERSONAL CHOICES = INSECURITY OPPORTUNITIES

7. Our culture – media mania: Women long ago only compared themselves to women in their towns, jobs, friend circles, or churches. Women today can compare themselves to any woman on the planet, 24/7. We live in a veritable competition fest. Models, movie stars, and swimsuit-clad *Sports Illustrated* stars all become our daily competition as we sit on our couch wearing our stretchy pants and eating a Little Debbie before bed. Studies show the more images of other women that are around a woman, the less confident she feels about herself. We don't just feel inferior to our best friend or the next-door neighbor anymore. Oh no, we feel inferior to thousands of women. All. The. Time. Oh, and something I forgot to mention,

there is no longer a generation gap either. A fifty-year-old woman feels the same pressure to fit into a certain size as a sixteen-year-old girl does. No matter her age, the amount of kids she has had, her current level of metabolism, or even if she is facing the onset of menopause can give her any excuse for not being the perfect size 6. Nope. No excuses, no hall passes. Just an immense pressure to look just like *her*. Being in tune with yourself enough to know when an insecurity is triggered will be key to your overcoming this one. When you feel that competition kick in and that old comparison trap loom before you, switch on the light. Just as roaches scatter when the light comes on, so will the lies and comparisons when the light of truth hits them.

So, let's talk about *her* for a moment. We all have a *her* on our social media feed. You know the one. She is tiny and cute and is married to a dream boat who writes her poetry and sings her love songs. Her kids hit home runs and have clean rooms and they eat green leafy things without an epic meltdown. These same green leafy eating kids are also smart and obedient and write 'thanks, Mom' on Post-it notes around the house. Her hair is so good, she does hair tutorials, and her clothes so cute that she posts where she bought them, because she gets *soooo* many questions about them. Her house looks like it stepped out of an HGTV show, and her job fulfills her completely. #yeahright. You have one too? #eyeroll. We all do. Let me tell you a little trick when you feel threatened by a *her*. Pray for her. No, I mean it. Really. Pray hard for God to bless her and for Him to help her and encourage her. If you know her well, ask her what prayer requests she has, and then pray for her. You will be amazed at how that honest and heartfelt prayer will disarm those old feelings of being threatened. Try it. I dare you.

8. Pride: Many other roots of insecurity are from without, and we can't control their presence in our lives. But, this one, well, this one

is true for all us. Actually, it is *in* us, and how much of us we allow it to control is all up to us. This may be a new concept for you to think about, but pride actually feeds insecurity. At first glimpse they look like polar opposites. But that simply isn't true. We live in a culture that is inundated with pride and self-centeredness. Phrases like 'me time,' 'self-care,' and 'look out for #1' are peppered in our commercials and in our way of thinking. But when did God ever promote 'self' anything? In fact, the Bible promotes the exact opposite of self-esteem. It promotes other's esteem. Scripture says we are to esteem others better than ourselves in Philippians 2:3–5. This doesn't mean we self-hate or take abuse or become a doormat for others to tread upon. It means we are not distracted, focused, or consumed with 'self' anything. You see, focusing on our flaws, our imperfections, our weaknesses, or our have nots is still *focusing on self*. Satan doesn't care whether we are focused on how superior we are or how inferior we are, as long as we are focusing on *self*. Whether we are bragging or berating matters not to him, as long as we are focused solely on us and no one else. Thinking too much or too little of ourselves isn't the name of the game for him. The name of the game is that we are thinking about us no matter what. Whether you spend all your time thinking how much better you are than *her* or how much less you are than *her* accomplishes the same thing. Your mind is completely preoccupied with thoughts of *self*. And let's be honest, we aren't thinking thoughts of kindness and love toward her no matter if we are feeling superior or inferior. So, here's how this works:

We aren't the best, and that hurts our pride.

We aren't better than or as good as _____, and that hurts our pride.

We don't make the cut, and that hurts our pride.

We aren't the first ones to be picked, and that hurts our pride.

We don't win the game, and that hurts our pride.

We aren't in the click, and that hurts our pride.

We don't fit into a size _____, and that hurts our pride.

They didn't stay true to us, and that hurts our pride.

Pride doesn't look like insecurity, but on the deepest level it is. Pride drives in a car with the bumper sticker 'deserve' on the back. You may feel like you deserve the most or the least, but deserve drives you either way. We all have a need packed in the trunks of our hearts to be loved, adored, cherished, and accepted. God actually made us that way. He created us with a God-sized hole in our hearts, and He did it on purpose. This need was intended to drive us to Him. Well, we allow it to drive us, alright, but to all the wrong places. This is where the train goes off the tracks, so to speak. We seek this love, approval, acceptance, and cherishing from all the wrong sources. We get performance and service all mixed up in our minds. We were made to serve, not be served. We were made to worship, not be worshiped. Pride screams for us to perform for approval, but God instructs us to perform out of our approval.

Insecurity makes everything about us. Everything. Years ago, when I was in the seventh grade (a grade where insecurities abound) I noticed a note being passed around class. I caught a glimpse of my name and the name of the cutest guy in class, who I just happened to have a massive crush on. In my insecurity-driven mind, the note had to be about my liking him and the whole class was laughing about it. So, what did I do? I marched right up to the person who currently had the note at the time and ripped it out of their hands. Triumphantly I stomped to the trash can and proceeded to tear it up into tiny little pieces. That ought to show them not to exploit my seventh-grade crush on the most popular guy in school! That's when I noticed that the tiny pieces revealed the note wasn't about me at all. It was about another girl named Amy and her run for class president against Mr. Popular. I slithered back to my seat in defeat. It wasn't about me. No one was talking about me. No one was focusing on me at all. And somehow that realization was worse than when I thought they were!

SIDE EFFECTS OF INSECURITY

Have you ever been watching TV and along comes one of those new medicine commercials? By the end, the commercial has shown all the ways this new medicine could possibly help your condition, and you are just about to be convinced that you need to call your doctor and see if you can get this amazing new medication, that is until all the side effects are listed just as the commercial comes to an end. I saw one the other day where the narrator said 'side effects may include sudden death or paralysis.' Umm... I think I will just deal with the blood sugar issues, or the gastrointestinal issues, or the itchy skin issue that I have, thank you. The 'sudden death or paralysis' is enough to deter me from trying that new medicine for whatever issue it is that I have at the moment. And so it should be with insecurity. We are getting ready to go over that long list of side effects that can come along with regular doses of insecurity.

Insecurity side effects may include all or some of the following:

1. Insecurity causes us to excuse or accept things that are not healthy, normal, or godly at all. Not only will we will accept them, but we will stay quiet about them, or even participate in them just to avoid being shunned by the people whose approval we are so desperately seeking.

2. Insecurity can make you act wrong when it comes to any sort of relationship. Behaviors that are clingy, needy, possessive, or obsessive will cause all manner of woes no matter the relationship.

3. Insecurity can make a mom be controlling and manipulative.

4. Insecurity can make you think another talented person is a threat to you.

5. Insecurity blinds us to our blessings.

6. Insecurity keeps us from venturing out and trying new things.

7. Insecurity can make us do things we really do not want to do.

8. Insecurity makes us give a terrible impression to others. (This impression can be anything, from snobbish to painfully shy or quiet or anything in between.)

9. Insecurity makes us over-compensate.

10. Insecurity makes it hard to accept compliments and even harder to accept love.

11. Insecurity makes our perception to be distorted and skewed.

12. Insecurity makes us lie to ourselves and often to others. Ever said you were busy and you weren't? Or weren't busy when you really were? Or said you knew what someone else was talking about, or knew whom someone was talking about when you really didn't? Or have you ever said you would be happy to help with _____ when you really were anything but happy to do so?

13. Insecurity makes us fake. We put on a persona that we think that others will like while, all the while, the real us is hidden behind a mask.

14. Insecurity will keep us from taking any risks.

15. Insecurity will make us settle for a less than existence.

TRIGGER HAPPY

Everyone has insecurity present in their life to some degree. Everyone. We will react to its presence in one of these two ways: 1) give into it over and over again or 2) try to hide it until something triggers it.

Let's talk about those triggers, shall we? We all have them. Triggers can be so small that we fail to even realize they are even there. Let's list a few so that you can get used to looking for them:

- a reprimand at work

- a new competition arrives in your life that you perceive as a threat

- your mom gives you that look, or sighs that sigh again

- you don't get a text back immediately

- your ex has a new hottie of a girlfriend

- a failure

- disinterest from your spouse, boyfriend, or a friend

- a significant decline in your appearance, such as a bad haircut, weight gain, or a scar from a surgery

- a betrayal

- a rejection.

Triggers cause the flood gates to open, and we become a raging, weeping, stalking, clinging, crazed maniac, and all it took was a hot second after the trigger occurred.

When a trigger happens, and it will, we can decide to keep our dignity or we can decide to voluntarily give it up. What a high price to pay! In that split second after a trigger, we decide to keep our integrity intact or to trade it in for much pain, regret, and loss. You see, that split second comes with a gift, and it is a gift we have seen before in this book. Remember the 'we don't get to choose our 'what is,' but we do get to choose our 'what now' gift' from the grief chapter? Well, that same gift is presented to us in the split second after a trigger. It is the gift of choice. We do not have to react the way we always have. We choose to react that way. Over and over and over again. But what will you do the next time, now that you are aware of this gift of choice that you have? Will you dare to make a different choice, one that will let you retain your dignity and your integrity? We cannot help *feeling* emotions at a trigger, but we can choose not to *act* on those feelings. With time and targeted obedience, God can enable us to overcome those emotional triggers, even to the point of not having those painful emotions anymore when they occur. But, until then, we must choose to walk in obedience in our actions *and* in our reactions despite the emotions we are feeling. This is called retraining your reacting. It will take time, intentionality, and dedication. But it will happen.

STEPS TO SUCCESS

The first step to victory over insecurity is to be *aware* of it in the first place. Being authentic to the point of getting real with yourself about your own insecurity is step one. No other steps can be happen until this one is made.

The second step is to be *deliberate* in your decisions. These decisions will be the opposite of what comes naturally. You will have to think about them, deliberately choose them, and then act on that new and very unfamiliar choice. It won't be easy, but it will get easier as you do it more and more often.

The third step is to be *brave*. Choosing a different course of action, or a vastly different reaction, takes guts. It is the road not taken by you. Ever. Taking a deep breath and exhaling a prayer after a trigger will help you to make the brave choice. Being brave will enable you to make a different behavior choice than you have ever made before.

The fourth step is to choose to live in *victory* over a vicious cycle. This means your new brave choice will have to be followed by a million and one other brave choices that back it up. Making that first brave choice is winning a battle; all the other choices after that will win the war.

We must recognize our triggers, pray over them, journal about them, trace them back to where they started, follow them through to where they will lead, and then choose to release them. Targeted praying will be key in your victory. Praying head-to-toe prayers over yourself beginning with the mind, followed by your eyes, ears, mouth, shoulders, hands, heart, knees, and feet cannot be stressed enough here. If you are unfamiliar with head-to-toe praying, I strongly encourage you to go to www.pbckannapolis.org and order *A Woman, A Warrior*. This is also available on Amazon. When I wrote this prayer journal a few years back, I had no idea the impact it would have on my prayer life and the prayer lives of so many women all over the country. This little journal will revolutionize your prayer time by helping you to pray powerful head to toe prayers over yourself and your loved ones. You will learn to confess from head to toe, ask God to empower from head to toe, and pray over the ones you love from head to toe. You will learn how to pray specific scriptures over these areas and how to target your prayer time so that you can pray more effectively. Insecurity is definitely an area you can target with prayer. While approaching your prayer time in this manner, being unaware of your insecurities will no longer be an option. Trust me, God will reveal truth to you while you are on your knees before Him.

'Pray – Process – Practice.' This is the mantra you will need while tackling this area of your life. Pray over your insecurities, your mind, your perceptions, your emotions, those that you feel threatened by, your actions, and your reactions. Ask God to reveal the truth about these areas to you. Ask Him to reveal a better way to handle those triggers. And ask for healing for those deeply rooted insecurities that plague you. Let's be honest, have you ever actually asked God to heal your insecurity? That's a convicting and sobering question, isn't it? Most of the time we just resign ourselves to living in our weakness instead of praying for God to enable us to overcome them. Next, process what He reveals to you and what you learn about yourself. Finally, practice the truths you have learned in this chapter.

In your journal write out what your patterns are when it comes to insecurity and then document them. Here are some common patterns in women when it comes to trigger reactions. Do you:

1. get overly defensive?

2. act superior or arrogant to cover for your insecurity?

3. binge-eat?

4. binge-watch movies, shows, etc.?

5. binge-read for hours?

6. withdraw?

7. head to a mind-numbing addiction?

8. rage or rant?

9. endlessly question loved ones?

10. give the silent treatment?

11. cry hysterically?

12. resort to self-harm?

13. turn to a habitual self-gratification coping mechanism such as pornography or sex?

14. shop or overspend?

A trigger happens – a thought process follows – your emotions kick in – and then a behavior choice is made. What is your chosen behavior pattern from this list? If you are having trouble seeing your go-to, journal a recent trigger and then what happened next. Do this several times, and the pattern will soon become clear. The next thing to journal is what the biblical response should be. Search Scripture and see how God outlines for you to act/react when this type of thing happens. What behavior does God expect? Follow a Bible character's life and see what they did with a similar trigger. How did that work for them? Was God pleased with their reaction? What type of conduct did Jesus have when faced with a similar trigger?

In a nutshell, we must *uncover* our pattern, *discover* biblical truth, and *cover* ourselves in prayer. After all that, it is time to *recover* our behaviors.

DRAWING THE BATTLE LINES

We have spent much time on the importance of our thought life throughout this book, and unfortunately, it is no different when it comes to defeating insecurity. The battle of our mind must be won before we can move onto the battle of our emotions, our behaviors, or our words. We are all familiar with Philippians 4:8, which says, "Finally brethren, whatsoever things are true, whatsoever things are honest, whatsoever things are just, whatsoever things are pure, whatsoever things are lovely, whatsoever things are of good report; if there be any virtue, and if there be any praise, think on these things."

I want to hone in on just one word out of that sizable list. That word is 'true.' In order to help us understand fully what is 'true,' we need to spend some time uncovering what is *not* true. First of all, *intuition* is not true. Intuition thoughts sound something like this: "I feel like they…." In order for something to be true, it must be *provable*. Intuition is based solely on feelings, and hence it is not provable; therefore, it cannot be considered to be true. Allowing your thoughts to obsess and focus on thoughts that are purely intuition based is to allow yourself to think on untrue thoughts that, as a result, are not biblical.

Another way of thinking that isn't true is when we have thoughts that are based on *perception*. This type of thinking sounds like this: "It looks like they…." These untrue and unprovable thoughts are founded solely on our own viewpoint, which is limited and biased at best. The way we *perceive* a person's actions or intents may or may not be true. Many of us have wrongly judged a person based on faulty information, incomplete knowledge, or biased opinion. Once the whole truth was known, we had to adjust our judgment of this person. Beware of faulty perceptions that are lurking in your thought life.

The third type of thinking that is not based upon truth is *suspicion*. These kinds of thoughts sound like this: "I wonder if they…." These thoughts are based solely upon conjecture and many times they will color our viewpoint in a completely incorrect way. We assign malicious intent to people in our lives as we assure ourselves that this person 'meant' something by what they did or did not do. Meanwhile, the person is completely clueless as to what you are thinking and assigning to them. They are not deviously out to harm us in anyway. Their actions, or inactions, had no malicious intent toward us. In fact, they weren't thinking about us at all. They were just going about their day without any evil schemes or plans at all on their part.

The last type of thinking that isn't based on truth is *speculation*. These thoughts sound like this: "I bet they…." You show me an insecure woman, and I will show you one whose thoughts are absolutely filled with speculative thoughts. That type of thinking will then lead to faulty emotions that will end in some sort of destructive behavior. God did not call us to speculate. He called us to calculate. Calculate the facts before acting, calculate the facts before we allow emotions to brew, and calculate the facts before we dole out judgment, jump to conclusions, or jump into a mess that stems from a wrong behavior.

THINK ON THESE THINGS…

Ok, so we have looked at what isn't truth, and, if you are like me, you probably discovered that there are a lot of falsehoods that have been given way too much real estate in your mind. Now we need to see what truth really is, so that we can make sure that truth becomes the owner of the vast majority of available real estate in our minds.

Truth is God's perspective on things. His viewpoint, His opinion, and His Word are truth. Period. What He says goes. It is absolute, and it is unchangeable. The falsehoods we discussed earlier color our perspective of others and also the perspective we have of ourselves. So, just how does God view me? How does God view you? How does God view other women in my life?

Psalm 45:9 and 13 let us in on those answers. He views us as 'honorable' women. He views each of us as a king's daughter (which, in fact, we are). He views us as all glorious within and gorgeously arrayed with royal apparel without. He sees us as strong and, once again, honorable. This is your truth. This is my truth. This is each woman's truth who has ever been born again. Even if we don't feel honorable, strong, or gorgeously arrayed within and without. These are also the truths of each and every woman who has asked Jesus into their heart. These truths are unchangeable come what may. They are *facts* displayed by the One who created us and therefore gave us our worth and our value. According to Psalm 139, God divinely designed us perfectly imperfect, just the way we are, on purpose and for a purpose. He is very aware of our flaws but chooses to love us completely and totally anyway. He hasn't been duped or had one pulled over on Him. He is perfectly aware of our imperfections, and He deliberately gives us His perfect love and acceptance anyway. He chooses us. As we are. And He doesn't ever experience buyer's remorse. Making sure our perspective is clear as we look into the mirror, or across the church aisle at another woman, is vital to moving forward and making progress in our journey to the other side of insecurity.

We have seen the importance of thinking clearly and perceiving clearly. Now, let's take a look at the third thing that will be of utmost importance as you proceed forward, and that is praying clearly. Without complete honesty with yourself and with God, you simply will not cover any ground in the area of insecurity. Denial, excusing, and ignoring won't accomplish a thing and will only cause you to remain stuck.

I don't know about you, but I am tired of losing ground in this area of insecurity. The same week that I was writing this chapter, I had a major meltdown centered around insecurity. It's the same issue that I have had meltdowns over for my whole married life. I experienced a trigger and I felt myself spiraling down into a sniveling, needy, desperate woman in need of assurance from an outer source. Afterwards, I got angry. I mean, good grief! I am writing a book on emotions and insecurity has a whole chapter in there! Shouldn't I have this down? Shouldn't I be further along than this? As I prayed about it, I felt a rush of insecurity about my insecurity (yes, that is a thing), and that's when God whispered in my heart the following answer: "Amy, the fact that you still struggle with it is the very reason I want you to write about it. Being real is what helps people. Being transparent is what gives people hope. Be real. Be vulnerable. Be you, as I made you to be."

So, let's write out an honest, not-so-pretty, prayer, shall we? Don't expect a, "now I lay be down to sleep" kind of prayer. That kind of prayer just won't do. The prayer I am talking about is raw and real and wonderfully effective. I encourage you to take this prayer and make it your own. You can even use it as a guide to write out your own insecurity prayer. Pray it aloud and pray it often. Journal your way through it if you want to, but whatever you do, don't forget it. Don't close this book today and forget that these words are here. Dog-ear the page. Underline, highlight, photocopy, or rewrite it. But whatever you do, pray it. I want you to know, ladies, I am writing this prayer for me. I want to regain some ground that the enemy has taken from me. Then I want to cover new territory that I haven't even stepped foot on yet. I want victory, and I have a sneaking suspicion that you do to. So, here goes...

Dear Lord, I come to you so very weary of the path I am walking, named Insecurity. It robs me of my dignity, my surety, and my peace of mind. Today, I am making a declaration. No more! Not one more inch of real estate in my mind, my heart, or my behaviors will I give up to this vicious enemy. I am a daughter of the Most High God. You are my Abba Father. I am Your child. I am Yours and You are mine. You created me for more than this. You created me to live life more abundantly. You created me to be more than a conqueror. You created me to live a life more abundantly than insecurity allows. I can either live up to that calling or live down to Satan's bidding. So, I choose today to live up to the calling that You have placed upon my life. I refuse to live a less-than existence that comes from believing I am a less-than person.

I am calling on you, as Jehovah Rapha, God my healer. I am asking You to heal my broken thoughts and perceptions that lead to broken behaviors. Heal my broken thoughts, Lord. Thoughts that are not based on truth are lies. Reveal these to me. Show me the wayward thoughts that are so camouflaged in my mind. Shine the light of Your truth on them, I pray. Help me to bring those thoughts into captivity to You today and every day. I reject the fears that crowd my mind and feed my insecurity. You have not given me the spirit of fear, Lord. You have given me a sound mind. That's a promise and that is my birthright. I now choose to start living up to that birthright and all the blessings that come with it. Today I choose strength, clear biblical thinking, power, love, and sound thoughts.

You touched blinded eyes while on this earth. I ask you to touch my eyes and heal me from distorted perceptions of myself and others. I am beautiful, cherished, worth much, whole, complete, accepted, and adored. Right now. As I am. There is nothing I can be or do to earn any more of Your love. There is nothing I can do or not do to lose any of Your love. Not only am I all those wonderful things on that list but so are all the other women I know. They are not my competitors. They are not greater than or less than me. To see them as such means I have bought into the lies of Satan. Another woman's strengths are not my weaknesses. Her victories are not my defeats. You love her and You love me. You have good for her. And You have good for me. Help me to lift her up in prayer and mean it. Help me to be for her and not against her. Help me to see her as You see her—precious, worth much, and lovely. Bless her, Lord. Help me to bless her in my thoughts, attitudes, and actions, I pray.

You touched the ears of those that couldn't hear clearly while You were on this earth. I am asking You to touch my ears so that I can hear You clearly above the noise of this world and the society that I live in right now. Help me to turn down the noise of this toxic society and to tune into Your still small voice today and every day. Help me to detect the half-truths and outright lies that Satan pushes on me daily. May they not get in me. Help me to weigh them against the truth of Your Word.

You touched tongues that were bound and could not speak, and You healed them. Lord, help me to speak truth and not be bound to lies. Help me to speak truth to myself, over and over again. Help me to speak truth to others in love. May I not have corrupt communication that compares, criticizes, or tears down another. Instead, help my speech to be helpful and never harmful. Help me to edify and uplift, encourage and challenge others to go farther in their walk with You.

Lord, I pray over my heart today. My emotions are directly tied to my insecurities. I pray over my triggers and my weak areas, Lord. You know what they are, but I want to name them. I need to name them and be completely honest about them. Here they are, Lord. My triggers and my struggles when it comes to my emotions and insecurities are: _____

_____

_____

_____

_____

_____

_____.

I need You to touch my emotions and heal my broken way of feeling that is such a pattern and a cycle, in my life. Deliver me, not just from hell, Lord, but from myself. Greater is He that is in me, than the me that is in me. Save me from myself, my destructive cycles and ways of thinking and feeling. I don't have to keep living this way. I choose victory. I choose obedience.

Lord, I pray over my shoulders today. In the temple, You healed a woman that was all stooped over. She couldn't stand up straight. For years she was bowed low under the control of a crippling disease. Lord, many days I live like that. I am all stooped over under the infirmity of insecurity. It keeps me from standing upright in dignity and freedom. You spoke the words "Woman, thou art loosed from thine infirmity" to that woman so long ago (Luke 13:12). Speak it over me today. Help me to be loosed from my infirmity of insecurity. According to this passage you laid your hands on her and straightened her. Do the same for me. I invite you to put your hands on the areas of my life that are feeding my infirmity.

Lord, you touched withered hands when You walked among men on this earth. Today, I lift my hands up to You. Insecurity disables me. It keeps me from doing for others, serving You, giving, and completing tasks. It keeps me from trying new things or from taking risks. Insecurity makes my hands hold a magnifying glass over my flaws and the flaws of others. Insecurity causes me to be needy and clingy instead of strong and giving. It keeps me from applauding the accomplishments of others or offering a helping hand to someone in need. Help my hands to be free of insecurity so that they can be busy doing what You have called them to do instead.

I pray over my knees today. May they be bowed to living life the way You designed it to be lived. May I surrender to Your will, Your truth, and Your way. For too long, I have submitted to society, to others, and to the enemy. I have bowed to the altar of false gods named 'beauty,' 'success,' 'power,' 'achievements,' 'applause,' 'approval,' 'money,' 'control,' 'addictions,' 'unhealthy coping mechanisms,' and 'sin cycles.' I ask You to supernaturally enable and divinely empower me to destroy and to rise above these idols. Help me not to put any other god before You.

Lord, You healed many lame feet while on this earth. Insecurity cripples. It maims. It halts progress. It stops us in our tracks. I admit that I have walked the path of insecurity so long that there is a very deep and well-worn rut by now. It will be hard to turn left when I have always turned right. I know that. But I also know that You do not call a person to do what You won't enable them to do. Lord, do a miracle. Change me. Empower me. Enable me. Equip me. Whatever You do, Lord, don't leave me the same. God, do a wonder in me from head to toe. Do exceeding abundantly above all that I can ask or think concerning my insecurity. Do great and mighty things which I know not, God. In the mighty name of Jesus, I pray, Amen.

GOD'S ALARM SYSTEM

Not long ago, my family got an alarm system. It was new to us. We were used to just opening a door whenever we wanted to with no thought at all. Now, all that had changed. Honestly, we did pretty well for a while, and then someone—I won't name any names—got careless and went back to her old ways. This particular someone decided one night that she needed to open the door so she could take a picture of the moon before climbing into bed. The moon that night was so amazingly bright and beautiful that she didn't even think before she opened the door. Her husband was in bed already, and so were her children. Now, when you open a door after the alarm has been armed, a countdown begins. If you punch in the code quickly, you disarm the alarm and all is fine. But, if you don't, then the alarm goes off (quite loudly, I might add), and the voice from CPI demands that you identify yourself and give the all-clear code word. Well, after opening the door upstairs, I (yes, it was me) didn't even hear the countdown begin at the keypad located all the way downstairs. And so, a few seconds later, a very loud alarm sounded. My poor girls thought a criminal had broken into the house and we were all about to die. I had never seen my husband move so fast down a flight of stairs! All I could do was say over and over, "But I didn't hear the countdown! What happened to the countdown!" Well, it took quite a while for us to settle back down and go to sleep after all that. Needless to say, I am no longer allowed to even approach the balcony door in our bedroom anymore!

The security alarm was triggered as soon as the motion sensor detected an open door. Much like a home security alarm, we all have sensors factory installed on our own personal 'security alarms.' These sensors detect movements here and there, and when it is triggered, we have just a few seconds to key in a code before a meltdown of epic proportions happens. The code we can all punch in when this happens is this: T-R-U-T-H. No matter the trigger, no matter your personal wiring and personality, there are a few seconds that we get to disarm the alarm before it goes off for all to hear. What we do in those few seconds can spare an entire household the loud screeches and ear-piercing wails, if we will only pay attention and punch in T-R-U-T-H.

Our triggers are events that cause our 'security sensors' to go off. A word was said, or not said; a text was snippy, or not returned at all; a look was given; someone sighed loudly; an invitation wasn't offered; or a comment was posted, and that was all we needed for our sensors to be tripped. Beep, beep, beep, beep. The countdown begins. The tripped sensor triggers an emotion to immediately follow on the heels of said tripped sensor. But the alarm (meltdown) doesn't have to happen. If we punch in T-R-U-T-H and make ourselves heed it, the alarm can be disarmed, and the household can go to bed in peace.

TRUTH ROOTS

Scientists say that the strongest and heartiest of plants have root systems that grow below ground exactly the same measurement as the plant grows in height above ground. For example, if a plant is three feet tall, the roots go down three feet into the ground. A root system for a plant is made up of two kinds of roots: surface roots and tap roots. Surface roots are for the collecting of rainwater and water from the watering cans of gardeners. But a plant cannot survive with just these roots alone. The plant must have tap roots that go way down deep and tap into the water reserves underground. These roots supply the plants with water during harsh dry seasons or seasons when the gardener is a lot like me—forgetful and neglectful of their plants.

The problem is we put out only surface roots for our security. This causes us to depend on our situations, our people, or our surroundings to supply us with the necessary water to survive. But, as you are well aware, sometimes drought comes, and sometimes growing seasons don't have enough water. Sometimes temperatures soar and the ground gets hard and dry. Sometimes gardeners forget, or just don't care, or go on vacation and forget about the plant altogether. So, it is with our lives. Hard, dry times come. People don't care and they walk away, taking their watering cans along with them. If we do not have tap roots deeply planted and in place, girls, our security just won't make it. It will shrivel up and die. But if we send a tap root way down deep into truth reserves, we will have what we need in spite of missing watering cans or hot, dry days that just keep coming. The fact of the matter is, their leaving or their neglect may make you feel injured, but it doesn't have to make you feel insecure.

Tap roots seek our identity, our worth, and our value from the deep and unchanging truths of God's Word. They do not seek these things from situations going our way or friends being with us along the way. Are we firmly rooting our security in God and His word, or in other people and our circumstances?

COMPETITIONS AND CHICKENS

Have you ever caught yourself sizing up the competition when you meet another woman for the first time? Have you ever watched a group of teenage girls all vie for the attention of one guy in the group? We all have. Trying to outdo or one-up other females is just as natural as breathing to most women. Competition culture is at an all-time high right now, especially now with social media. Instead of falling into this toxic mindset, how about we live in the realization that we are not against one another? How about we choose to be *for* each other instead? All it takes is a difference in perspective and perception to go from competing, comparing, and criticizing to cheering, clapping, and showing compassion along the way.

Chicken farmers have always battled the common problem of when chickens gang up against and attack an injured chicken. If a group of chickens see blood, an exposed wound, or anything colored red, they gang up on the poor, misfortunate bird and mercilessly peck it too death. In other words, they find an exposed weakness and pick at it until the bird could no longer survive. Girls, I am afraid we have become nothing but a group of merciless and mean-spirited chickens looking for a weakness to exploit. Once we sense what it is, we all gang up on the poor, unfortunate woman and we mercilessly peck, peck, peck.

To keep this terrible thing from happening anymore, a desperate farmer invented an unusual product. It was odd and made fun of at first, until it was proven unbelievably effective by the results. The clever man created tiny little red sunglasses that he put on each chicken and secured it with a band so that they covered their eyes. Now, when the chickens looked at each other, all they saw was red. Even when they looked at themselves, red was all they could see. Because of this, the chickens' behavior changed. Since everyone was now red, wounds didn't stand out and the merciless pecking and ganging-up stopped. The farmer became quite rich as a result of his creative thinking and wounded chickens everywhere rejoiced.

Ok, so we aren't chickens living on a chicken farm, but the idea still carries merit with humans, especially female ones. Could we not figuratively place red glasses over our eyes each time we were around other women? Could we not see them as flawed, imperfect, and hence wounded, just as we are? Could we not realize that there are not levels of worth and value? Could we not see we are all on the same very same struggle bus named 'Womanhood'? Could we not give them and ourselves some grace and stop being so brutal when we see an exposed wound or weakness? We could and we should and we can, if we will make the deliberate choice to change our perspective and our perception of other women. What a difference that would make in our friend circle, our churches, our workplaces, and our society as a whole. Just the simple act of viewing others as wounded and hurting and raw and in desperate need of kindness completely disarms the need to one-up them. Because we realize that we are her and she is us.

TRACE THE TRIGGER

Behind each and every trigger is a force named fear. When your insecurity meter is running high, stop and ask yourself, "What am I afraid of right at this moment?" The answer to that question will lead you to the root of your trigger point. Follow the fear.

For example, one of my biggest fears has always been becoming a widow. I am not an overly independent woman, and my husband is a very capable and strong leader. My passive nature allows him to do all the things that I don't want to do. For me, that is the business side of things. I hate all things math and am terrible at all things numbers. These just don't come naturally to me, so our roles have always been very defined. He manages the money, and I spend it! I am perfectly happy with that arrangement. The problem is, if anything were to happen to him, I would be completely at a loss as to how to manage the household funds. That's my fear. A trigger might be being in the company of a widow, or reading about a horrific accident that left a young widow behind, or possibly even attending a funeral. My fear sounds like "I could never" or "what would happen if" or "how would I ever manage that." So, I have uncovered the fear that feeds my insecurity and I have forced it out into the open. Now, let's follow the fear to the end.

Ok, so what if my husband did suddenly pass away and I am left behind shattered and broken? What then? I plan the funeral with the help of family and friends. What then? I walk through the details in a fog numb with shock and pain. What then? I survive the funeral. What then? I survive the day after the funeral. What then? I awake to new mercies, unfailing compassions, and great faithfulness each and every day that follows. What then? I get out of bed and do the next thing that needs to be done. What then? I love my kids and fix supper and clean the house and do the laundry. What then? I ask someone to help me understand the business side of things. What then? I organize and come up with a plan that works for me. I pray and I lean on the Lord and not my own understanding. What then? I discover that day by day, month by month, God is enough. He holds me when I cry, He strengthens me when it is just too much. He grants grace and peace and help on an hourly basis. What then? I experience the great grace and peace I have heard so much about when other widows shared their testimonies. I get to know my Jehovah Rapha and my Jehovah Jireh on a whole other level.

Now, I must ask myself, after that excruciatingly hard exercise, "What now?" Is there something I can do *now* in order to help what could be a difficult *then*? The answer is 'yes.' I can sit by my husband's side and have him show me the ropes of the monthly business called 'The Edwards Household.' Each month I can sit and I can ask and I can slowly learn how to do what he always does. This practically equips me if I ever do have to walk through that terrible trial. It disarms my trigger that is fed by my fear. So, we *find the trigger, force out the fear*, and *face the fear as we follow it to the end*. Finally, we *fend off the fear* by finding a practical solution to the 'what if' fear. 'What if' has no control over a woman who is at peace with 'what now.' In my scenario, I have no control over my 'what if.' But I do have some control over my 'what now' as I sit and learn and grow and become.

The exercise of following your fear to the end is a particularly power-ful one. I strongly suggest completing this exercise at some point in your own private journal.

If I ever have to face _____, then God will _____. Here are some verses and examples that you can fill in the end blank with.

- God will perfect what concerns me (Psalm 138:8).

- God will work it all out for the good of me (Romans 8:28).

- God will empower me (2 Corinthians 10:4).

- God will supply all my needs (Philippians 4:19)

- God will give enough grace to me (2 Corinthians 12:9).

- God will be strong enough for me (2 Corinthians 12:9).

- God will do and be more than enough for me (Ephesians 3:10).

These are *facts* that will help you overcome or face the *fear* that is feeding your insecurity at its very core.

Making It Personal

Answer the following questions in your journal:

1. What are your insecurity triggers? Name at least three.

2. In each instance, what event happened immediately before the trigger?

3. What were you thinking and feeling before, during, and after each trigger?

4. What behavior happened as a result of your insecurity being triggered?

5. What fear is feeding or fueling your insecurity?

6. Follow the exercise outlined at the end of the chapter and follow your fear through to the end using the 'what if,' 'what then,' and 'then God' methodology. Then include a 'what now' section that outlines any and all practical things you can do *now* to disarm your fears about those scary 'thens.' You can use the verses provided or dig in and find different verses to fit your own personal fears and needs. It will be challenging and extremely difficult to write out your biggest fear, but you will find that God will help disarm your fears as you face them one by one. Trust me when I say it was incredibly difficult when I journaled mine several years ago, and even more so when I shared it with you. But the exercise has brought much liberation to me, as it has disarmed my deep insecurity that was fed by my own particular fear.

CHAPTER FOURTEEN

Joy

Happiness – "an emotion in which one experiences
feelings ranging from contentment and
satisfaction to bliss and intense pleasure"

Joy – "a feeling of good pleasure and happiness that is
dependent on who Jesus is rather than on who we are or what
is happening around us. Joy comes from the Holy Spirit,
abiding in God's presence, and from hope in His Word."

A s I have mentioned in an earlier chapter, I grew up working at a daycare center that my mom directed for the church, where my dad pastored. My whole life I helped entertain, provide crowd control, wipe noses, feed snacks, and sing songs with every child who came through those doors. It's a wonder I ever had any children of my own! There were some activities that we did that some of the kids loved, there were some activities that only a few loved, but there was one activity that all the kids loved. That activity was chasing bubbles. It didn't matter if they were in the two-year-old room, the three-year-old room, or the four-year-old room; they all loved it. When things got sketchy, every teacher knew to pull out the bottle of bubbles and those kids were good to go for quite a while. At first, being a novice, I tried to blow the bubbles. Well, as you can imagine, blowing a couple of bubbles in a room full of two-year-olds, who are completely convinced that every-thing belongs to them, was a disaster. No way was that going to work because those kids only had eyes for the bubbles and ended up running headlong into each other. Several boo-boos later, I figured out the solution to our bubble dilemma. Place the bubble wand in front of a fan. (This was before the invention of the little bubble machines you can get in the dollar section nowadays. I should have patented my idea and then I would be writing this book from a beachfront house somewhere warm and sunny.) The result of my bright idea was bubbles galore, enough for even a roomful of selfish two-year-olds. They chased those bubbles around and around and around. Each time that they would actually get one, it would pop and disappear before their very eyes. But then I would dip the wand back in the bottle and the fan would create a whole host of other soap bubble possibilities. Not once did those kids ever come to me and say, "You know lady, I think I have caught onto the gimmick. I will never be able to catch the bubble, so you may as well stop distracting me with all these spherical shaped films of soap." Nope. Not one time. The typical response, no matter how long we did it, was "ooooh bubbles… I want one!"

I feel like much of my life has been spent chasing the soap bubbles labeled 'happy.' If I can catch this one, then I will finally catch happy. If I can do this or achieve that, get married or have kids, buy this or live in that, then happiness will finally be mine. You get the picture. In fact, in my mind, I am kind of getting a picture of Satan holding the bubble wand in front of a cosmic fan somewhere, and all of us gals are running around wasting our lives, maybe even running headlong into one another, all trying to chase happy. Let me illustrate.

The first part of my life I chased acceptance. If only I could get that popular girl to be my friend or get to be a part of that cool friend group, then I would have finally caught my happy. As I matured into a very immature teen, I began to think that the opposite sex held my happy. If I could just get that cute guy to give me the time of day, then I would finally be happy. College came and my happy bubble turned into achievement. Not that I didn't keep chasing after those cute guys! A girl can multitask, you know! Finally, the day came when I walked across that stage and held that achievement in my hand. Pop! Happy didn't come. So, I moved onto a wedding ring bubble. Mr. Right would make me happy. He was what I had been searching for all along. The hunt began in earnest, and the bubbles *popped right and left. Finally, the right one did come along and that wedding ring finally became my reality. But as wonderful as he was—and still is—my bubble still popped. He didn't hold my happy after all. He wasn't perfect, didn't meet my every need, and couldn't possibly love me the way I had constructed in my mind, thanks to Harlequin romance novels and the Hollywood film industry. Having children became my next happy bubble. If I could just have kids, then I would be fulfilled. And so, I began chasing down that bubble. Each month, another busted bubble. Month after month after month after month dragged on with no happy baby bubble.*

    It was during that time that the Lord began to deal with my heart about my salvation. I knew something was off. I had watched my husband closely since we had gotten married. He was so fulfilled. So content. So, dare I say it, happy. What did he have that I didn't? Had he somehow caught the elusive happy bubble? One night we attended a revival about an hour away from our house, and on the way home Mike put in a preaching tape. (Yes, I am that old.) The preacher was preaching a very strong and clear message about the reality of hell. I was shaken to the core. Of course I had heard countless messages similar to this one, but never had I ever felt like I did that night, sitting in the passenger seat, going down that dark country road. My husband never even realized the war going on in the seat beside him. After we got home, we talked and I began to ask questions. Slowly, God peeled away the pride and the pedigree that had blinded me for so long. I was a pastor's daughter and a preacher's wife. I was a Christian school teacher for Pete's sake! How could I be lost? But lost I was, and I now knew it. So, at about 11:50 pm, sitting in the back bedroom of that old rental house on Yates Road in a little town called Faith, (ironic, wouldn't you say?) North Carolina, I asked Jesus to save me. I was twenty-six years old. I almost missed the whole thing.

    The next morning I woke up still in shock over what had transpired the night before. I got up and sat down with my coffee on the couch to read my Bible like I had done every morning since I could remember. But this time… well, this time, it was totally different. I actually felt His presence. I heard His voice speaking through the words on the pages. I experienced Him. For the first time ever. As I went through the day, I noticed the bird's songs were sweeter than ever before. The sky was bluer, the air fresher, and the sun brighter. Peace filled me. Awe inspired me. All because God was now in me. What a difference! The emotion I was feeling wasn't happy. It was joy. Go back and reread the definition of joy. It is an emotion based on the presence of God and the person of God. Without God, you have no joy, and that was why I had felt such a void my whole life. I had tried everything I could to fill that void but to no avail. It is a God-sized void only He can fill. And when He does, joy is the result.

Now, I am sharing this with you while sitting on my couch almost twenty-three years later. My Bible is sitting by my side, and yes, my coffee is here too. While I do not feel the elation, the wonder, and the awe as intensely as I did that very first morning, He is still here, I still hear Him speak to me through the words of Scripture, I still feel His presence, and I still experience Him. There are times when He is quiet, but He is never absent. Therefore, all these years later, I still have joy. That bubble has never popped. It has been my constant because He is my constant. Yes, there have been some hard times, some very hard times, but His person has never one time left me or failed me. Joy is mine for the taking each and every day because I have Him, the giver of joy, in my heart and life.

SO, WHAT DOES JOY LOOK LIKE, ANYWAY?

You may have found yourself surprised when you turned the page and found that a chapter on 'Joy' was included in this book. All the other chapters have dealt with emotions that are hard and have to be managed and controlled. Joy doesn't seem to fit with all those other emotions. I agree, it is vastly different. All the other emotions we have and don't really want, although we desperately need to learn what to do with them. This one, well this one, we want but don't seem to know quite how to get it. As a result, this chapter will need to be approached differently. This chapter is not going to teach what to do with joy or how to manage joy when you have it. It will, however, tell you how you can manage to get joy and then how you can keep it. And yes, there is a special key that unlocks the door to joy. Stick with me, and do not skip this chapter simply because you don't see the need to manage the emotion called joy. Actually, learning to manage this emotion is the key you need to help you manage all the other pesky emotions we have talked about thus far.

In doing some research for this chapter, I did what I often do and googled it. I sometimes get a kick out of what the world says about stuff. As is often the case, the world did have some insight into this emotion but had absolutely no idea that a lot of what they were saying could be found in Scripture. I found an article entitled "Five Qualities of a Joyful Life." Keep in mind, this was a secular article. According to the author, joyful people have five characteristics that they all have in common. Characteristic number one was that they viewed joy as being constant. These people all realized that their joy wasn't tied to circumstances, it didn't come and go, it could come and stay. No matter what. The second characteristic was that their joy inspired creativity in these people. They enjoyed doing… something. They allowed the joy inside them to come out in some way that was beautiful and beneficial. Characteristic number three was that they understood that their joy was often unreasonable. What did the author mean by that? These people knew that their circumstances were sometimes bad, maybe even downright awful, and to experience joy wouldn't make sense at all. But yet, joy was theirs for the experiencing. True joy didn't follow the 'rules,' and others weren't going to understand it. These people got that and were at peace with it. The fourth characteristic these people had in common was that their joy was untroubled. To them, joy wasn't confined by the laws of nature. Joy was supernatural. Lastly, the author concluded that joyful people felt that joy was enough. Period. Joy sustained them. Joy didn't need anything else. How amazing it is that each of these characteristics is a truth taught in the Bible? The author was backing up Scripture and didn't even know it.

Now, let's look at each characteristic through the lens of God's Word. In John 16:22, Jesus tells His disciples, "And ye now therefore have sorrow: but I will see you again, and your heart shall rejoice, and your joy no man taketh from you." In other words, He said, boys, this is hard and going to get harder, but your joy is 'untakeable.' No person on this earth has permission to take it from you. It is 'unstealable.' No thief can rob you of it.

No circumstance can sneak up and suck it out of you. It. Is. Constant. Jesus knew these men were getting ready to walk through the darkest days of their lives. Calvary was looming and they would be thrown into a faith test like never before. Jesus also knew that Satan would take some things from them. Their leader would be gone. Their direction would be taken. Their idea of what the Messiah was supposed to do would be shattered. All their plans for their future were going to be stripped from them. He knew they needed to know that even when Satan had permission to take all of those things, He didn't get permission to take their joy. The same is true for you. Satan may have had a hand in taking your ministry, job, relationship, home, or finances from you, but he cannot take your joy. In order for him to do so, he would have to be able to take the person and presence of God away from you. And that, girls, is a no-go. He simply cannot do that.

What does the Bible say about joy inspiring creativity? Well, I would say the ark was pretty creative, how about you? The temple? Creative to be sure. Defeating the enemy with nothing but pitchers and torches, well, that takes the creative cake, doesn't it? How about defeating a mighty fortress of a city by doing nothing but silently marching and then shouting really loud? God is the God of creativity. Just look at nature. His creativity knows no bounds. Hebrews 12:2 says, "Looking unto Jesus the author and finisher of our faith: who for the joy that was set before him endured the cross, despising the shame, and is set down at the right hand of the throne of God." Nothing is as creative as the redemption of mankind. Jesus endured all the horrible of Calvary because of the joy salvation would bring. No one saw the cross and the empty tomb coming. Their idea of redemption was earthly and far smaller than God's idea. God has a way to redeem your situation. He has a creative solution to the problem you are facing. We can face the hard with joy, as Jesus did. Jesus knew that the Father would redeem His death. We can be assured of the same. God has a redemption plan for your situation. I don't know what has died in your life, but I do know that God never ever pens 'the end' at the grave. There is always a 'to be continued' at the graveyards of our lives. His plan isn't finished yet. And, trust me, you won't be able to script what He has in mind. There is much joy in knowing our difficult doesn't mean God is done. We can rest assured that He is quietly creating in the background of what is happening in our lives. That quiet assurance can step up to any fear and unrest and say, "Shhhhh, peace be still."

1 Thessalonians 5:15 gives the command, "Rejoice evermore." That means our joy will be quite unreasonable at times. Your friends won't understand and your family won't get it. And that's ok. Circumstances cannot dictate our joy. Situations cannot control our joy. They simply do not get that power. They do not have permission from heaven to steal it. How empowering is that? It is ok to be ok when everything isn't ok. Let that sink in. Let that hold you up. Let that help you out. Look your situation in the eye today and say, "You know what, I am alright even when it isn't alright. My joy is intact when my life isn't. So, my evermore isn't what I thought it would be. I can rest in the fact that it will be exactly what He wants it to be. So hear me well, circumstances. Today, I rejoice because to rejoice is a matter of choice. Take that, circumstance! So there, situation!" You may need to repeat those words over and over again each day that you are in your trial, but my, what power comes with those words! What power comes with the realization of what those words really mean! What a release! We can be released from the idea that everything has to be ok in order for us to be ok. That's why I think it is called 'joy unspeakable and full of glory.' We can't explain it. It just doesn't make sense. I get to choose joy in the middle of the difficult circumstances that I didn't get to choose.

Psalm 118:24 says, "This is the day which the LORD hath made; we will rejoice and be glad in it." See that choice? Our Joy is untroubled. It is unfettered with issues, problems, and circumstances. Our joy is unearthly. It is heavenly, constant, and unchanging. I don't know about you, but in a world that keeps changing at lightning speed, a constant is incredibly comforting. I need it because sometimes a 'day' can change everything. I can draw strength from this truth as it wraps around me like my warm blanket here on my couch. Do you notice the wording 'we *will* rejoice…'? Sometimes we have to 'will' our rejoice. There are going to be days when this will be a sheer act of our will. We need to know that there will be moments, days, weeks, or maybe even years when our joy will have to be chosen by sheer willpower. But never has our will had more power.

Romans 15:13 says, "Now the God of hope will fill you with all joy and peace in believing, that ye may abound in hope, through the power of the Holy Ghost." I could write reams of paper on this one verse alone. We are never hopeless because the God of hope is in me. To be hopeless is to be Godless. And a child of God can never ever be that. We can be down, we can be sad, we can be discouraged, and we can be beat up. But we can never ever be hopeless. This God of hope can fill us with joy and peace that comes from believing. This is where faith separates the men from the boys, so to speak. Believing in the easy, the comfortable, and the routine isn't going to fill us. Nope. But believing in the hard times, the lean times, and in the unexpected, well that is another matter altogether. That's when God steps in and fills us to the brim and even to overflowing. Our joy and our peace that come from our belief spill out into every area of our life and circumstance. They fill our minds with quiet and rest. They fill our heart with peace and calm. They fill our words with kindness and patience. They fill us, thrill us, and heal us. Simply put, they are enough. They enable us to live out Philippians 4:4: "Rejoice in the Lord alway: and again I say, Rejoice." Many times our 'alway' situations aren't very conducive to rejoicing, are they? We don't feel like rejoicing anyway in our alway. But notice that this verse is a command. We have to realize that we aren't commanded to rejoice in our circumstance or our situation. The reason we can rejoice *in* our 'alway' moments is because of what we are commanded to rejoice in and that what is a Who. He is what we are supposed to be rejoicing in, not in getting our way, or having what we want, or life being good and easy and going according to plan. And that is why our joy keeps coming up missing. If we tie it to circumstances, it will disappear when our circumstances go rogue. We keep getting happy and joy mixed up. They are not one and the same.

Happy is soap bubbles. Joy is something we have and can hold onto forever. Big difference. Happy is never enough, never satisfied, always popping as soon as we get it. Joy never fades, never pops, and is a constant in our lives. Joy is a choice, whereas happy is a feeling. Joy is obedience. It is following a command, instead of following an emotion. Joy is a constant, while happy is all over the place. There is nothing wrong with happy. I like it. I want more of it. But to mix it up with joy is to mix up a concoction for misery and discontent. That's why so many Christians look like they have been sucking on lemons. That's why choirs all over the country stand in beautiful buildings and sing wonderful words of life without a smile anywhere near their faces. That's why those same choirs sing to churches full of people checking their watches and thinking about all they have to do on Monday instead of worshipping the God that is being sung about. But if we were to go visit a church in Pakistan, where they meet in secret and sit on dirt floors, we would notice these Christians sing with a smile so wide that it nearly splits their faces in two. We would see underground churches filled with people hungry for God's Word and just grateful to be a part of something as wonderful as a church family. No checking watches, yawning, and distracted minds would be found there. What's the difference? Their joy is tied to the Savior they are so happy to have, and ours has been assigned to our situations and circumstances.

Ladies, aren't you ready to finally get this right? I know I am. In order to do so, we have to uncover the secret to having and maintaining true joy. For the remainder of this chapter, we are going to discover and explore the key that unlocks our joy and our ability to rejoice evermore in our alway. Here it is. Are you ready? Drumroll, please. The key to joy is *gratitude*.

HEAD, SHOULDERS, KNEES, AND TOES

Living a life filled with gratitude doesn't just happen. It will require every last part of you to work together for a common goal. For example, your *mind* will have to choose to think grateful thoughts instead of hateful thoughts. Your mind must *decide* to choose gratitude over and over and over again. You won't just gravitate to gratitude. I wish I could tell you differently, but I can't. Gratitude will not be your default mode. But, perhaps, it will be one day, if you make a calculated decision every day that you *will* be grateful, no matter what. Not thinking about being grateful has gotten us to where we are today, a selfish, self-centered, self-serving, demanding, generation of Christians who are filled to the brim with entitlement. Deciding to be grateful means every thought that harbors bitterness, mulls over wrongs, lays out comparisons, or sings 'woe is me' must be kicked out before it takes root. This will take a boatload of effort and will be a round-the-clock job, especially at first. Rewiring the brain to think 'thanks' is a big job. The goal is for gratitude to be your default mode— your factory-setting mode. The one you go to without thinking. Your knee-jerk reaction. I can say with almost 100% certainty that for nine out of ten women this is not their current default mode. How do I know? I know women. I know emotions. I know sin. I know me. For most of us, 'critical' is our default mode. Or perhaps, 'complaining' is your factory setting. 'Never have enough' is another popular one, along with 'I have it worse than everyone else' mode. What's your mode? Waking up each day with the determination that you will be grateful is the first step toward living a life of gratitude. The mind, you will find, is where gratitude is born or where it will die.

Next, we move to the *eyes*. These will have to determine to *focus* on the goodness, faithfulness, power, and presence of God instead of the harshness of your circumstances. Making yourself look for blessings will be key to reaching your goal of gratitude. Our *ears* also must be involved in this team effort. Listening to the lies from Satan will most definitely not lead you down a path of gratitude. He will hiss some things that probably go like this: "You deserve better," "Why me?" "Why not me?" "Where's God?" "God doesn't love you, just do what you want. You have to look out for number one." Any of those sound vaguely familiar? Your ears must be dedicated to tuning into that still small voice that often gets drowned out by the noise of our emotions, details of our circumstances, and the sin in our own hearts. Making yourself listen for the still small voice that we know is His will be absolutely vital to our success in this endeavor.

Next, we need to talk about that body part that needs lots of prayer—our *mouth*. Remember when Moses and the Children of Israel ran down to the waters of Marah hot, thirsty, and on the brink of dehydration? What did they discover? The water was bitter there, toxic actually. God showed Moses how to heal the waters and make them clean and healthy again so that the people could drink and be refreshed. Our words are the water that comes from the deep well of our hearts. According to Scripture, out of the abundance of our heart, our mouth speaks. Our words show us, and everyone else around us, just exactly what is in our well. Do we have sweet water or bitter water? If our words are spewing anger, negativity, criticism, complaints, whininess, comparison, or bitterness, then we have toxic water that needs healing. If our words are filled with praise, thanksgiving, compliments, encouragements, kindness, truth, love, and hope, then our waters are sweet. I was reminded of this the other day as my daughters and I were playing the game Phase 10 with my mother in law and sister in law. Now, to play a game with my crew you have to realize that we want to beat you and we want to beat you badly. We are brutal and we show no mercy. There is a lot of smack talking and wise cracks enough to go around. As we were playing my daughter Sarah was so aggravated because she couldn't seem to get off of a particular phase during the game. I was laughing, joking, and poking fun of her relentlessly. Now, my sister in law Christy, she was saying things like, "you will get it next time," and "it's ok, don't worry." Then when she finally did get her phase and won the next round, Christy said, and meant every word, "Great job! I am so glad you won that one." All the rest of us just stopped and looked at her, like are you for real? But we all know that was exactly what she was being because that is just who she is. She has a well that runs deep and sweet and her words were giving each of us a clear view of her well. Do your waters, or your words, need healing? If so, then let's move to the next part of you that must cooperate in order to become a grateful woman. That's the *heart*. The heart is the seat of our emotions in our culture. If your heart is filled with toxic emotions, gratitude will not stand a chance. Allowing an emotion to drive you, control you, fill you, engulf you, strangle you, or blind you is actually completely up to you. You do not have to surrender to that emotion. Making a conscious decision to be grateful in the midst of hurt brings healing. You may not have many circumstances that you can be grateful for right now, but you can always be grateful for your God. Choose to spend time meditating on His love, His goodness, His kindness, His mercies, His forgiveness, His provision, and His blessings. You have all that. Even in your tough circumstance. Take those emotions, rein them in, and make them bow to the God who saved your soul. Take them to Calvary. That will heal those bitter waters and make them sweet again.

Now, let's talk about our *shoulders*. How can your shoulders be grateful? They can choose to cast instead of trying to carry your burdens. They can lay down the load and be grateful for the place provided for us to lay it and leave it. They can be grateful that they don't have to carry the heavy burden that was just too much. They can be grateful for His shoulders that are all powerful and designed to carry your every burden. When our shoulders are freed up, then our *hands* will be free to raise in praise. A lifted hand in worship is a beautiful thing. Your hands will now be able to count your blessings instead of your complaints. They will even be able to help a brother or sister along the way. They can uplift others and help them take their load to Jesus. They can now be free to give instead of always taking now too.

Our *knees* have an assignment too, and it is a very important one. Their job is to do exactly what they are designed to do. They are to bow. They are to surrender and submit to whatever it is God has designed for your life. They are to bow to their God and King. When one knows one's place before a Holy God, gratitude comes easy. When one doesn't have that realization firmly in place, gratitude can scarcely be found.

Finally, our *feet* get in on this assignment with the all-important task of following the leading of God in our lives. Allowing God to direct our steps shows that we know who is in charge and who holds our tomorrows. Resting in His perfect timing and His ability to make no mistakes will fuel gratitude, even in those waiting times. Grateful feet won't lead us wrong. Whether it is being still or walking by faith, obedient feet are grateful feet.

Just keep on walking toward anything that leads you closer to Jesus and you won't go wrong.

HOW FIRM A FOUNDATION

Gratitude is the foundation upon which every aspect of a victorious Christian life is built. Just try to live a life of faith without gratitude or try loving like Christ loves without gratitude. It won't take you long to realize gratitude is at the heart of every aspect of a victorious and obedient Christian life. You will never serve as Christ served without having a grateful heart. Giving of yourself, sacrificing, and having a generous spirit cannot thrive apart from gratitude either. Gratitude, now that I think of it, is kind of like salt. Let me explain.

I love cooking shows, especially the competition ones. I love to watch the master chef teach the novices a thing or two about cooking. I love watching the teachable moments when an expert imparts wisdom to a willing student. The seasoned chef always tells them about flavor profiles and spices and which food pairs well with another. In every show, however, there is one student who refuses to listen to instructions and inevitably under-salts his dishes. The chef then fusses and fumes and maybe even throws things in frustration. You see, salt is a natural flavor enhancer. It brings out all the flavors of the dish and amplifies them. No salt, no flavor. Period. Salt brings out the best in everything it touches. Come to find out, gratitude is the salt of life. It enhances everything it touches. It brings out the best in us and in others. Without it, life is flat and missing something vital and important.

Want to improve your looks? Try gratitude. I am sure you, like me, know a woman who if she would just smile, her face would appreciate it. I once knew a woman who was not beautiful by the world's standards at all, but she had the most beautiful smile ever. And she wore it often. Even when her husband received a life-threatening diagnosis. Even when her bank account was empty because he could no longer work. Even when a near and dear to her heart loved one died. This woman was always the first to praise God when the preacher asked for a testimony and she always did so with that beautiful smile firmly in place. One day my youngest daughter and I were talking about true beauty. I asked if she could tell me the most beautiful woman she knew. This lady's name was one of her first replies. Amazingly, she was the very one I was thinking of too! What a testimony! Every once in a while, tell your face that you are redeemed. Let your expressions know that you aren't under the judgment of a holy God anymore. Send your facial muscles a memo that says you are loved, forgiven, cherished, and divinely designed by the God of the universe. It will be the best beauty treatment ever. If Revlon could bottle it up and sell it, they would make a fortune. A grateful heart makes a smiling face.

Want close, healthy, and thriving relationships? Try gratitude. When you were a kid, did you ever have that science teacher that taught you about magnets? I did. In seventh grade, I had the best science teacher ever. He was a left-over hippie from the sixties that never quite got the memo that the hippie movement was over and done. He even brought his guitar to class and strummed tunes to help us pronounce deoxyribonucleic acid. One day he handed out magnets to everyone. Each student got one on their desk. He let us play around with them for a bit before he ruined our fun with a science lesson. After he explained the poles of a magnet and the rules of how they repel and attract, he let us pair up and see how this worked in action. My partner (who, to my dismay, was not the cute boy across the aisle) and I flipped our magnets this way and that. Amazingly, the law of attraction proved true. Flip the pole of the magnet one way and it attracted, flip it the other way and it repelled. You couldn't see anything, but you could sure feel when it repelled the other magnet. There was an invisible, but very evident, force literally pushing the other magnet away. I think I would be right to say that each one of us probably knows a woman like that. She has an invisible force around her that repels others. That force can't be seen but it sure is felt. Instead of a magnetic field it is a negative field, a whining field, a critical field, an ungrateful field. Whatever you call it, it repels. I also think I would be right if I said that we all know a woman whose 'pole' attracts. Her field is grateful and kind and joyful. She attracts. People are drawn to her, to her smile, to her laugh, to her beauty that has nothing to do with the cosmetic counter at Belk. I want to be her, don't you? How about we purposely flip our poles to the positive side? Let's change our attitude and outlook field and watch how others are attracted to our new found smiles, gratitude, and positivity.

GREEN BEANS AND GRATITUDE

When my oldest daughter was about six years old, I decided to surprise her with a Thanksgiving meal in July. She had loved eating the special Thanksgiving dishes in November, and I wanted to do something special just for her. So, I cooked and cooked and was so excited about the reaction she would have to her unexpected surprise. To my dismay, when she looked at her plate, she exclaimed, "Ew… green beans!" I was more than a little disappointed and frustrated. The next morning, God nudged my heart about how many times I had done the same thing to Him. God loads the plate of my life with so many wonderful things. I guess we could call them mashed potatoes and gravy blessings, if you will. Right beside that glorious pile of goodness we will find our plates stuffed with the stuffing of God's goodness and mercies. Next, we find the sweetness of His love in a big pile of sweet potato casserole. Mmmmm, sounds good, doesn't it? Tender, juicy turkey smothered in the gravy of those unfailing compassions and great faithfulness can be found on that plate too. Don't forget the warm buttery roll that is comfort food at its best. It shows us the Comforter and His warm presence when we need it most. And then, we bump into that dreaded pile of green beans. The one thing that has some sort of nutritional value! The one thing that may benefit us in some way. The one thing that we won't regret eating later, by the way. Well, that small spoonful of something good for us represents that something we don't like on our plate but will benefit us in some way. That pile of green may not be our favorite thing, but it is a good thing. When God dishes up those things on the plates of our lives, what is our response? Are we guilty of the "ew… green beans" response? If so, then God must feel exactly how I felt that day. Disappointed, hurt, and a little angry at the ungratefulness of my child. Lord, help us to focus on the blessings and realize that the piles of green beans in our lives are good for us and were dished up with as much love as the mashed potatoes were! That day I was hoping for a "Wow, Mom, what a surprise! Thanks! I can't believe you did all this for me!" Something tells me that God desires that same kind of response from us.

Philippians 2:14–15 says, "Do all things without murmurings and disputings: That ye may be blameless and harmless, the sons of God, without rebuke, in the midst of a crooked and perverse nation, among whom ye shine as lights in the world;" Our green beans could be characterized as our 'all things' according to these verses. In other words, we are to be grateful for the green beans. Sarah had a plate full of goodness. There were lots of wonderful things that she could have focused on, yet she chose to focus on the *one* thing she didn't like. She honed in on it so much that it was all she could see. Those beans actually eclipsed all the other good things around them. Boy, isn't that exactly what we do in life? Most of our 'plates' hold so many wonderful things and usually only one or two small portions of something we do not want. Yet, if we are not careful, we will focus so intently on the one or two things we do not like, that we no longer even see all the other wonderful things that God has given us. Statistically speaking, most of us have 80% of good on our plate and 20% of bad. But that 20% of bad tends to get 80% of our attention, words, emotions, and thoughts, doesn't it? That leaves the 80% of good only getting 20% or our attention and gratitude. Now, I am not a math whiz, but even I can see that that is way out of proportion.

Time passed and getting Sarah to eat green beans became a battle. She would fuss and whine and plead and beg to get out of having to eat them, but her dad and I knew she needed what green beans had to offer. If it had been left to her, she would have existed on a diet of mashed potatoes and rolls. But, according to Scripture, foolishness is bound in the heart of a child. So, we stood our ground. She didn't know what was best for her.

We did. So, the great green bean battle began. She begged. We stood firm. She refused. We stood firm. She was not allowed to leave the table until the small pile of green beans was gone. Her response? She sat for over an hour staring at what she hated. Those poor beans were now cold and nasty. She resorted to tears. We still did not back down. She even tried stomping, which just got her a spanking and a seat back at the table with the now even colder green beans. Finally, a couple of hours, lots of tears, several gags, and lots of little-girl drama later, she got them down. Man, did she make that harder than it had to be!

Are you feeling as convicted as I am? How many times do we beg, plead, cry, stomp our feet, and flat-out refuse to partake of what God has dished up for us? I am here to tell you, He will stand firm. He won't back down. We aren't going to change His mind, no matter how much drama and theatrics we pour on. If green beans are on our plate, they are there for a purpose. They will somehow benefit us. There's something they bring to the table that we need. In other words, we need to eat our vegetables, girls. And we need to do it without murmurings and disputings. Oh, what a difference it would make in our mealtimes, for all those around our tables! Our tables are set in crooked and perverse world that would greatly benefit from a single solitary glow from a light of gratitude, submission, and true joy. We need to understand that our ingratitude and stubbornness are harmful, not only to us but also to everyone around us. Are we blameless here? Are we being harmless here? Sobering questions, to be sure.

THE INGREDIENTS OF GRATEFULNESS

Gratitude cannot exist without three key ingredients. There must be an *awakening* to the many blessings and benefits that we have received from the hand of God. We must open our eyes and realize where our blessings come from. They are not luck, coincidences, or chance. Each one has a purpose and a reason for being in our lives, even the ones we don't particularly care for. Perhaps we need to reevaluate how we define 'blessing.' Oh, we have a preconceived notion of what that word means, let me assure you. We see a beautiful big house, complete with a white picket fence. We envision happy and healthy kids who do great in school while achieving MVP status on the team. These smart, healthy, talented overachievers have no ongoing issues and make us look good at every turn. Blessed means our husbands read from the Hallmark movie script we have carefully written for them and meet our every need—before we even know we have them. In order to be blessed, we must have a fulfilling career that has lots of digits on our paycheck each month, our coworkers are like our second family, and our boss appreciates us. Our bodies? Well, they are slim and healthy with no aches and pains and definitely no sags or bags. Yes, I believe I just described 'blessed' as we see it here in the good old USA. But, if we could see 'blessed' from a heaven's-eye view, we would see that a cancer diagnosis can actually be a blessing. It could be the very thing that brings our wayward child to their knees in repentance or it may become the bridge that closes the distance between the two of you. Losing a job may be a blessing if it causes you to stop missing church so often and allows you to spend some much-needed time with your family. An unexpected delay of what you felt would be your next thing could actually be the protective hand of God shielding you from unforeseen harm. Blessings one and all, as each one had something in it that we needed, much like the vitamins in a green bean.

Next, we must have an *awareness* that God is the ultimate giver of every good gift. We do not earn it or deserve it. We can never be entitled to it either. With this awareness must come a humbleness and a realization of how undeserving we really are and how merciful and wonderful He really is. This awareness comes bearing gifts as it gives us a willingness to let go of things we used to hold so tightly to. Generosity is born and a love for giving to others becomes our new normal. We seek out ways to be a blessing because we now have a proper understanding of what a blessing really is. Our joy now comes from anonymously meeting a need instead of receiving more than we need. The verse that says it is more blessed to give than to receive is not only *the* truth; it becomes *our* truth.

The third ingredient is verbally *acknowledging* our gratitude. Hebrews 13:15 says, "By him therefore let us offer the sacrifice of praise to God continually, that is, the fruit of our lips giving thanks to his name." Did you see how clearly God worded that? He expects to *hear* us *say* thank you. He expects our praise to be verbal. In other words, we need to do more than just 'think thanks.' We need to say it. How would it go over if we just said 'thank you' mentally to our spouse? What if they did a kind gesture or showed love to us in some way that was out of the way and when they asked if we appreciated it or noticed it, we said, "Oh, I said thank you in my mind." I don't think that would fly, do you? Well, God doesn't want to read our thanks in our thought bubbles. He wants to hear it in our spoken words. He longs to hear you thank Him for the many blessings and benefits He bestows upon you daily. And who can blame Him? Not me. When I do something special for someone, I want to hear that it meant something to them, don't you? God is no different, and it is time we realized that.

PROVIDENTIAL PET PEEVES

As you read through Scripture and get to know God, you will find there are some things that get on His holy nerves, so to speak. One of those things is an ungrateful heart. We see this very clearly in Luke 17:11–19 when Jesus tells the story of the ten lepers who were healed. All ten were living with a terrible disease that was going to make them die a very slow and painful death. All ten had a very legitimate need. Ten asked. Ten received. Ten were rescued. Ten were spared. Ten now got to enjoy health and a future. Ten got their lives back. Ten got their families back. Ten now had hope and freedom. But ten didn't say thank you; only one did. Why? Were the other nine terrible people? Were they all infamous ingrates that had always been ungrateful? Somehow, I don't think so. I honestly believe these men were very grateful. I think they realized what a gift they had been given. I think they realized it was no ordinary man who had given them their healing. So why the lack of gratitude? Why the breach in manners? Why the breakdown in polite protocol? The answer to all those questions can be found in one word: distraction. These men became distracted with other things. Those things took their attention from what was most important in that miraculous moment. It is important to note that those attention stealers weren't terrible things. They were actually good things, like running home to embrace their wives and children, getting back to work, changing into clean clothes, becoming a functional part of society again, going to the Temple, volunteering at their children's school, fixing the things around the house that had fallen into disrepair, or maybe even becoming head of the committee that oversaw the donations to the local leper colony. Get the picture? This story gives us a powerful visual of the verse we looked at earlier concerning our lips giving thanks. These men were grateful—in their hearts and minds—but that's where their gratitude stopped. These men allowed other things to steal away the opportunity to give thanks with their lips to the One that saved their lives, the One that rescued them from an awful and painful death, the One that gave them hope and future, the One that blessed them with health and a family, and the One that shielded them from so much physical and emotional agony. These nine men didn't run out and do sinful things; they just failed to do the most important thing.

This brings a whole new perspective to this story that we have read in Luke so many times. Truthfully, I have always condemned the nine and passed judgment on them. I have pictured them as ingrates that had always been that way and always would be. But now that I really think about it, I am them. And so are many good people who are saved and serve and volunteer and go to church three times a week. In fact, I am convinced churches are filled with 'the nine.' We are grateful. We know He saved us from an awful fate. We appreciate the life He has given us. We know apart from Him we would never have had it. We know whom we owe it all to. But we get distracted. We get busy. We get so involved with other things, good things mind you, that saying 'thank you' to the You that gave us all those things somehow gets lost in the shuffle.

A great illustration that shows this comes to us in the story of how the Taj Mahal was built. The great king, Shah Jahan, was suffering from inconsolable grief. His beloved wife had passed away a year earlier after giving birth to their fourteenth child. The following year he decided to commission the greatest monument ever built in honor of his great love. After years of construction, the king became consumed with the massive project he had undertaken. Never was this seen so much as the day when he was walking the construction site and accidentally stumbled over an old wooden box that was sticking out of the dirt. Angrily the king ordered the box to be removed and destroyed. Later the king discovered that the old wooden box was actually the casket of the very one he had set out to honor in the first place. Distractions. They steal our focus. They rob us of what we set out to do in the very beginning. They take our time, our focus, and our energy away from what is really important. These seemingly innocent distractions divide our devotion, our drive, and our dedication.

I believe those men meant to say thank you. I believe they wanted to say thank you. I believe if you asked them later, they would tell you they were grateful and would even give Jesus all the credit for their healing and the happiness they now enjoyed. I would even go so far as to say that they may have even believed that they said thank you. Has that ever happened to you? You did something big and meaningful for someone and they failed to say thank you for it. It bugged you to the point that you called them on it. Their response? "Didn't I say thank you? I thought I did." Or even worse, they say, "But I said I liked it." You didn't want to hear "I like it." You wanted to hear "thank you." Have you ever written a text and thought you sent it, only to find out later that you failed to hit 'send'? You took the time to construct a text to that person, but you never communicated it to them. Why? You failed to hit 'send.' Ladies, have we hit the 'send' button on our gratitude to heaven recently? Or is it still in the message field waiting to be 'sent'?

We are all familiar with Ephesians 5:16, which says the famous phrase, "Redeeming the time...." I looked up the word 'redeem,' and it means 'to rescue.' Wow! We desperately need to take to heart the meaning of that word. Our time needs rescuing, and it needs rescuing badly. To see how much time you need to rescue, check your screen time on your phone. After you pick your jaw up off the floor, a concerned realization needs to set in that our time is being taken hostage to a small device that fits in the palm of our hand. I have come to the conclusion that I cannot have my quiet time or my prayer time with it beside me anymore. Something pops into my mind and I find myself picking my phone up to answer that text, put that item I forgot to order in my cart, check the weather, the latest headline, or some such thing. Time and attention stealers. We must 'praise-oritize,' and no, that is not a misspelling. We must make sure that we prioritize our praise. We also need to make sure we thank other people whenever a service is rendered or a kind deed is done for us. Cultivating gratitude must be made a priority or, like everything else, it simply won't get done.

Notice that only one leper made gratitude the proper priority in his life. The other nine thought whatever it was that grabbed their time and attention was more important than returning to the source of their blessing and saying thank you. But the one grateful leper received something the other nine did not. Jesus looked at him and said, "Arise, go thy way: thy faith hath made thee whole." I know a lot of people who have faith, but their faith hasn't made them whole. The other nine had faith and that faith made them well. Last time I checked, well and whole are not the same thing. The word 'whole' means 'complete, entire, not defective, unimpaired, unbroken, uninjured, sound, not hurt or sick, restored.' The nine only received the 'not hurt or sick' part of this definition. I believe this one man received the rest of the definition. I believe his mind, heart, body, soul, behaviors, and relationships were all restored. The rest went home physically healthy but still broken spiritually, emotionally, and behaviorally. I know many people who are healed from being a sinner on their way to hell but are still very much sin-sick. They are healed but not whole. Gratitude was what made the difference between healed and whole. One man who decided to make Jesus a priority by cultivating gratitude, practicing gratitude, and speaking gratitude went from being made well to being made whole. How many *whole* people do you know? A *whole* person is complete. They are unimpaired, unbroken, sound, and restored. That unimpaired doesn't mean they have never been impaired; it just means that they aren't currently operating impaired. Impaired means 'weakened or damaged.' Whole means this person isn't living life in their weakness, impaired by it, held back by it, hindered by it, or limited by it. They used to be, but not now. Well, hallelujah! What got that one fella freed from his flaws, his weakness, his issue, his brokenness? Gratitude. Ladies, I know a lot of saved people, but I don't know a lot of whole ones. And if I am correct, you can probably say the same thing. I don't just want Jesus to deliver me from hell, I want Him to deliver me from a lot more. Things like busyness, idleness, selfishness, distractions, worldliness, habits, cycles, weaknesses, and all sorts of emotional traps and tendencies. Whole people have allowed Jesus to deliver them, not just heal them. Gratitude, little old seemingly insignificant gratitude, is the key to experiencing 'whole' deliverance.

GRATITUDE KILLERS

The number one killer of gratitude is *unrealistic expectations*. When we walk into a situation or a relationship expecting far too much, we are doomed to live in disappointment. We will then find ourselves always longing for more and living in the sorrow of what we think could have or should have been. Discontent and gratitude cannot coexist. One is the other's nemesis. So, let's evaluate, shall we? In the area of your marriage, are you living in disappointment and discontent or are you living in gratitude? In the area of parenting, at which address can we find you? 207 Frustrated Avenue or 207 Grateful Court? How about your job? Are you going into work grateful and everyone knows it, or are you going in hateful and everyone knows it? What about your living conditions? Are you content with your house/apartment as is, or are you constantly longing for something better? Disappointment is the dirt in which ungratefulness thrives best.

The number two killer of gratitude is when we suffer from *memory loss*. The word 'remember' is mentioned 144 times in the Bible. God is constantly reminding His people to *remember*. Each time His children forgot, they became hardened and sinful and began to live lives full of wickedness and wrong choices. Harsh judgment and punishment were always the result of such actions. When we make ourselves remember God's goodness, faithfulness, power, and never-ending mercies, we will remain tender hearted, aware, reverent, and thankful. This will then lead to living an obedient and surrendered life, and who doesn't want that?

The third killer of gratitude comes in the form of four little words that represent an overall attitude of ingratitude. These words should cause warning bells to sound in our hearts and minds. They are *deserve, earned, rights*, and *entitled*. When we preface something with 'I have every right to…,' we can rest assured that we aren't in the right. Beware of this killer as it is running rampant in our society today. We will never be truly grateful for something we feel we 'deserve' or somehow 'earned.' When we fall prey to this dangerous attitude, we will stop viewing our blessings as gifts from God and we will begin to start expecting, even demanding them. After all, we 'earned' them, right?

The last killer of gratitude is *comparison*. Longing to be 'better than' keeps us from being 'grateful for.' You can quote me on that. It's an Amy original. Here's another one: appreciation cannot thrive when comparison is alive. Beth Moore, eat your heart out. Wait a minute, I think I just did what I was warning you not to do! See how easy it is to fall in this trap? When we run around with a measuring stick, seeing how much 'better than' or 'worse than' we are, Satan has already won the battle. He doesn't care which one you focus on as long as you aren't focusing on Christ.

BUT WAIT, THERE'S MORE

Have you ever watched an infomercial? By the end of a good one you are convinced you cannot live without whatever product they are selling. Well, at this point, I feel like I am trying to convince you of the fact that you cannot live life fully without adding gratitude to the mix. If I could, I would hire actors and actresses, and some of them would even wear lab coats and have impressive credentials by their name in my gratitude infomercial. I would have a studio audience and share lots of personal testimonials and before and after pictures trying to convince you of the amazing power of gratitude. Right at the very end of my thirty-minute infomercial, I would pull out the big guns and I would say, 'But wait, there's more.' And then I would show you something really amazing.

We have arrived at that point in our infomercial. You have heard the testimonials. You have seen the evidence, but now you need to witness one last thing in order to convince you to take the gratitude plunge. I would then stand centerstage and tell the audience that I had one more expert to interview on the matter. His credentials were long and impressive. The audience would ooh and ahh when I called God onto the stage. "Welcome, God. I am so glad you took time out of your busy schedule to join us here today. We all know you are an expert on this subject and an authority in the field. What would you say to someone out there that is still on the fence about the importance of taking the gratitude plunge?" God would then direct the audience's attention to the screen at the front of the stage and say that we are about to see how He views ingratitude. We are going to get some rare footage of what a lack of gratitude looks like from a heaven's-eye view. A hush falls over the audience as they anticipate what they will see in this never-before-seen footage.

To their amazement, the footage is simply 2 Timothy 3:1–5. Take a moment and read those verses in your Bible, if you will. I could type them out for you, but I want you to get the full effect. These verses are talking about the end times when the world gets incredibly wicked and sinful. God writes a long laundry list of grievous sins that will be present in the last days on this earth. With each one, we sadly shake our head and agree that we are seeing them in our present world. Let's take a look at the list for a moment, shall we? I have looked up several of the words the Bible uses and written definitions of some of the words on the list. For some, I used the modern-day word so that you can receive the full impact of this awful list of sins. In the last days people will be: self-centered, covetous, boasters, proud, blasphemers, disobedient, rebellious, unholy, sexually perverse, deceivers, dishonest, powerless, mean, haters of anything good or holy, traitors, rash, quick to believe a lie, full of self-conceit, lovers of pleasures more than lovers of God, and last, but not least, people will deny that God even exists or that He has any power. Oh, wait, I forgot one. Nestled in between disobedient and unholy is the word 'unthankful.' Oh my! God put being ungrateful in a list alongside such things as being sexually perverse, lying, and atheism. Bet the studio audience didn't see that one coming.

In this passage we find unthankful listed among some pretty heavy hitters. God doesn't view this sin as no big deal. If we are to become a grateful person, we must understand the seriousness and the consequences of being an ungrateful person. Then we must uncover the ingratitude that is present in our lives and uproot it by humbly confessing it as sin. Being ungrateful isn't a bad habit, an oversight, or a simple slip of our memory. It isn't even just being rude. Being ungrateful is sin. That has to be understood if we are ever going to be a truly grateful person.

Maybe you still aren't convinced about buying into this whole 'gratitude being the key to joy' thing. Well, I have one more list for you. Why is it so important to be grateful?

1. Being grateful is a command. 1 Thessalonians 5:18: "In everything give thanks: for this is the will of God in Christ Jesus concerning you." Do you remember when your parents used to answer you with the dreaded words "Because I said so"? When you were a kid, those words meant nothing to you. Now, as a parent, you understand that they mean everything. Why? Because of the position of authority that backs them up, that's why. Sometimes we need to just accept the authority of the one who gives the commands and simply do what they say to do. Think soldier. Think commanding officer. Think "Sir, yes sir!"

2. Gratitude benefits our relationship with God and others. I have decided that thankfulness is the sixth love language (see Gary Chapman's book *The Five Love Languages*), and it is most definitely the love language of God. Gratitude gets you close to God and keeps you there. It literally ushers you into His presence. Psalm 95:2 and 100:4.

3. Gratitude is key in having peace. Philippians 4:6–7. The peace of God that keeps our hearts and minds only comes when we pray and praise. So, for you mathematical people, prayer + praise = peace. This is one mathematical equation you really will actually use in life!

4. Gratitude has a 'no excuse policy' with God. 1 Thessalonians 5:18 and Ephesians 5:20 remove any and all excuses we may have for not being grateful. We are commanded to give thanks in everything and for all things. These verses leave no room for 'interpretation.' God's word is very clear. He expects us to be grateful for all things and in all things. Now, I know that is hard. It can even seem unreasonable at times. But, once again, some things we do simply because He 'said so.' When life isn't just hard it is downright awful, we can always focus on being grateful for HIM—who He is, His presence, His person, His power, His plan, His providence, and His preeminence. Taking our eyes off of our 'it' and putting them on Him will allow us to cultivate gratitude even in the awful.

5. Gratitude is the will of God. Everyone wants to know what the will of God is for their life, like it is some sort of mysterious, mystical hidden thing. It isn't. God's will for your life and mine is plain old gratitude. Maybe if we would follow the revealed will of God (like being grateful), He would then reveal those hidden things we so desperately want to know.

6. Gratitude is tangible and visual evidence of the Spirit of God within you. Here it is in cotton patch language—a grateful person has a credible testimony. They are the 'real deal' and prove themselves 'authentic' to those around them who are watching to see if there is any merit in this whole Christianity thing. A grateful person's walk backs up their talk.

7. Gratitude makes you look like Jesus. Jesus was grateful. While on this earth, He said thank you quite a few times. Jesus is recorded saying thank you to God the Father for His plan and how He had orchestrated it. Now, remember this 'plan' He was thanking God for required Him to die a brutal death on the cross. He also thanked God for hearing His prayer in John 11:41 while at the tomb of Lazarus. And in three out of four gospels it is recorded that He thanked God at the last supper for the breaking of His body and the shedding of His blood that was facing Him in the very near future. Imagine that! He was literally thanking God for the horrible pain and torture He was about to endure. He knew every horrible and graphic detail of the brutality about to be His reality and He thanked God for it. He lived out the command of being grateful in and for all things right then and there. You see, God will never ask you to do something He hasn't already done or to endure something He didn't already endure first.

LET'S TALK NUMBERS

On paper, we should be the most grateful people on earth. Let me explain.

- Life expectancies have almost doubled in the last century.

- The average size of a new house has gone from 1,100 sq. ft to 2,300 sq. ft.

- The average Westerner is more prosperous than 99.4% of people who ever lived on this earth.

If numbers don't lie, and they don't, gratitude should be at an all-time high instead of at an all-time low. But look around. Do a survey of your surroundings. Take a census in your congregation. Do a gratitude check at church. Take an exit poll as people leave a Sunday morning service and you will find the numbers are just not matching up. We have more than we have ever had and we are the most miserable we have ever been. Even with all this amazing growth in stuff and wealth, the number of people who labeled themselves as happy is no higher than those who labeled themselves as happy in the 1950s. Why is that? Stuff doesn't equal happy. Wealth doesn't mean contentment. Great gains on quarterly reports do not ensure a grateful heart. We are living that reality every day. We sit side by side with it in church every Sunday. We wake up to it daily. We head into work with it. We go to sleep next to it each night. We look into the emptiness of it as we stare at our reflection in the mirror. Material possessions do not bring joy. Just ask the Hollywood crowd whose drug addictions, divorces, and suicides tell the true story. Fame is not the name of the game. Riches do not reflect our happy. Mansions aren't the measure of success. Money does not 'make the man' as they say.

So then what does? What on earth can make us happy? That's the problem. Nothing on earth can. Nothing of earth can. But the One who created the earth? Well, that's the One who holds true joy in His hands. Finally realizing this will allow us to tap into that Living Water Jesus talked about. He is the Source. Being grateful *to* Him and *for* Him is the equivalent of dropping our bucket into that well of Living Water and filling it all the way to the top. Trying to be joyful without this truth is the equivalent of pouring water into a bucket with a giant hole in it. It will never be full and neither will we.

IT'S THE THOUGHT THAT COUNTS

With gratitude, it is all about attitude. You have to purposefully choose to appreciate the little things, the big things, and all the in-between things. You have to be aware of them. According to James 1:17, "Every good gift and every perfect gift is from above, and cometh down from the Father of lights...." Don't you just love giving the perfect gift? My husband is notoriously hard to buy for. My family fights over who has to have his name at Christmas. My sisters always call around Thanksgiving time and ask what on earth they can buy him. I never have an answer because I am trying to figure out what I am going to buy him for Christmas. And to make matters worse, his love language is gifts! Talk about a challenge! The reason he is so hard to buy for isn't because he is hard to please; it is because he lives pleased. He doesn't want anything. He is the most content person I know and honestly needs very little to be happy. As he goes through life, he views everything as a gift and therefore doesn't really want any other gifts. I wonder what life would be like if we all lived that way. Amazon would probably go out of business if that became everyone's reality.

It is customary at our house to write thank-you notes when someone gives us a gift. My daughters know that when someone gives them a birthday gift or some such, a thank-you note is in order. After writing this chapter, I now think that that may be a great thing to do when it comes to God. How about we write a thank-you note every day to God in our journals?

Dear God,

Today I want to thank you for the good and perfect gift of _____.

My, my, how that would cultivate an attitude of gratitude instead of the one of entitlement and greed that so easily permeates our lives! Try it. Begin each day with a thank-you note to God. Do it each day for a month and just see if you don't end the month much more joyfully than you started it.

What sort of gifts should we say thank you for? There are spiritual gifts like salvation, forgiveness, peace, hope, comfort, rest, direction, wisdom, daily mercies, unfailing compassions, faithfulness, conviction, a verse or a message just when you needed it, an answered prayer, and so forth. The list could go on and on and on. Then there are physical gifts like a new car, money to pay rent, an unexpected financial gift from someone, a doctor bill that was lower than expected, a good deal on a purchase, health, an all-clear medical test, the physical ability to carry out a necessary task, a person God blessed your life with, a healthy birth, a sunny day to run errands on, a close parking space on a rainy day, a raise at work, or a new insurance package that covered a major surgery you had no idea would be facing you this year. How about mental and emotional gifts? Goodness, there are a lot of those too! Healing and freedom from mental and emotional strongholds, strength and the capability to problem-solve, the ability to overcome fears, an enablement and empowerment to overcome weaknesses, hurts, past issues, and present failures. When we make ourselves slow down and really think about these good and perfect gifts, we cannot possibly name them all. Perhaps this is what He meant when He told us to be still and know that He is God. When we finally get *still*, we will *know* and be aware of the Godness of God in our lives. Gratefulness can't help but come when we get a good glimpse of God.

We know that a failure to write a thank-you note is rude. So, let me ask you, how many times are we rude to God? How many countless gifts do we receive a day and yet we fail to say thank you? We wouldn't let our children by with such rudeness, but we are guilty of it ourselves! A rude person is a presumptuous person. Have you ever gone out of your way for someone only for them to just presume you should have, or that they deserved it, or that it was no big deal for you to do a big deal kind of thing for them? It doesn't take us long to tire of a person who acts this way. And before long, we will not want to do for them anymore. I imagine God feels very much the same way.

The truth is, we have more gifts in a day than we can number. Psalm 68:19 says that God loads us up daily with benefits. If we have more benefits in a single twenty-four-hour day than we could possibly even count, imagine how many we have in 365 of those days! Now take all those years and count them up in your lifetime. Ladies, I think you will agree with me that we are way behind on our thank-you notes to God.

IN CLOSING

Don't you hate it when a speaker says 'in closing' and then keeps going on and on and on? I feel like this chapter may be approaching doing just that. I need to wrap it up, but there is so much more to say. In the words of this chapter, I have tried to speak of what the Bible refers to as 'joy unspeakable.' I think if you could take this whole chapter and boil it all down to just one sentence, it would be this: Joy is a choice and not a feeling. We can each choose joy on rainy days and Mondays. We can choose joy while sitting in chemo treatments or divorce courts. We can choose joy when we are thirty pounds overweight and feeling less than. We can choose joy when we are passed over and left out. We can choose joy when hardship comes and decides to stay. We can choose joy by choosing gratitude. I hope you have seen that proven in the pages of this chapter. So, what now? Well, now it is time for this chapter to end and your life of gratitude to begin.

Making It Personal

It is now time for you to take the gratitude plunge. For the next thirty days, you are tasked with writing a thank-you note to God each and every day. (I am over halfway done with this assignment, and let me tell you, it has made the biggest difference in my outlook, my inlook, and my uplook.) You can do this in a journal, a notebook, or on actual thank-you notes. What you choose to thank Him for each day is up to you. While working on this assignment, I found that I would wake up many mornings with a song on my mind. It was a lyric of that song that I would end up writing my note to God about that day. For example, if I woke up singing about the deliverance of God, I wrote a thank you for a personal deliverance I had experienced. It was uncanny how many times a song reflected my heart's gratitude. This exercise caused me to actually wake up grateful. You may discover along the way that you have some thank-you notes you may actually need to write to other people in your life as well. Please make sure you do so. A person who is grateful to God is also grateful to others. A good exercise to do alongside this one is to have the goal to write one thank-you note a week to someone you know. It could be a note to a high school math teacher who made a difference in your life, or a friendly bank teller who is always so cheery on Monday mornings. Maybe it is a lady at church who is always so kind and caring to you, or your child's Sunday School teacher who works so hard to make class fun and interesting for your little one, or perhaps it is your pastor who works so hard to lead your church and love his congregation. The goal is to set out each day to be grateful on purpose. Begin each day in prayer, asking God to help you to become a thankful and grateful person as He reveals to you the many blessings and benefits in your life. Then, all that's left to do is to watch your attitude of gratitude transform your life into one filled with true and lasting joy.

Gratitude Challenge:

> Write one thank-you note to God each day for thirty days in your journal.

Write one thank-you note per week to someone who has made a difference in your life.

To be completed after the thirty-day challenge:

1. What did I learn during the thirty days of gratitude challenge?

2. How did I see my life change during this time?

3. Did I notice more joy in my life as I became more grateful?

4. What did this joy look like and feel like?

5. What do I need to do in order for this change to be permanent and ongoing?

6. How would I rate my joy before I started this exercise?

7. How would I rate my joy now?

CHAPTER FIFTEEN

That's a Wrap

Years ago, I bought a workout DVD by a lady named Leslie Sansone. Anyone remember her? She made lots of money by simply helping people walk miles and miles and miles in their living rooms. I got those workouts when I was pregnant because I could easily and safely exercise while expecting and also while recovering from having my little one. Leslie smiled and encouraged and helped me walk countless miles when it was difficult to do so, when I had every excuse not to do so, and when it was quite comical at times for me to even try to do so. For a while it could have been a waddling DVD instead of a walking one!

I feel that in this chapter I am the the equivalent of your own personal Leslie Sansone. Instead of a physical walking workout I am leading you in a spiritual and emotional 'walk' workout. I am going to smile and encourage and cheer you on. I am going to say things like she did. I can even hear her voice and see all those perfectly white teeth as she smiled and said, "And we march, we march, keep on marching, ladies. Walking burns calories, you can do it!" I may not be as perky as she was in that DVD, and I definitely don't look as good in spandex, but I believe in what a healthy walking regimen can do for you. No, I am not talking about getting us into shape physically, but I am talking about us getting into shape emotionally and spiritually. Stick with me and you will understand what I am talking about.

LACE UP THOSE WALKING SHOES

2 Thessalonians 4:1–4 and 7 say, "Furthermore then we beseech you, brethren, and exhort you by the Lord Jesus that ye have received of us how ye ought to WALK and to please God, so ye would abound more and more. For ye know what commandments we gave you by the Lord Jesus. For this is the will of God, even your sanctification, that ye should abstain from fornication: That every one of you should know how to possess his vessel in sanctification and honor; For God hath not called us unto uncleanness, but unto holiness." I emphasized 'walk' on purpose. God came out with a walking program long before Leslie came on the scene. This entire book has been a daily walking plan for our emotions. We want to "walk and to please God." Why? So that we can abound more and more. This book is meant for you to read through once and then certain chapters will need to be read and reread as needed. When you are battling anger or some such emotion, go back and reread that chapter. Dig deep in God's Word and read about whatever particular emotion you are currently struggling with. Through your study you will get your marching orders and, as any good soldier will tell you, you will need to follow them. In Scripture, God lays out very clearly how you are to walk while dealing with each and every emotion.

In the book of Joshua, he received some very interesting, if not absolutely insane, marching orders. Now, Joshua was a soldier. He was used to giving and receiving orders. He knew how to fight. He had studied warfare and could lay out an effective battle plan. But God blew his mind when He gave him his marching orders for the battle of Jericho. In Joshua 1:2–3, God shows up and gives Joshua a charge to get up and get to stepping, so to speak. "Arise, and go over this Jordan...." Moses was dead and the children of Israel had been stuck in the same place while they mourned the passing of their great leader. Moses was gone and they didn't have a clue what to do next. That's when God showed up and let them know they had been still long enough. They had been sad long enough. It was time to get up, get moving, and cover some new territory. I feel as though God has that same message for a bunch of us reading this book along the way. 'ARISE, AND GO….' We have been stuck in grief, in anger, in bitterness, in fear, or insecurity, long enough. It is time to regain territory the enemy has gotten control over. It is also time to gain some new ground and cover some new emotional terrain, girls.

In Verse 3, God tells Joshua, "Every place that the sole of your foot shall tread upon, that have I given unto you." There it is. If you walk in obedience to God, the victory is yours for the taking. God has already given it to you. We just have to get up and go get it. In Verses 4–7, God gave Joshua some amazing promises and reassurances. Isn't that just like God? He gave this overwhelmed and intimidated man exactly what he needed in order to follow the command he had been given. He promised victory and His never-failing presence. He also gave him a charge to be strong and courageous. God then tells him how to go. He specifically explained to him what that 'go' looked like in Verse 7. "… do according to all the law… turn not from it to the right hand or to the left, that thou mayest prosper whithersoever thou goest." In Verse 8 He goes on to tell him what the key to his success will be. Obedience to the Word of God would be the key to winning this military campaign and it will be the exact same key for our success in the emotional victory we are seeking.

In Joshua 6:2–5, Jesus Himself shows up to Joshua and gives Him face-to-face instructions on how the troops were to defeat the massive stronghold of Jericho. They were to silently *walk* (this keeps popping up, doesn't it?) around the city once a day for six days. Then they were to silently *walk* around the city seven times on the seventh day. At the end of the seventh lap, they were to listen for the loud trumpet blasts from the priests and then they were to shout. Loud. Then, and only then, would those impenetrable walls collapse, making way for the troops to march in and win the victory.

Now, I am not a soldier, but those are some very odd battle plans even to my untrained eye. March. Be quiet. March some more. Be quiet some more. Keep going even when the way gets long and you want to quit. Then, at the exact moment God tells you to, shout and God will do the rest. Girls, I am here to tell you that in order to cover some new emotional territory, you are going to have to follow some very odd marching orders at times. They won't make sense. God's going to tell you to be kind when kind seems very odd. He will tell you to be quiet when all you want to do is shout. He may even tell you to shout and fight a battle when all you want to do is run and hide. Amazingly, the battle plans given to Joshua worked. The impenetrable walls fell down flat and the Israelites won the victory, just as God said they would. You see, the power wasn't in the marching, it wasn't in the silence, or even in the shout. The power to win the victory over a massive unbeatable stronghold came through each step of obedience.

We all have strong, intimidating emotional strongholds. These have been built over years and years of hurt and hard and all the times we incorrectly dealt with all the stuff that the hurt and the hard brought with them. Massive walls have been erected one brick at a time over the years. Those bricks come from heaps and heaps of emotional baggage that has resulted from our wrong choices, hurts, stuffing, ignoring, renaming, and excusing, not to mention all the wrongdoings and mistreatments from others in our lives. Trust me, there is no shortage of building material in our lives. Piles of bricks labeled culture, society, pop psychology, and worldly logic lie around and are plentiful for the taking when it comes to emotional stronghold building. And let's not forget the generational sins, inborn flaws, and weaknesses, along with family and all the baggage that can bring.

But, as usual, God has a lot to say about how we are to fight these battles. Emotional strongholds aren't impenetrable. It's just that the battle plan won't make sense or follow logic a lot of times. In fact, the world will tell you that you have every right to do exactly the opposite of what God asks. Your own nature will say to do it differently. Well-meaning friends and family will jump in with their opinions along the way too. But when God gives you a battle plan and a promise of victory, you will have to walk in obedience in order to achieve it.

Jericho was no small city. Those walls weren't the flimsy fences that you can buy at Lowes either. Oh no, those walls were big and thick and well built. In fact, there were actually two walls that surrounded Jericho.

First, there was an outer wall that was about 6 feet thick, followed by a 12–15 feet of space, then an inner wall that was 12 feet thick. Those strong walls weren't just thick either as they towered 30 feet high in the air. As you can see, that's no small wall! No wonder Joshua was intimidated! Located on the wall was a massive watchtower that was 30 feet wide at the base, with walls that were almost 5 feet thick. Records have been found that at the tower alone took eleven thousand workdays to finish! That's 2,200 five-day work weeks!

Sounds suspiciously as big and thick as our emotional strongholds that have taken years upon years to construct. We know how big and thick our walls are because we have tried to chip away at them with the ice picks labeled 'will power' or' New Year's resolutions' and finally one that says 'determination'. Ok, so some of us have pick axes and not ice picks, but no matter which we have in our hands, we can only make a dent in such massive strongholds.

2 Corinthians 10:4–5 says, "(For the weapons of our warfare are not carnal, but mighty through God to the pulling down of strong holds;) Casting down imaginations, and every high thing that exalteth itself against the knowledge of God, and bringing into captivity every thought to the obedience of Christ." Did you see that our weapons aren't conventional weapons? Did you also see that we must bring our thoughts as prisoners of war into captivity to the obedience of Christ? You see, that's where the victory is. Our mind is where obedience begins. Without obedient thoughts our feet will never take obedient steps. Our minds are the command centers of our bodies. If we want to march right, we have to think right.

It has been calculated that it was about a 1.24-mile walk around Jericho. This probably took about an hour to walk around one time. That means for an hour a day the Israelites silently marched around that city enduring jeers and sneers from those on top of those menacing walls. Talk about difficult! They couldn't set the record straight. They couldn't even defend themselves. They just had to hold their tongue and take the next step of obedience. Their job was not to correct the wrongdoers. Their job, for now, was to march.

Now there are typically 2,500 steps in a 1.24-mile walk. So for about 2,500 steps a day for six days they had to silently endure mistreatment and misunderstanding. Each of these days they took 2,500 steps in obedience toward their victory. Each step they took was an investment in that victory. Not one step was wasted or useless. It is important to note that while taking these steps, they didn't see much progress. They didn't see even a tiny crack in the foundation, or even a small chink in those big old walls. How discouraging!

Then day seven came. I am sure you have heard of the song "Mama Said There'd Be Days Like This." Well, day seven was one of 'those days.' Have you ever noticed that some days, well, they are just harder than others? It is on those 'some days' that God just seems to require more from us. There's no other way to say it than that. That seventh day God asked more of them. He required *seven* trips around that city. So, that's 17,500 steps that day! For approximately seven hours they endured the heckles and the jokes and the laughter of the inhabitants of Jericho. Altogether they would have marched approximately 32,500 steps. And you know what? Not one of those steps was any more important than the other. Their day-seven victory would never have happened without a day-three obedient march. Without step number 11,414 of obedience, they never would have experienced the victory that happened on step number 32,500. Each and every step they took in obedience was an investment in the victory they got to experience on that final day with that final step. Oh, we all want to take that final step and experience victory, but very few of us want to sign up for all the marching that gets us there. Ladies, I don't know how many steps of obedience it will take in order for your emotional stronghold to crumble and collapse, but I do know that every step you take in obedience is important because it is progress. Each step matters. Victory will come if you keep marching in obedience and keep following the orders God has laid out in His word.

THANK YOU FOR FLYING THE NOT-SO-FRIENDLY SKIES

Those of you that have flown in a commercial airplane have heard the little safety speech that the flight attendant gives before each flight. If you are like me, you are probably too busy digging through your purse or carry-on in order to find that all important snack or perhaps a book to pay any attention at all to what the poor flight attendant is saying. But what he or she is saying is actually important. They are trying to get a group of distracted, impatient, and selfish people to listen to something that could save their lives if the plane were to encounter some serious trouble.

We have now come to the portion of the book where I am giving that same safety speech. I know you are almost to the end of the book and are ready to stop thinking about emotions. You may even be tempted to start digging around in the bottom of your purse, searching for a stale treat that fell down into that dark abyss long ago, am I right? Nevertheless, I will give my speech anyway. While I give it, please pay attention, as your safety could depend on it. The first little preflight speech I am going to give you is a sample one that you would hear if you flew on Delta or American Airlines today. The second one is a more, ahem, appropriate one for those of us who fly the not so friendly skies sometimes. So, pay attention, and stop trying to discreetly stare at the stranger who just sat down beside you. And will you please stop glaring at the noisy kids who are sitting in the row in front of you? Here we go:

> *Ladies and gentleman, I would like to thank you for flying with us on _____ airlines today. Please pay close attention as we will now go over some important safety procedures. In case we encounter turbulence, the seatbelt light, located above your head, will come on. If this happens, please return to your seat and remain seated with your seatbelt firmly fastened until the seatbelt light is turned off, at which time you may freely move about the cabin. In case of an emergency, please familiarize yourself with the location of the emergency exits.*

In the unlikely case of an emergency change in cabin pressure, oxygen masks will deploy from their compartments above you. Please secure your oxygen mask firmly in place over your nose and mouth before trying to assist anyone else with their mask. Once the oxygen mask is in place, remain calm and breathe normally.

In case of a water landing, your seat cushion can be removed and used as a flotation device.

Please power off all devices as we prepare the cabin for takeoff. We hope you enjoy the flight and as always thank you for making us your choice in flight.

Now, I know you may be wondering how any of that applies to emotions. Well, I am about to give you the emotional preflight safety spill.

Welcome ladies, we would like to thank you for choosing to fly with Emotional Struggle Bus Airlines today. Please pay close attention, as we will now go over some important safety procedures. Expect to encounter turbulence—lots of turbulence during your Emotional Struggle Bus flight. When this happens, you will need to sit down and buckle up, Buttercup, because it is going to be a bumpy ride. When the seatbelt light is on, you better sit your tail down and don't even think about moving around this cabin freely. Got it? Good. Before takeoff, please look around and see where the emergency exits are located. You know the ones with the big glowing red EXIT signs? If you would put your phone down and look around, you would see them. In case of an emergency, there is no need for you to panic. Calmly move toward the nearest emergency exit while everyone else on the flight will totally be panicking. No screaming, pushing, yelling, or trying to get in front of other people, because what is rude when things are going just peachy is rude when things are getting kind of crazy.

When we experience a not so unexpected spike in cabin pressure, oxygen masks are going to fall down from up above. It is important to fix your mask first, so that you can breathe, before you try to fix someone else's mask. Your passing out ain't going to help anyone! Oh, and in case we crash-land in the ocean, before you drown, or a shark eats you, take the time to rip your seat off and it will act as a life preserver, no worries at all! As always, thank you for flying the not so friendly skies with Emotional Struggle Bus Airlines today. Enjoy your flight.

I had to giggle as I typed that. But there really are some pretty good truths tucked in there when it comes to our emotions.

1. Expect turbulence. Expect it. Teeth-jarring bumps and 'bottom dropping out of your belly' dips will be encountered. Life won't always go smoothly, neither will marriage, parenting, jobs, or friendships. Turbulence happens in all of those. Expect it, prepare for it, so that you can make concessions and then adjustments when it does happen on your flight. In every plane, on every seat, is a little thing called a seatbelt. It is a restraint that was put in place in order to keep you safe before you ever encountered that turbulence. Emotional seatbelts are the restraints, or the rules, put in place. Seatbelts restrain you from moving out of a safe place. They keep you in your safe place and out of harm's way. God's Word is full of rules and restraints that are there for our safety. Use them.

2. Emergency exits are in place and are well lit and clearly marked. 1 Corinthians 10:13 says, "There hath no temptation taken you but such as is common to man; but God is faithful, who will not suffer you to be tempted above that ye are able; but will with the temptation also make a way to escape, that ye may be able to bear it." God gives us emergency exits, ways of escape, when we are tempted to blow it emotionally. Escape hatches, I call them. They are well lit

and clearly labeled, if we will just look for them. No one can *make* you do or say a thing and no one can make you act or react in a certain way. You do have a way out. That's a promise from God. It has been my prayer that this book will better equip you to seek out that way of escape and to use it instead of falling into the same old sin pattern time after time.

3. Power off your devices. Girls, we are going to have to put our phones down. There will be seasons when we need to get off social media for a while. Powering down the distractions is vital so that we can power up through a careful focus on prayer and God's Word. Pay attention to screen time. If it encroaches on your quiet time or your family time or your rest time, power down so that you can power up.

4. If you experience an unexpected increase in the pressure of life, make sure you work on what is wrong with you before you try to fix what is wrong with someone else. If you keel over from lack of oxygen, you can't help anyone. Take in what you need to take in before you try to make sure others are receiving what they need to receive.

5. If life plunges you in deep water that is over your head, what held you up earlier when everything was fine will also hold you up in deep waters. Cling to your God and His Word tightly instead of frantically flailing about trying to keep your head above water in your own power.

If anything does go wrong during a flight, the airline attendants go into a well-trained machine-type mode. Everyone knows what to do and what they are in charge of. They do not panic. They simply follow procedure. Why? They have been trained to do just that. They have practiced and gone through drill after drill in order to equip them in times of emergency.

In other words, before the emergency ever happened, they learned what to do and exactly how to proceed.

This book is chocked full of your emergency plans. Every chapter has drills—activities, verses, and psychological truths concerning each emotion. While things are calm and your flight is going smoothly, that is the time to study, prepare, and go through training so you will know what to do when an emergency does come. Reading a book isn't training. Training includes reading *and* interacting, cooperating, journaling, praying, obeying, trying, failing, trying again, determining, and implementing what is learned in order to be a successful training program. I strongly suggest rereading the chapters in the areas where you struggle. Form your battle plan. Journal your predetermined responses. Make those declarations. Locate your emergency exits. Run some drills. Complete the activities. Train and then when the inevitable does happen, you will be ready to put into practice all that you have learned.

Ladies, I have loved every minute of this journey we have been on together. Goodness knows we have laughed, cried, and been absolutely mortified at each other's honesty while we have been together. What has happened in these pages has been very raw and real. I feel as though we have walked on some holy ground, me and you. Absolutely nothing has been off limits and nothing short of full disclosure has been required of us both on this trip. I can honestly say that I truly love each and every one of you. We are in this thing together. I hope you know that as I have poured out my heart in these pages, I have prayed for you and I have prayed for me too.

Life is hard. Emotions are hard. But hard, well, that is where God shines the brightest, isn't it? Maybe someday, up in heaven, we can sit down and have a nice long chat. You can tell me your embarrassing seventh-grade stories or your awful girls'-locker-room moment. We would laugh together and maybe even cry a form of holy heavenly tears together as we talk about all we learned when we finally got real about our raw emotions. And we both know where our conversation would end up. We would talk on and on and on about Jesus and how good He was through it all. But until then, we will have to be content to do all that through the pages of this book and your own private journal. Until then, I will leave you to it. Love you much!

How to Have a Personal Relationship with Christ

If you are reading this, you have taken the first step toward salvation. Realizing that salvation isn't a result of going to church, being a good person, or believing there is a higher power out there somewhere is the very important first step. Understanding that you aren't saved is what has to happen before you can ever get saved. Religion isn't the answer. Relationship is. So, how exactly do you get saved?

Let's go to the Bible to find that answer. Romans 3:23 says, "For all have sinned, and come short of the glory of God." This means everyone who has ever been born has sinned and unfortunately, it just takes just one sin to be a sinner. What exactly is sin? Sin is anything that we do that is wrong or against God's standard of holiness. Now, this poses a big problem. Because God is absolutely holy and righteous, He cannot allow unholiness into His presence in heaven. As a result of our sins, we simply cannot get into heaven. But, thankfully, the story doesn't end here.

Romans 5:8 says, "But God commendeth his love toward us, in that, while we were yet sinners, Christ died for us." Here's the good news. God sent his only Son, Jesus, to die for our sins on the cross of Calvary. Because Jesus was perfect, holy, and sinless, His death atoned for our sins. He was the perfect sacrifice that redeemed us from our sins.

Romans 6:23 says, "For the wages of sins is death; but the gift of God is eternal life through Jesus Christ our Lord." Have you ever bought someone special the perfect gift? You went to great lengths and expense to get just the right gift that you knew they would love. But what if they never came and got it from you? Did they receive that gift? Did that gift ever do them any good? No. The same is true for the gift of salvation that was given to every person on Calvary. You have to receive it for it to do you any good. Realizing you are lost and realizing you need His salvation is key to ever receiving salvation. Realizing you *need* to be saved is the first step toward salvation. So, if you are ready to receive this gift of salvation, keep on reading.

Romans 10:9–10: "That if thou shalt confess with thy mouth the Lord Jesus, and shalt believe in thine heart that God hath raised him from the dead, thou shalt be saved. For with the heart man believeth unto righteousness; and with the mouth confession is made unto salvation."

Romans 10:13: "For whosoever shall call upon the name of the Lord shall be saved."

These verses let us know exactly what we need to do to get saved. First, confess that you are a sinner and that you need to get saved. Next, declare that you believe that Jesus is the Son of God who died on the cross and rose again so that you can be saved. Lastly, just ask Him to forgive you of your sins, come into your heart, and save you. That's it. That is how to receive Jesus as your personal Savior, according to Scripture. If you would like to do that, simply pray something like the prayer below and mean it with your whole heart:

"Dear Jesus, I confess that I am a sinner and I don't want to be a sinner anymore. I believe that Jesus is the Son of God and that He died on the cross and rose again so that I can be saved. Please forgive me of my sins and come into my heart and save me. Thank you for saving me. In Jesus's name, Amen."

I am so very glad you have made the choice to ask Jesus to save you! If you made this decision, I would love to hear from you. Please contact me through our church website, www.pbckannapolis.org so that we can rejoice with you!

About the Author

Amy is an author who has a passion to reach and teach Christian women of all ages. She is the author of many Bible studies and devotional books written from the perspective of a woman to other women. Her desire is for her books to challenge and encourage women to grow and walk in victory. Her practical and applicable style of writing has equipped women around the world to become students of God's Word for themselves as they dig deeper for the truths that apply to their lives. Amy currently lives in Kannapolis, North Carolina, with her husband, Mike, and daughters, Sarah and Anna. She and her husband serve together at Piedmont Baptist Church, which they founded in 2001. Her books are available on Amazon and at www.pbckannapolis.org.

Other Books by Amy Edwards

Women of the Word: This extremely popular three-volume series is an in-depth Bible study about each of the women in the pages of Scripture. This interactive study takes a deep dive into not only the life of each woman we meet in the Bible but also your own life. Each day you will learn fascinating new facts as you explore the culture, the life, and the times of these women who lived so long ago. *Women of the Word*, Volumes 1–3, is available on Amazon, or you can order from www.pbckannapolis.org.

A Woman, A Warrior: This interactive prayer journal for women combines praying Scripture and the powerful head-to-toe prayers that are mentioned in this book. You will learn to pray bigger, deeper, and much more meaningful prayers for yourself and your loved ones. This journal is a game changer for your prayer life. *A Woman, A Warrior* is available on Amazon and also at www.pbckannapolis.org.

Reflections: This four-volume series is a 365-day devotional for women that will challenge you to read the Old Testament once and the New Testament twice, all in one year. Each day has your assigned scripture reading along with a written devotional based out of the assigned verses for the day. *Reflections*, Volumes 1–4, is available on Amazon or at www.pbckannapolis.org.

The Marriage Ring: In this book, Amy cowrites with her husband as they tackle the common issues that every marriage will face. Each chapter begins with a realistic, and often comical, scenario in the home. The chapter then moves on to discuss helpful tips and many practical ways to work around or through the problematic issue discussed in the chapter. At the end of each chapter you will find questions that are designed to encourage open and honest communication between husbands and wives. *The Marriage Ring* is available on Amazon or at www.pbckannapolis.org.

The Princess Project: This is a fun mother–daughter Bible study designed for moms and little girls ages six to twelve. It is based on the original Grimm's fairy-tale princesses, such as Snow White, Cinderella, and Sleeping Beauty. The elements of human nature that are portrayed in these original stories will take your little girl straight to Scripture to find timeless truths that will help her when she faces a similar situation. Each week you have an art project, a lesson, a recipe, and a devotional for mom that goes with the original princess story you will read that week. You and your little princess will be in for lots of giggles, quality time, and lifelong lessons as you complete *The Princess Project* together. *The Princess Project* is available on Amazon and at www.pbckannapolis.org.